ENDORSE

MW00562152

Compilation books of this nature can lack focus, as they tend to be an interesting assortment of diverse ideas. On the other hand, they can be a priceless collection of testimonies and insights by key leaders that is sure to have profound impact on all who read it. Laura Taranto's book, *Take Your Place in the Harvest of Nations,* is the latter. She has collected the stories and testimonies of many European leaders who are participating in a move of God currently reshaping the continent—a continent that many thought was lost forever. These men and women of great courage stood up in faith and declared, "Not on my watch!" The fruit of their stance is undeniable. With careful stewardship, Laura has recorded the powerful ways the Gospel of Jesus Christ is spreading through a unified church to a hungry world. As you read this book, you will encounter inspiring stories of humility and boldness that will awaken your heart with hope and insight for all that God is doing around the world.

BILL JOHNSON
Bethel Church, Redding, California
Author of *Born for Significance* and *Hope in Any Crisis*

Take Your Place in the Harvest of Nations by Laura Taranto is a collection of amazing testimonies of God's power currently manifesting throughout Europe. The lost are coming to Jesus by the droves as believers say "Yes" to the vision God has given them for the harvest! These incredible stories will build your faith and inspire you. Join the movement that is already sweeping the nations!

EVANGELIST DANIEL KOLENDA
President/CEO Christ for all Nations

The writer of Hebrews 11 gives us a stirring record of heroes of faith ending with a charge for us to continue in their example. In the same spirit, Laura has compiled testimonies of men and women of our day who have been shifting the atmosphere in Europe. We are energized by their example to run with endurance into the harvest fields of Europe.

BEDROS NASSANIAN
Noor Global
Geneva, Switzerland

Jesus is the Lord of the harvest. A bride is Calvary's reward. He is longing for the nations to come into His love. I'm thankful for servants like Laura who are giving their lives to Jesus and His Gospel. May this book bless your heart and ignite a fire in your soul for Jesus Himself.

MICHAEL KOULIANOS
Founder of Jesus Image

"Africa is no longer the 'Dark Continent' of the world. It's Europe and it's because Europe hasn't had a significant spiritual awakening in almost a hundred years," I heard Reverend Billy Graham say this at a missions conference, and it was the very first time that Europe even registered on my radar. This was before God called me to the Netherlands. The Spirit of the Lord is moving across the earth and, praise God, it's Europe's time! The stories in this book will inspire you. They also show that it takes courage and perseverance to be one whom God uses to bring change. God still moves, and He can use you—all you need to do is be available! Well done, Laura Taranto, for writing this book!

DR. ARLEEN WESTERHOF
Founder and Leader, Netherlands Prophetic Council
Co-Leader, European Prophetic Council

Laura Taranto brings to you a treasury of faith-filled stories of how God is moving in Europe and in the nations. At many times, I've seen that the biggest moves of God begin with a cloud the size of a person's hand. As we are faithful, stewarding the flame, the flame will become a furnace that will burn through nations and generations. This book carries that anointing to set your heart aflame for an unprecedented move of God resulting in worldwide harvest. Read it and be stretched in your faith.

TEOFILO HAYASHI
Founder, Dunamis Movement
Senior Leader Zion Church

It is God who spreads the waves of Awakening, and He raises people to announce, proclaim, and reveal it. I feel that the launch of our beautiful sister Laura Taranto's book is an omen of Awakening in Europe. In recent years, much has been said about reduction of the number of Christians in Europe. Then I see this beautiful book arguing that it is our time now to "take our place in the harvest of nations," because God gave each one wonderful and unique gifts and talents. I believe that this book will soon become a bestseller; it will encourage millions of people all around the world. I would like this book to be translated into Russian, so our pray-ers could learn, as it is said in the book, to dream big with

God, to get wisdom from seasoned leaders, experience unity in the body of Christ, and to entrust Awakening in Europe to our Lord. I thank God for these amazing stories proving that there is nothing God cannot do. And I am sure this book will be an effective motivator for numerous churches in Russia and all former Soviet states.

SERGEI RYAKHOVSKII
Lead Bishop, the Russian Union of Christians
of Evangelical Faith (Pentecostal)

Laura interviewed various European spiritual leaders, all of whom, through their faith, wisdom, and openness, can serve as great examples. Having worked as Heidi Baker's assistant for many years and having witnessed what God can do, it is Laura's wish to use this book to pave the way for a mighty move of God in Europe. Along these lines, it is her heart's desire that each and every believer finds and bravely takes his or her place in God's wonderful plan. When reading this book, it felt like I was hearing Elijah's servant call, "The rain is coming!"

CHRISTOPHE DOMES
Lead Pastor, diekreative BERLIN

"May they be one as We are One." This is one of the few prayers of Jesus where we know the content, and it's perhaps the most important—united in love, vision, and mission. This book is a must-read for all who rejoice in the unity of believers. For others, it's a powerful encouragement to seek unity in the service of a vision. Thank you, Laura, for enriching us with these testimonies.

THIERRY and MONIQUE JUVET
Founders of the Global Institute of Honor
Switzerland

Laura is a woman in love with Jesus, and she carries the call to wake up and serve the church. In this book we are encouraged to dream big with God and to understand that we need divine wisdom to guide us through a revival process and the necessary barriers to overcome to create unity in the church and the courage to face disbelief, disappointment, and generalized discouragement to motivate ourselves to believe that a revival is possible in Europe.

RODRIGUES PEREIRA
Director, European School Supernatural Ministry
Builder Bethel Leaders Network

Listen! There is such a gentle and warm island breeze in these pages inviting us to intimacy with Jesus. Listen closely! There is a living heart pulsing everywhere in this book. The Father's heart striving for you. Yes, whatever your broken past, as His dearly cherished son or daughter, join Him in loving back home all those God-orphans in Europe. Hear the sound of these testimonies—a beautiful Gospel song with such diverse voices, amazingly united in Spirit. A sound of worship, intercession, true heart relationships. And above all, the sound of many footsteps—the King walking in Europe, your steps following His, in your own personal shoes with His empowerment. If you will.

PAUL HEMES
Theologian, Pastor, Physicist
Switzerland

TAKE YOUR PLACE IN THE

HARVEST
of NATIONS

Revival Stories from Europe that Will
Ignite Your Faith for Awakening

LAURA TARANTO

DESTINY IMAGE® PUBLISHERS, INC.

P.O. Box 310, Shippensburg, PA 17257-0310

"Promoting Inspired Lives."

This book and all other Destiny Image and Destiny Image Fiction books are available at Christian bookstores and distributors worldwide.

Cover design by Eileen Rockwell
Interior design by Terry Clifton

For more information on foreign distributors, call 717-532-3040.

Reach us on the Internet: www.destinyimage.com.

ISBN 13 TP: 978-0-7684-5826-8
ISBN 13 eBook: 978-0-7684-5827-5
LP ISBN: 978-0-7684-6154-1
HC ISBN: 978-0-7684-6155-8

For Worldwide Distribution, Printed in the U.S.A.
1 2 3 4 5 6 7 8 / 25 24 23 22 21

Acknowledgments

First, I thank Jesus. Your love and mercy changed my life. I pray this book will encourage many to boldly follow with all their hearts and live their lives for Your glory.

Next, I thank each person who shared their story with me. This book is a collection of interviews from men and women who live their lives with passion, dedication, and fiery love. Your love for God and for people is evident and beautiful. During each interview, I was inspired afresh in my own pursuit after God. I am grateful and humbled by the way each of you vulnerably and openly shared what you have learned on this journey of faith.

I also thank Pierre Bader who came up with the concept for this book. Thank you for trusting me with the vision, working together, and encouraging me along the way.

Thank you to Jean-Luc Trachsel for your courage to believe God for the continent of Europe and call so many others to join you, including me. I am grateful for your support and honored by your friendship. Starting and leading this movement, empowered by the Holy Spirit, is not an easy assignment. Your devotion to Jesus, commitment to unity, steadfastness in the work of the Gospel, and vision for Europe inspire many. You never give up, always trust God, and no matter what comes your way, you continue to believe and declare, "Europe shall be saved."

Next, I personally would not be the woman I am without Heidi Baker. Thank you for teaching me, speaking into my life, and praying for me continuously. Worshipping Jesus, reaching out to the poor in the farthest villages, and ministering to people around the world with you dug a deep foundation of faith in my life. We have been stranded at sea, almost shipwrecked, hungry, very well fed, sunburned and tired, treated with luxury, filled with mourning, and filled with laughter. In every season and every situation, we fix our eyes on Jesus the Author and Perfecter of our faith. God writes every story, and I am so glad our stories intertwine.

Thank you, Larry Sparks, for championing me and affirming me in my writing and communication skills. Thank you for giving me opportunities to write for Destiny Image—working with you is an absolute joy. You collate many voices to present a full, clear picture to the body of Christ with such honor and integrity. You love to find new voices and give them the platform. You show no favoritism; your mission is always to honor Jesus and lift Him higher. I greatly appreciated your support as I embarked on this journey of writing my first book. Thank you for helping me share this collection of powerful testimonies with the world. I believe it will inspire many to wholeheartedly follow Jesus and dream big with Him.

CONTENTS

FOREWORD

By Heidi Baker

God is moving powerfully around the world. It is an incredible time to be alive. We have the choice to either concentrate on the conflicts and extreme challenges or to totally trust in Jesus.

We can focus on the problems or we can focus on what God is doing in our midst. When we look to Jesus, we will see that He is beautiful, holy, and full of love. He is working in and through His body in the nations. The hungry are being fed, the lost are encountering Him, and many are being touched by His love. God is looking for friends who will worship Him and fix their eyes on Him at all times. He is looking for those who will go wherever He calls them to reach people with His love and transform this world.

Take Your Place in the Harvest of Nations is a collection of interviews with fifteen inspiring leaders ministering across Europe in their united passion for the Gospel. Each person gave God their yes and did not look back. Laura Taranto does an excellent job of capturing their hearts as she shares where their stories began, how they overcame challenges, and what they are believing for right now, both personally and for the continent of Europe.

Several of the leaders interviewed are my close personal friends, so we have prayed and ministered together for many years. It is my joy to be a spiritual mother in this movement. From the first Europe Shall Be Saved roundtable until now, I am standing with them in faith for what God wants to do in Europe. We all believe John 17 is a key passage for the body of Christ. It is time to minister in unity, love one another, and learn from each other.

I believe that as you read these testimonies, you will be encouraged to press into God and pursue God's dreams for you. If your heart is saying "yes" to Jesus and to His invitation to love the lost and the broken, *Take Your Place in the Harvest of Nations* is a powerful resource for you. Take this book as an invitation into intimacy and adventure with God. Some are called to other nations, while others are called to their own hometowns. Wherever you are, you can stop for the one to share God's love and faithfulness.

The Great Commission is for all of us. *Take Your Place in the Harvest of Nations* is about what happens when you give God your yes, no matter the cost. God gives us visions from His heart. Our part is to believe with Him, pray, and take one step at a time. Like Mary, we say, *"Let it be to me according to your word"* (Luke 1:38). When it feels hard or even impossible, we don't abort. We continue to trust and believe. God is raising up many men and women from all around the globe who will walk in this same spirit of faith, perseverance, and total dependence on God.

Sometimes the leaders interviewed in this book did not feel like they had much to give. The vision for Europe felt too big for them. But just like the little boy with five loaves of bread and two fish, they offered Jesus whatever they had for His glory. They watched with wonder as He did what only He can do. He took their offerings with joy and multiplied them over and over again. In Mozambique, sometimes we also feel so small when we see the need around us. Then we remember that we have a mighty God, and nothing is impossible for Him. We watch in awe and wonder as He pours out His Spirit time and time again. He provides for the poor and the needy as we partner with Him. So, if you feel too small or inadequate, fear not. You are in the perfect position to see God move through you. He is the One who empowers your dream.

I truly believe it's Europe's time. God is moving in powerful ways across the continent in many denominations and nations. God is calling Europe back to her roots, back to the place of being connected to the Vine, to Jesus. At times Europeans have thought they could do things on their own and continue to prosper no matter what. That might work for a time, but we can only truly thrive when we are connected to the Source of life.

I see God leading His people and reconnecting them to Himself. There is a huge harvest in Europe. It is a partnership between God's plan and our participation. God has determined this revival in His heart, and we have the privilege to participate with our prayers and our lives.

It is time for men and women of God to wake up and not be silent. It is time to cry out to God for the continent He so deeply loves. We win this battle on our knees. We win it on our faces. We draw close to God in intimacy, connected to the Vine, then we go out and love the ones who don't know Him yet. The men and women in this book are doing exactly that. Will you join them in prayer and action? Will you give God your "yes," no matter the cost?

Laura Taranto wrote this book to encourage others to rise up in their callings with courage and faith. I know her heart is to bless you, inspire you, and help you step into all that God has for you. Laura is a spiritual daughter. She ministered with me in Mozambique and around the world, giving her yes and her life for Jesus. She is a passionate lover of Jesus, and she walks with great honesty, integrity, and creativity. She is a shining one.

As you read each interview, let God increase your faith for your life. Whatever your dream is, remember that all things are possible with God. You are a son or a daughter, loved by your Father God. He is calling and equipping you to make a difference in this world for His glory.

HEIDI G. BAKER, PhD
Cofounder and Executive Chairman of the Board
Iris Global

Introduction

This book is written for you and your story with God! The testimonies and wisdom on the pages to come are meant to inspire you and give you strength and courage to continue moving forward with everything God puts on your heart. His plans for you are even better than you could ask or imagine. Each Christian is part of God's plan for this world. God loves us so much that He sent His Son Jesus to die, rise again, and save all who believe in Him. Our primary calling is to love God and love people with this same powerful, selfless love. We are then commissioned to share Jesus through our lives with our words and our actions.

We are all created in the image of God, and we all look completely different. This means when we are fully ourselves, we express His beauty and love in exactly the way He created us to do so. God has a great plan for your life, and your story has the power to impact many for His kingdom. Each one of us is uniquely positioned to reach those who do not know Him yet: in our families, preaching on the streets, through media, with new songs, at work, or by any other method imaginable. As we pursue God, dream with Him, and take our places in the harvest, He will use our lives for His glory in the nations.

This book shares about the lives of men and women who are being used by God in their spheres of influence. Each one started out with a little seed, an idea God put on their heart, without a full plan or strategy in place. It was often inspired by something that touched their lives first. Their powerful God stories unfolded step by step, chapter by chapter as they trusted God, took risks, and believed Him for more. The Bible says *"Worship God! For the testimony of Jesus is the spirit of prophecy"* (Revelation 19:10). That means when we testify, or tell others what we know about Jesus and what we have seen Him do in our lives, it is the spirit of prophecy. In other words, it is a picture of what God can do in their lives too. My heart in writing this book is to showcase what God is already doing in Europe and raise expectations for the more to come. He has great plans, and we have only seen a small measure of all He wants to do among us in our day.

It is truly Europe's time, and we see Him moving powerfully all over the continent. It is not just in one denomination or one country—the stories we hear are coming from all directions. We have also heard those old rumors, like maybe you have heard, that Europe is hard and dark, not open for the Gospel. But in our opinion, and in our experience, the exact opposite is true. The family of God is growing rapidly and spreading His glorious love far and wide.

Prayer is increasing, people are meeting Jesus and getting discipled, many are running after God with great passion, and worship is rising with a new sound all over the continent. We feel great hope, joy, and expectation when we hear the testimonies of what God is doing. Through each story in this book, we want to share with the whole world, especially with those living in Europe, what's possible with God. If it's possible for the people in this book, it's also possible for you!

In creating this book, I interviewed people from all over Europe who are seeing God move in their lives and their cities. I had help from Pierre Bader with two interviews in French; and in fact, this book was his idea. I absolutely loved the vision to share the stories of leaders in Europe and inspire others to run forward in their callings, so I agreed to write it. During the interviews, we asked questions about how they got started on their journey, why they are doing what they are doing, what they learned along the way, how they overcame discouragement, and what they see Jesus doing in the continent of Europe.

In each chapter, I include key points and personal questions for you to apply the lessons they learned to your own life. Let their advice sink in, and let their victories inspire your story. Again, I wrote this book for you, so open your heart to dream with the Lord. Be encouraged; be provoked; be filled with hope for all God has for your life and your nation. He has a unique purpose for you that only you can accomplish. You are called, and it's your time!

Part I

IT'S YOUR TIME

1

Jean-Luc Trachsel's Story

Jean-Luc Trachsel is one of the most passionate people I know. He is most passionate about Jesus, family, and the harvest in Europe. Jean-Luc champions others and wants to see every Christian take their place in the harvest. He especially loves when people join us in his beloved continent of Europe. His heart is for everyone to work together in unity. God gave him vision for many ministries to come together and develop strategy to reach the continent. That started a movement called Europe Shall Be Saved. Every person and every ministry have unique giftings and strengths. Unity is a major theme throughout this book. When I asked how we can pursue unity, most of the interviewees, including Jean-Luc, referenced Jesus's words in John 17. Jesus prays that we may be one as He and His Father are one. That is also our prayer.

There is room at the table for everyone, including you. On the following pages, you will read Jean-Luc's story in his own words. I believe it will inspire you to pursue your calling and follow Jesus with passion. I hope it encourages you to love and honor your Christian brothers and sisters from every denomination. We believe as we work together in unity and bring our strengths together, we will see revival and awakening!

THE VISION

Jesus died and rose again to make a way for us. He paid the highest price for you, for me, and for the nations. There are multitudes and multitudes standing in the valley of decision right now, people who do not know Jesus as Savior. We need to reach them. Each one of us is needed. No person or ministry can bring in the harvest alone; we must work together. We live in a strategic time. God is moving across the earth. My heart is personally burning for Europe, but I also believe the globe shall be saved. God is moving in every nation.

This book is not just for Europeans. It is for every follower of Jesus who is longing for more. Each person written about in this book, including me, longs to walk in the fullness of what we read in the Bible. Through trials and victories, we press on to run the races marked out for us. As you read, seek God about your personal calling and destiny. Run your race; bring your strength, and take your place in the harvest.

In Europe, many ministries are joining together in unity, as family. We don't want to work alone or build on our own; we are committed to strategizing and building together. As we do, God is moving across the continent. Europe is being saved. We honor each person and ministry as we work together for one vision: to preach the Gospel across Europe and reach the lost for Jesus.

As we prayed together, the mandate God gave us was for 100 million souls. We desire and believe for 100 million people to begin following Jesus in our generation in Europe. To reach this goal, we need to lay down our egos and logos and work together. There are many denominations, many styles, and many giftings, and each one is needed. Unity is not about proving we have the right method. It is about honoring one another and lifting up the name of Jesus. This is the heart behind the Europe Shall Be Saved movement.

As human beings, we want to defend our theology and our methods, but that is not how we will win this continent. Unity requires humility, and it requires love. Paul defines love in this way:

> *Love is patient, love is kind. It does not envy, it does not boast, it is not proud. It does not dishonor others, it is not self-seeking, it is not easily angered, it keeps no record of wrongs. Love does not delight in evil but rejoices with the truth. It always protects, always trusts, always hopes, always perseveres. Love never fails...* (1 Corinthians 13:4-8 New International Version).

When we relate to one another with this kind of love, we will experience unity and breakthrough.

We will not agree on everything, but we do agree that Jesus Christ is the Son of God. *"For God so loved the world that He gave His only begotten Son, that whoever believes in Him shall not perish but have everlasting life"* (John 3:16). Jesus came to the earth to save those who are lost, deliver, heal, and give abundant life. We want to see Him alive in Europe, not an intellectual Jesus that we study in books or sing about on Christmas and Easter, but the real Jesus who is living with us through the Holy Spirit. When we keep Jesus at the center, our secondary differences can be set aside to achieve the higher goal of bringing many into the kingdom. It is all about Him.

Many pastors and ministries have been working very hard in Europe for decades plowing the ground very faithfully in what felt like a desert time in Europe. We honor all those ministers and pastors who have sown so much seed into this ground. Several years ago, something began to shift in Europe. We started to see more fruit and experienced something sovereign of God. Thousands of people started following Jesus across Europe. We believe this is just the beginning. We are going to see the multitude of multitudes coming to Christ. Again, this will come through unity and working together. We need a collective strategy to win this continent and make Jesus King of Europe again. This is not about me or my vision, it is much bigger than my life or my capacity. It is about each person taking their place.

Throughout this book, you will read the testimonies of many others with the same fire and passion for this continent. We are all full of faith and anticipation that Europe shall be saved. As you read, be inspired to follow Jesus with your whole heart, live in the fullness of who He created you to be, and do everything He shows you to do on this earth.

JEAN-LUC'S STORY

I gave my heart to Jesus when I was just 5 years old. I am from the 5th and 6th generations of born-again Christians. My father is a pastor, and my grandfather was a pastor and songwriter in the Brethren choir. At the age of 6, my parents asked me if I wanted to receive the Holy Spirit, though this was not common in our denomination. We prayed a simple prayer, but it felt like Heaven opened. I felt a fire coming from the top of my head to the soles of my feet like 10,000 volts of electricity. I can still remember the feeling today. I felt this call of God on my life to go to the nations and preach the Gospel. I heard a voice, almost audibly, so clearly that I can still repeat it today, even though I was only 6 years old. I heard the phrase, "Europe shall be saved."

As I grew up, my heart burned to see revival in Europe, to see salvations, healings, signs, and wonders, and to see people cry out for Jesus with the same passion we saw in revivals in South America and Africa. My greatest inspiration was (and still is) my spiritual father and mentor, Reinhard Bonnke, a German evangelist who had a powerful ministry in Africa. I treasure every moment I spent with Reinhard; our relationship deeply impacted my life. He taught me that we need to hear the voice of God for continents. I first met him when I was a young boy. He came to Switzerland each year to share about his work in Africa. I still remember him playing his accordion and carrying the fire of God to our small church in the mountains. As I grew up, we became closer and started organizing events together.

In 1987, Reinhard invited me to the Fire conference in Frankfurt, Germany, with people from nations all over Europe. That conference made me hungry to see more. As Reinhard was sharing his vision for Africa, we declared, "Africa shall be saved." I declared that the first time because I love Reinhard; but the second time I shouted, "Europe shall be saved!" I had this conviction that God would do what He has done in Africa in Europe too. When I came home after the Fire conference, I was ready to rent a soccer field to preach the Gospel. I was so passionate to see revival in Europe. But God told me it wouldn't start with a big event; it would start in the place of prayer. Reinhard also birthed everything in prayer with intercession, before, after, and during all of his events.

Prayer

A few friends and I started a group to pray for revival in an intentional way. We prayed fervently and faithfully in a cold cave in a Swiss village every Saturday morning from 4 a.m. until 8 a.m. I met my amazing, beautiful wife, Josianne, in those meetings. We prayed for ten years every Saturday morning, and once a month from Friday at 8 p.m. through Saturday 8 a.m. We prayed for souls, for the region, and for Europe. This is where I started to get vision for the continent. I do believe what I am experiencing today is what I saw in those prayer meetings. I know prayer was a significant key in the breakthrough we finally entered.

During the same time period, we were working hard in the field trying everything we could think of to share the good news of Jesus. We went to the streets, the bars, the discos, preaching everywhere. We knocked on doors and planted churches. My friends and I went to other ministries to learn new evangelism tools. We tried many techniques and methods.

Then when I was 18, I started having my first miracles and healings services in our little village. About 80 local residents came, and ten or fifteen were saved for the first time. Today, some of those people are leaders in the church. Throughout that time period, people did receive Jesus, but we wanted so many more to encounter Him. Nothing we did brought the major breakthrough we longed to experience.

Then in the year 2000, I went to Lagos, Nigeria, with Reinhard for a historic gathering, his largest crusade. I could hardly believe my eyes when I saw more than 200,000 people on the field they had cleared for the event. I had never seen so many gathered together in one place before. It turned out, that was only the training and prayer meeting for the team that would help with ministry and follow up. That was day one. The next morning, I woke up and looked out my window over Lagos, an expansive city. I could see a big cloud of dust far away, which I later found out was the highway of people making their way to the crusade. The place was absolutely packed. It was incredible.

On the last evening, I walked the grounds to count the people with Peter Vandenberg, the right hand of Reinhard and vice-president of Christ for all Nations (CfaN). They have a very technical and precise way of counting, and we counted more than 1.6 million people, making it the largest gathering in the history of CfaN. Reinhard preached the ABCs of the Gospel and gave a clear altar call for salvation. There were 1,093,000 people who said yes to Jesus and filled out decision cards that night. As they raised their hands, I was crying like a baby. Then the Lord said to me, "One day you're going to see that in Europe." That moment marked my life forever and showed me what was possible.

Reinhard also believed with us for Europe. We spoke about that many times throughout our nearly thirty years of friendship. Reinhard supported me from the very start of my ministry and also when we launched the International Association of Healing

Ministries (IAHM). He came to our first healing conference and many other events. He sowed financially into events and renting stadiums. He was very excited about and proud of what was happening in Europe. He often said that God will do what He did in Africa in Europe and in the United States. He declared along with us, "Europe shall be saved." He died too early, but I do believe in John 12:24: *"unless a grain of wheat falls into the ground and dies, it remains alone; but if it dies, it produces much grain."* What Reinhard carried is being multiplied through thousands of other evangelists like him who are going to shake the whole world. The fruit of his life continues in his legacy.

Going back to my story though, after years of plowing hard ground, finally, a few years ago, something started to shift. In past seasons, when we had meetings in places like France, about twenty people attended. We had to push to get one person to raise her hand for salvation, and it was a little old lady—the same one each night. We went to so many places without seeing much fruit, but we kept preaching and sowing seeds.

Now things feel open and ready in a new way. People are hungry and thirsty for God. The presence of God is more tangible, and people are getting saved, one by one, but also by tens, hundreds, even thousands. Churches are growing, and we see breakthrough in many new regions. Many European leaders affirm that they also feel the shift. They also experience more fruit and more impact. God is moving, and it truly feels like His sovereign time for Europe.

I believe the plowing of so many for all those years in prayer and in faithfulness to keep preaching, no matter how hard it felt, is the reason why we now live in the breakthrough. For me personally, it started in that prayer cave contending for what I walk in today. Prayer is a massive key to revival.

Unity

Another key ingredient I can point to is unity. At first this was painful for me as an evangelical because like most denominations, we tend to think our way of thinking is the best way. As humans, we want to convert people to our theology, to our truth. But I began to realize it is not about one denomination, it is about different denominations coming together to bring the Gospel with power.

When I started working with other streams, I received a lot of criticism. People especially did not understand how I could work together with Catholics. Reinhard supported me and encouraged me to preach the Gospel wherever the door is open. Other spiritual fathers also helped me understand that to bring in the harvest, unity and love for the others is vital. When we travel for ministry, we come with humble hearts, not to teach others what to do, but to help bring the Gospel. We invite everyone to work together, and most people want to. Now, almost everywhere I go, we have some Baptists, Catholics, Mennonites, and others on the platform. Coming together brings strength. Jesus makes this point in John 13:35, *"By this all will know that you are My disciples, if you have love for one another."* Unity strengthens the Gospel message. It is a major key to fruitfulness.

As I worked with many others, and we all experienced the shift in Europe, I began to think more about the continent as a whole. I started to speak with key leaders asking, "We are seeing something fantastic, now what is your strategy to reach Europe?" With full respect for all my friends, no one was working on a continent-wide strategy, including me. All of us had a strategy for our own ministry or a strategy for church planting or for our city, but no one had a strategy to reach Europe. How was that possible? In all of history, a king or an emperor never took a city or a country without a battle plan. I suggested that we sit around a table together and discuss the strategy to reach Europe. Almost everyone was willing to join the conversation, but no one wanted to organize it.

At first, I didn't feel the capacity to take the lead on something so large, but I knew it was God's time for Europe. Then, in 2016, I humbly called together key leaders for a round table meeting focused on strategy for Europe. We had leaders from all around Europe as well as revivalists from other nations. I started with close friends who knew my strengths and weaknesses and ministered with me in the nations. In this heart after unity and strategy, I included a reformed pastor, a Catholic theologian, and even an officer general of the army. I also invited some of my close friends including my pastor, Werner Lehmann, Mattheus van der Steen, who we jokingly call "my twin brother," as well as Paul Manwaring, all the way from the States, and Ben Fitzgerald from Awakening Europe. I invited everyone to Switzerland, and we spent two days praying, seeking the Lord, and sharing our hearts. It was fantastic.

I wanted to hear from every person what they sensed and how we could reach the continent. I shared what I received from the Lord about developing a strategy for Europe, but it was really a collaborative initiative. Powerful ministers, very busy people including Heidi Baker, Daniel Kolenda on FaceTime, Paul Manwaring, Peter Wenz, and Johannes Hartl, said, "We lay down our egos and our logos to work together to reach Europe."

The mission God showed us at the round table was to reach 100 million souls for Jesus in Europe. This vision that came out felt like a birth, and we were the midwives. I believe the seed was planted when I was baptized in the Holy Spirit and fire at age 6, when I first heard that declaration, "Europe shall be saved." This was something prepared by God and in place already, but it became clearer when we came together in those meetings.

Europe Shall Be Saved

We started forming an evangelistic movement, Europe Shall Be Saved, not to be like an organization or denomination that already exists, but to gather the forces together to reach this continent for Jesus. Our focus is on the harvest, and we want everyone to bring their strength. We organized meetings where different groups could come together, build strategy, and share vision. This included evangelism, worship, media, business, and many other areas. The first area we really focused on was prayer, the spiritual Air Force. No army can win a battle or a war without the Air Force. The same is true in the spiritual reality. We know that without prayers, we can never have revival and breakthrough.

The vision for the Air Force actually came to me many years ago when I was in Pemba, Mozambique. Heidi Baker is my spiritual mom, and I love her very much. She invited me to minister in their school and on outreaches. While I was there, I had a powerful vision. I saw 10,000 people with different skin colors from different backgrounds—Chinese, Africans, many Europeans, and also Americans. I heard the sound of these people praying for revival in Europe, asking God to open the doors for Europe. It was not a dream; it was an open vision. When I asked the Lord about it, I sensed Him saying, "That's not the goal, it's just the birth of a major prayer movement in Europe, and that's the way you're going to start, with 10,000 people."

At the strategic round table, this open vision came back to me, and we decided our first initiative should be united prayer. Dr. Johannes Hartl, a general in the spiritual "Air Force" of Europe, agreed to take the lead. He is a Catholic theologian and one of my closest friends. He runs an influential and inspiring 24/7 house of prayer in Augsburg, Germany. Johannes began to intentionally gather other prayer leaders to unify the prayer movement and create vision together for the continent. In March 2017, we called people across Europe to 40 days of prayer and fasting, and more than 10,000 joined us for this powerful time. I firmly believe revival starts with prayer.

The other most important elements of the Europe Shall Be Saved movement are family, unity, and the urgency of the hour. We all love each other. We don't focus on our differences. We enjoy our diversity and work together for our Lord. God is a Good Father, and we are all sons and daughters. God has millions of children, and He loves all of us. He is willing to use all of us. It takes humility to look at our brother or sister and see that though they don't minister like we do, they carry something we don't have, something we can learn from. It takes humility to see others higher than ourselves, but this is exactly what Jesus asks of us.

I sense God is building a family army where every child can sit at the table and express who they are, just like a natural family. My own children are all different, some are quieter, some are noisy, some are more creative or intellectual. When we are together, each one shares and expresses himself or herself. Everyone has a place. On the army side, each person and ministry are vitally needed because there is a huge harvest. There is a multitude of multitudes standing in the valley of decision, and to reach them is a battle. It is very important, especially in this season, that we all seek the Lord about our place.

If we are humble, we will recognize we are not everything. I'm sad when some people think they can be an apostle, a prophet, an evangelist, a teacher, and a pastor. They want to be the whole body of Christ all alone. That is a problem, and it causes division. We need to recognize and give space for each person or ministry to run in their specific giftings, take their places, and be all they are called to be. We need to help, encourage, pray for, and bless each other.

If you are wondering how to join this evangelistic movement and be part of reaching the harvest, it's almost impossible not to join. If you follow Jesus and fulfill His commandments, you will start to love the others, and not just the ones in the same church. You will realize that others with different understanding and different revelation still love the same Jesus. They are your brothers and sisters. When we love each other, it's impossible not to hear the same call of God telling us to go to the harvest field. Go and preach together. Jesus is clear in Mark 16:15-18 when He says:

> *Go into all the world and preach the gospel to every creature. He who believes and is baptized will be saved; but he who does not believe will be condemned. And these signs will follow those who believe: In My name they will cast out demons; they will speak with new tongues; they will take up serpents; and if they drink anything deadly, it will by no means hurt them; they will lay hands on the sick, and they will recover.*

This is our mission, and today it is resonating from Heaven.

I encourage you to pray about your place in this family army and bring your strength. Ask God to show you where He is leading you and what to do. Then join with others and work together in the harvest. When we work together God multiplies our efforts, and we are much more effective. Connect with others in the same city and nation. Learn from each other, support one another with First Corinthians 13 love. If you are a great evangelist, intentionally invite people to help you train and make disciples. Work with others who have different strengths. That's the privilege of being in the family of God. Each one of us will receive something fantastic and unique; and if we give what we have and make it available for others, not just for our own projects, we can reach this continent for Jesus.

Whatever you are doing for God's kingdom, remember that everything starts with prayer. You need people to pray for you before you go, when you're going to work, and when you're preaching the Gospel. In Europe today, I see and experience strong spiritual warfare. To have victory, prayer is a vital key. It is not just the Air Force that is called to prayer. Every believer needs to pray and to consider prayer a privileged discipline. God's presence comes when we pray. We need the Holy Spirit to define the strategy for every city. We need the revelation of God. Let's be like Joshua and Caleb. They saw the fortresses and the giants, but they believed God was bigger than the enemies. If God is for us, who can be against us!

We all need to be prepared and participate. I see the heroes in Hebrews 11. There is a list of men and women of faith who served God and did everything He asked of them. We don't want to go back to the desert and even worse, to go back to Egypt. We want to go to this promised land; and if we have faith, we're going to see it. If we want to be part of this list, some of us will finish as martyrs for the Gospel. Some will overcome and see major breakthroughs in cities and nations. Be strong and courageous and remember Hebrews 12:1-2:

> *Therefore we also, since we are surrounded by so great a cloud of witnesses, let us lay aside every weight, and the sin which so easily ensnares us, and let us run with endurance the race that is set before us, looking unto Jesus, the author and finisher of our faith, who for the joy that was set before Him endured the cross, despising the shame, and has sat down at the right hand of the throne of God.*

The cloud of witnesses is stronger and closer to us than ever before. They are giving us the baton to run, in my opinion, the final race. They are cheering us on, praying for us, and encouraging us. I also feel it's a reset time when we need to get our priorities right and go back to our first love, the Lord. We need to stay focused. One of the top priorities for every believer should be to share the Gospel. There are so many people who need to hear hope; they need to hear that Jesus is alive. He's the answer. They are desperate. Let's follow the heroes who went before us.

Let's be men and women of great faith who see the strongholds and the walls in Europe—and know that God is bigger than any opposition. God is with us, and in Him we are victorious. Do not give up. Run your race. Europe shall be saved!

Part II

VICTORY STORIES FROM EUROPE TO INSPIRE YOUR STORY

Interviews from the Harvest

We live in a special time when God is moving in unprecedented ways. Through the challenges we face globally, we have the great opportunity to be salt and light on this earth. People are ready to receive God's love like never before. As we embrace our role and step boldly into who we are called to be, we will shine like stars in the sky holding firmly to the word of life, as Paul writes about in Philippians 2:15 (New International Version). We are created to shine. You are created to shine.

In the next part of this book, you will read interviews from people in different denominations and European nations. They all said the same thing: God is moving powerfully in this continent, and they are full of hope. Something shifted, and the family of God is growing in a new way. The seeds sown over generations are bearing great fruit here and now. Whether you are from Europe, called to Europe, or just passionate to see God move through your own life, we know these stories will inspire you. They will increase your faith for the continent of Europe and activate you personally in your calling.

When Jesus called Peter and Andrew to be His disciples, He said, *"Follow Me, and I will make you fishers of men"* (Matthew 4:19). They were already fishermen, but now they would "fish" for people. No matter what you are trained in, you are qualified to be a disciple of Jesus. He uses everything in our lives for the purposes of His kingdom. We all have different strengths and passions, which is why we are meant to work together. The body of Christ is made of many parts, each one with its purpose. We are all different; but ultimately, we have the same goal: for people to know Jesus and worship Him together. The methods we use and the styles we enjoy do not have to be the same, instead we honor each other in our diversity. As we all do our part, we will reach many.

We are believing for a movement of people running together, championing one another, and declaring, full of faith, "Europe shall be saved." Many people have seen visions of a huge net gathering in the harvest. We see this as many ministries knit together, pulling in harmony, and bringing in the greatest harvest. Jesus prayed in John 17 that we would be one as He and the Father are one. Let's be the answer to His prayer.

The men and women you will read about trusted God and took Him at His word. When they read the Bible, they knew it was not just a story of the past, but a guidebook for how we are called to live our lives. God is so good. His plans and purposes for each one of us are beyond all we could ask or imagine. Jesus paid everything for us, and we are created to walk in the fullness of His victory on the cross. He said to follow Him, and we would do even greater works.

Maybe you are already seeing amazing things, or maybe you are hungry for more. Maybe you have been a Christian for many years or maybe you just met Him yesterday. No matter what stage you're in, we believe there is always more to learn because there is always more in God.

After each interview, I share summary thoughts and questions to ask ourselves to receive the wisdom each person carries and apply it to our own lives. These are men and women who have seen and experienced powerful things in God. Let their testimonies prophesy hope and faith into your story. Let God move in your heart and fill you with hope for your glorious future. There are topics about your calling, relationships, walking in greater freedom, faith, overcoming disappointment, and so much more. I pray you will be ministered to exactly where you need it the most.

As you read these stories, dream big because nothing is impossible with God. Be inspired and take your place in the harvest.

2

JOHANNES HARTL

Organization: Augsburg House of Prayer
Position: Visionary Leader and Founder
Location: Augsburg, Germany

PERSONAL BACKGROUND

What is your favorite thing to do on your day off?

My favorite things are praying and traveling.

What is your favorite Bible passage or one you appreciate at the moment?

The Bible is a universe. It is a collection of countries, in which I live at different times of my life. If I have to choose one passage right in this moment, I choose Ephesians 2. It combines the view on the person of Jesus with a global and universal picture of God's redemptive plan for all creation. And it does that in very poetic and beautiful language.

Please share about yourself and your journey, including how you came to faith.

I was brought up in a Catholic family, and I had a positive view of Christianity and church. I would say that my first real encounter with God carried the trait of an encounter with beauty. I was not met primarily by the father love of God or by Jesus's word making sense to me, but rather with sheer fascination actually. When I was 14 years old, I was brought to a Christian meeting. I really did not want to attend and thought the meeting was terribly boring. At one point, they offered to pray for people, and I went forward out of sheer boredom. I figured if I had to be stuck there, I might as well receive prayer. I had zero expectations.

When I received prayer, however, I was awestruck. I was struck with a beam of fascination and beauty. I didn't understand what it was. If I can describe it, it was like meeting the most beautiful girl possible and falling in love with her, but there was no girl. This was my first step, and it spiraled me into this search for a way to maintain this fascination. My question was, how can I stay close to the Source of fascination? That brought me very, very quickly into the topic of prayer.

Prayer and a prayer life became my life journey early on when I was a teenager. Out of my prayer life, things started to happen. Other young people around me began to flock together and started to find Jesus too. I didn't intentionally plan to start a youth group, but somehow I found myself leading a group of about 100 or 120 teenagers. That same spark of fascination that had lit up my life was touching other people as well. Out of that, I would say, my life calling and life vocation began. I did my studies, but basically from that early moment with Jesus until what I am doing today, there is a clear trajectory in one direction.

Mission, Vision, and Lessons Learned Along the Way

How did you get from leading the youth group to starting the House of Prayer?

The question, "Where does the power come from?" never stopped fascinating me. Our youth meetings were growing, but we wanted to see more. We started with nights of prayer, 24-hour prayer chains in the late 1990s, and we experienced the sheer power of God. It was very interesting. We had a normal weekly meeting with around thirty teenagers. Then we had two weekend retreats where only our team gathered to fast and pray.

At our next normal youth meeting there was something different, the Holy Spirit fell. During the second song or so, people began to fall down, without anyone touching them. I was the worship leader, and I was actually rather shocked because it's difficult to lead a meeting if virtually everyone is falling down in the Spirit. This was out of my box. I've never been to Toronto. I'm a Catholic guy from Southern Bavaria. Yet there were people going through crazy things like deliverance and really heavy encounters with the Lord. We came to the conclusion that it had something to do with the prayer preparation.

By the early 2000s, since I had experienced the power of prayer firsthand, I already had in my mind that the source of effective evangelism, the source of missions, is prayer. It is definitely prayer. Around this time, I heard about other powerful moves of prayer including the International House of Prayer in Kansas City, 24/7 prayer in the UK, the Prayer Mountains in Uganda, the Prayer Mountains in Korea, and other expressions. I read about all of these movements, and that got me intrigued.

I come from a more monastic tradition. There is a Benedictine monastery founded in AD 766 in my hometown, which was part of my first exposure to Christianity. It is still active today, so it has been a house of prayer for almost 1,300 years now. The idea of people praying continuously in one specific place is not a novel idea, it's a pretty seasoned idea. The house of prayer model with worship and the free flow of prayer was a fresh expression of something ancient. When we started the Augsburg House of Prayer in 2005, it was still the same fascination at the core of it all, combined with my past and present experiences coming together. Then it just grew from there.

You said your first experience of God was an encounter with beauty. I also know you lead a conference called SCHØN, which means "beautiful" in German. Please share about that conference and the relationship between beauty, art, and the pursuit of God.

SCHØN, which means beautiful in German, is a conference of arts. This includes performing arts, video arts, graphics, design, classical music, rock and pop music, poetry, literature... all different spheres, even architecture. Then we have interviews about the interconnection of beauty and spirituality. The event is not so obviously, upfront Christian. We do pray together, but not all of the artists are Christians. We engage in a dialogue around questions such as: What does beauty point to? Where does beauty originate? What does it mean for you? What is the spirituality behind it? Most artists will say there is something bigger even if they don't call themselves religious or Christian...most artists are not atheists. Art can lead us in a very interesting way to ask the deeper questions, where then, as Christians, we claim to have very viable answers.

In terms of the relationship between beauty, art, and the pursuit of God, we see beauty everywhere in nature. It is fascinating to see that birds, flowers, sunsets, and oceans, are not just all gray and pale and ugly. They are tremendously beautiful. That is the first thing. The second thing is human beings create art wherever they come, wherever they go. Even from the prehistoric times, tombs have been found that are painted with artistic murals. From a Christian viewpoint, human beings are made in the image of God. This means human beings have an artistic sense, because they are made by an Artist, in the image of the Artist. Beauty is one of the clearest expressions of humans as image-bearers of God. It is no wonder all the old churches were built beautifully, and the old Bibles were painted in calligraphy. Sadly, in modern times we've lost something of that.

I do believe we have to reclaim beauty in two directions. First, beauty is a natural expression of our love for God. For me, excellence, even in the artistic senses, is where love meets matter. Love is something we can't see, but excellence and beauty are where we see love meeting the material world. This is incarnation. This takes place in real time and space.

Second, human beings have an innate sentiment or openness for beauty. Of course, beauty is not God. They are not the same. That being said, people who would say they are not religious, not interested in the truth, not interested in Jesus, might much more easily say they are fascinated by something beautiful. We have found, especially through the SCHØN conference, that the question of beauty is one of the pathways to open a very good conversation on the good and the real.

PRAYER FOR THE HARVEST IN EUROPE

You were part of the original round table with Jean-Luc to strategize about reaching Europe, and you led the first initiative calling people into 40 days of prayer. Please share about your heart to call people into prayer for Europe.

As a movement, our desire is to engage people with the bigger picture of Europe being saved, to focus on the harvest. We create different spheres of application, where people can be part of this mission. Prayer is an easy way to get involved. We found out it is far from normal for people to intercede for Europe. Many Christians don't even have a view for intercession. Either they don't even believe or don't even know that God actually answers prayer. He invites us to partner with Him in prayer, to join His effort of bringing His kingdom down on earth. Other people simply don't have a vision for Europe. They might have a vision for their own church, their own family, but not for Europe. Our goal is first to inspire and then to invite people into practical applications, like the 40 days of prayer for Europe.

We also provide resources for people to learn more and walk this out individually or as a group in their context. In the area of prayer, we teach on many forms of prayer. This includes declaration. Declaring is a form of prayer unknown to many Christians, the concept that we can declare something, not just petition God. We can also fast. We can ask for certain things. We can combine prayer with fasting. We can combine prayer with worship and with declaration of the Bible. There are many ways to pray and many things to learn together through intentional corporate prayer.

To summarize, as the Europe Shall Be Saved movement, we desire to work in unity, learn from each other, and join together in common initiatives that are relevant for the salvation of Europe. Prayer is a powerful area where this can be applied.

How does prayer connect specifically with evangelism?

In the parable of the sower in Matthew 13, Jesus used the metaphor of a farmer throwing seeds to teach about evangelism. If a farmer wants a good crop, he needs to prepare the soil. He can't just throw out the seeds or they will be eaten up. They will fall on rocky soil or be choked by weeds. He has to prepare the soil first, and this is actually what prayer does. Then the proclamation of the Word doesn't fall into a void, into an empty space, but enters an interaction with the constitution of a human person. This person might be more or less open. There are people who are ready, they've been waiting; and there are people who are not ready at all, they have no idea. Every evangelist knows the situation.

There is a difference between prepared and unprepared soil. An evangelist can go to a congregation or an event and sense whether the place feels prepared or not. This is what prayer does, it prepares the ground. We see this concept clearly in the Book of Acts. Paul prayed all the time. We see the early church praying all the time. In his letter to the Colossians, Paul wrote, *"praying also for us, that God would open to us a door for the word, to speak the mystery of Christ, for which I am also in chains"* (Colossians 4:3). This is interesting—isn't there always an open door? Obviously not. Obviously not if he asks them to pray for God to open a door for the word. Obviously, there are certain seasons.

Do you find that Christians can be overly focused on one area (such as evangelism or prayer), rather than seeing the bigger picture of working together?

I would say yes, it's true that people can be focused on one area. I do know many people who want to evangelize but underestimate the importance of prayer. I see that. Do I see a big prayer movement that is insulated from or unaware of the necessity of evangelism? Not so much. Because in the West, we are a very prayerless church. Our danger is not that we pray all the time and never evangelize. This is a very rhetorical, very illusionary idea. I would say rather the opposite is true. Once you pray, opportunities to evangelize will come naturally. Whereas if you only evangelize or only build churches, the possibility to lose spiritual depth is very high. That's when people burn out and people are shot down in the mission field, so to say. We need the combination of the active and the passive or contemplative. Church building, the missions movement, evangelism, and discipleship are more outward oriented, while prayer is more inward. We need to have a balance of both directions.

This is not just a consideration in Christianity, it is a normal human problem. In large organizations or companies, the salesperson doesn't always communicate with the accountant. They feel worlds apart, each in their silo. The church is also an organization. To ameliorate this, it is always helpful to understand the "why" behind the "what." The salesperson and the accountant both serve a customer who eventually buys a product, which is inherently good, in the positive. They need to work together toward this purpose.

As a movement, when we bring back the "why" behind the "what," everything makes sense. Of course, we pray because we want to see this continent change. Of course, we evangelize, but if we want to see this continent change, we are going to need prayer and evangelism working together, not one or the other. We will also need churches and networks of discipleship. Puzzle pieces fall back into place.

You discovered the power of prayer early on as a key to experiencing the power of God. Are there other keys you've discovered for those hungry for awakening and revival?

Yes, I can name several important elements from my experience. The first one is a positive view on a society. I am not suggesting we must say everything is fine in our society, but there are many Christians who are living in a bunker mentality. It seems like they are trying to never leave their own bubble. Even in the midst of crisis, there are real people out there, so let's engage with normal people and not isolate ourselves. Start a conversation. Don't just spend time with other Christians speaking Christianese. For me, it was a very important step to do my PhD in philosophy to actively engage with current culture. Our accessibility and language are key factors in relating to current society in a positive way.

The second thing, perhaps obvious, is we need to know our Bible. The first point was to be approachable by the culture, but the second point is we have to be strong in what we believe. There are so many Christians, especially in the West, who have been messed up with really bad theology. Many do not have the type of biblical formation that was common, say, one or two generations ago, especially in the United States. I have found the Bible is a well-hidden treasure that is so unknown to many people. So, knowing the Bible is the second key.

The third thing I recommend is excellence in leadership. Many Christians fail to strive for excellency, especially pertaining to the church. I don't really understand that. There is a double standard. In the professional world, we all expect each other (and ourselves) to excel and perform, in fact it is required. Then we go to church and expect to live a cozy life. I am not trying to be negative here, but I've seen church culture in Europe really suffering under almost the dogma of a lack of excellency.

There is a famous saying from the Jewish philosopher Martin Buber: "Success is not one of God's names." This is true, but in my opinion, it is one of the most abused quotes ever. Yes, success is not a name of God, but excellency might be one of God's names. If we never have success, if we never see fruitfulness, this is a very dangerous sign. If the things we are doing are not producing any fruit, we need to question what we are doing.

Then the fourth and final thing I would add is having a generous heart, a welcoming spirit, and a culture of friendship, honor, love, and unity. Unity is not the hesitation or the neglect of speaking out for what we believe, and it is not fuzziness in our theology. That is not what I am talking about. I would describe unity as majoring on the majors and not on the minors, being precise on what unites us, and leaving openness on the fringes. Sometimes we do the opposite. We major on the minors. We take small, small differences and make them big—big enough to separate us. What unites us is much stronger than what divides us. But living out unity has more to do, not with theology, but rather with a non-competitive mindset of servanthood and a culture of family. Those are the four keys I would name for awakening.

Wonderful. Will you explain more about excellency in the church? Are you referring to the church leadership or also the members? What would it look like to pursue excellency in the church context?

A leader always creates culture. When you lead something, excellency is your responsibility. Your core values and your working mentality will always determine the mentality and the culture of the company. That means if you want excellency, you have to start with yourself. If you don't know where to start, I suggest getting yourself a coach. I benefited from professional mentoring and coaching. Study companies and organizations. Get proper training. There is nothing wrong with learning from non-Christians, or Christians working in other industries, like business, politics, or the automobile industry. Be a better leader yourself. Learn what you need to learn. Excellence always creates an upward spiral of excellence, whereas lacking excellence always creates a downward spiral of bad quality.

Let me give you an example. Imagine there is someone in your church who is not a great singer or guitar player, but the person wants to lead worship on Sunday mornings. If you allow this, two effects will happen. First, those who are musically gifted will be appalled and leave. And then the only ones remaining are those who cannot tell the difference. They will feel emboldened to also demand a microphone, to also demand a position for which they are not gifted. This is the downward spiral of bad quality.

But there's an upward spiral of excellence as well. When people serve in the areas they are gifted and prepared for, two things will happen. For the sake of our example, now imagine a talented musician leading worship. Others will see that the person is very gifted and decide not to join the worship team if they aren't musically gifted. This is good. A clear evaluation of who you are and who you are not is just wisdom. The second thing is they will try to find out what they are good at and maybe even get some training. Now, we have an upward spiral of people who can tell the difference in quality, and others will flock to that congregation. They will notice there are gifted people, and they will want to bring their gifts too.

If you want excellence, you have to lead like that. But it will cost you. It will cost you some sympathy because people are not used to this approach. Some people believe in order to belong, they have to have a position. They have to hold a microphone on a stage. The reality is, no, they don't. They really don't. That's a mentality that doesn't have a lot to do with the Holy Spirit giving gifts to people. That's more of a position-oriented mentality.

FINDING YOUR PLACE

It is powerful when everyone finds their place and excels. Your calling seemed to come about in a very natural way, you mentioned a clear trajectory from your first encounter to the present. Please give advice for those who are still trying to figure out their calling or who have some ideas but are not sure how to get there.

My advice would be to look for one or two other people with a similar passion. Meet together once a week and read books or listen to teachings and get inspired. You can visit places to get inspired as well, like other ministries or events. Your group can be set up however you want, in person or online, but it should be a small, active group. That is how I started. The thing is, most people you meet, even most Christians you meet, will probably not be on fire. Most people just live their lives. But you can find one or two people who are on fire as well. If you gather and you keep the fire burning, you feed your fire with a constant flow of inspiration. Then the fire will grow, and eventually more people will come. At least that was my experience. Just maintaining the fire over the course of months and years is already a great thing to do. It is worthwhile.

Do you have a testimony to share from your life of stepping out in an initiative or project that felt risky or big, but went very well?

I will tell you the most recent story, which was the project Germany Prays Together. I was approached by two or three super prophetic people. They said, "Johannes, next week is Pesach and Easter, and we have to call Germany together." People have been telling me to bring Germany together in prayer for some years now, but I never felt like it was the Kairos moment. I didn't want to make a widespread call and end up with our little denominational stream. I spent several days praying about this and had the feeling now it actually was the right time. We started the project, Germany Prays Together, and within two or three days, we were overwhelmed by the positive reactions. The president of our state of Bavaria decided to officially sponsor the initiative and members of the German parliament joined us. It was on the front pages of two of the largest news outlets in Germany. Many joined from different denominations and movements.

It was very risky because once you step out, you get a lot of bad press as well and a lot of attacks. I think we were protected, but it was still a challenge. We didn't know how it would go. In the end, it exceeded our expectations. We assume up to one million people joined the prayer day (online), and people began approaching me on the street as "the guy from Germany Prays Together." Something remarkable happened. Then, on the same date as the prayer event, the COVID-19 curve started to go down in Germany. It was the first day the number of recovered people overtook the number of new infections. I don't claim this is because we prayed, that would be too simplistic, but we found it as a kiss from Heaven that things shifted on the day we prayed.

You mentioned something interesting, that in the past people approached you about a united German prayer initiative, and you pondered the idea, but it didn't feel like the right moment. Then, this time it was the Kairos moment. How do you know when it is the right timing for an idea?

There are two main things that have to come together for me to see there is a leading of the Holy Spirit. First, Jesus gives us peace, and second, He is constant. So, the first advice is you should never do something that you don't have peace about. I'm not talking about a good feeling in the moment, but remaining, lasting peace. That is one of the strongest evidences of God's leadership. I have felt God's peace even in decisions that hurt me or that I didn't like. They cost me something, but still I felt God's peace.

The second thing is normally God doesn't speak only once— He speaks through the mouth of two or three witnesses. Normally an impression comes over and over and over, and then I realize He is really trying to get my attention. I do believe if you pray enough, if you really have a prayer life, and if you listen to good counsel, and if you only go forward when you have peace, you will have a chance of maybe 80 percent of actually doing something good. We prophesy in part, so we'll never have 100 percent success. We always need correction and sometimes we miss it. That's normal. But we grow better the more we follow Jesus's peace and consistency.

Have you had an experience when you felt like you were going in the right direction and you thought that Holy Spirit was leading, but things did not go as you hoped?

In 2017, there were two very significant things that did not take place in the way I was expecting. The first one was a production for a secular mainstream TV network in Germany. The second was the purchase of a large piece of land close to our House of Prayer. Both things are not off the table forever, but in a matter of some weeks, both projects fell apart. Both were very, very, very promising. I thought we had heard from God, and this was really coming. Then in a matter of weeks, it was clearly not going to happen. The crazy thing is we had a peace about it; so it was a disappointment, but there was also peace.

Looking back, I would say these two things coming to pass back then would have killed me. Not literally, but it was not the right timing. Now, I believe it was a Divine stop, though I still don't have the answers. I don't understand why it happened the way it did. We really had the impression we had to push through and would see these things work out. But looking back, I'm pretty happy about the way things didn't take place. I've seen similar situations many times. Many times. For example, someone wants to buy a house, and he prays about it. He prays about it, but it's not happening. One month later, something else opens up, which is much better, and he is so happy he didn't get the first one. I've prayed long enough to be thankful for all the times when God didn't answer my prayers, because I've prayed for stupid things, as probably every Christian has. The Lord answers prayer, but sometimes the answer is no.

That's great advice and perspective. It sounds like you navigated those situations very well on a heart level, but sometimes disappointments really are, well, disappointing. We can become confused and frustrated even at God. What is your advice for people who are wrestling with disappointment?

The first thing is to realize that you've probably done nothing wrong. Don't beat yourself up because nowhere in the Bible can you find Jesus speaking about us never having to suffer if we follow Him, or saying God punishes us because we've done something wrong. Don't beat yourself up, be patient with yourself.

The second piece of advice is to take some time. Because for the human soul to go through a severe crisis drains a lot of energy. You need to be patient with yourself if you can't work properly or carry on as though nothing happened. Sometimes we are so cruel. We expect ourselves to work as if we were machines, but you are no machine. You're a sentient, a feeling being, so sometimes you just need time. And sometimes God also needs time. Yes, He's the Comforter, but the ways He comforts are different. Sometimes between the sadness and the comfort lies some time. He knows best why.

The third tip would be don't make big decisions in a moment of acute crisis. Don't make big decisions, and don't rewrite your theology. This is just bad timing to make big statements about your life and about God. Don't believe everything you think. If you're sad, if you're disappointed, that is how you feel. Feelings are not bad. We are feeling beings, but thoughts can be right and wrong. You should not believe every thought you think, especially if you're in panic mode, and especially if you're going through hell, you probably have thoughts that are not trustworthy.

Next advice: do not stay alone. Call somebody. If it is really heavy, get professional help. There is nothing wrong, there is nothing unworthy, nothing shameful in going to a therapist or getting professional help. Christians can go see counselors. This is just not a problem. If you don't need a counselor, ask one or two good friends to pray for you. These should be people with whom you can be really honest and completely open.

Last advice, inspired by Winston Churchill's quote, "If you're going through hell, keep going." Don't get stuck. Don't stop. Because the truth is, you might not see it in the moment, but this too shall pass. That is true. We have all been through a crisis; and looking back, we can often say it was an important time. It wasn't a nice time. But looking back we say, wow, it made me stronger.

The problem is we never know when it's going to end, so the only thing that we can do is try to live one single day. People put in isolation and jails as prisoners of war, in torture chambers, or in concentrations camps used this method. I met some of those people; this is how they survived. You survive one single day, and then you survive one single day. Looking back, you're probably going to say this time was not worthless. We are not always good at evaluating our own situation in the present moment. We are better at looking back. Looking back, we see God was faithful. God had His reasons. He didn't always do what we hoped He would do, but He was still faithful.

How do you stay connected to God in those moments when there can be a tendency to draw away or distrust the Lord in times of disappointment and confusion?

I've found that I'm far worse off without Him. You can do that, if you're already in desperation, if you're already in depression, you can try to do it without God, but I cannot recommend it. Many people don't understand how tender He is. Jesus didn't say, come to Me, all you who have no problems. Come to Me, all ye perfect. No. If you've messed up, if you're really overwhelmed with things that you've done wrong or people who wronged you or whatever else you face, He says, "Come to Me, and I will give you rest." That's what Jesus said. Sometimes we believe we have to be good enough to be pleasing to God. We think we have to get our act together before we can approach Him, but this is not right. We never get our act together without help, especially if we are really in a mess.

In the 12-step program of Alcoholics Anonymous and other addition programs, the first step is to admit that you're overwhelmed. I love that. It is a capitulation actually. It is saying, "I wave the white flag. I'm done. I can't control this anymore." The second step is to ask God for help, which is so beautiful. You don't have to get your act together. The Gospel is not for the perfect ones. It's really for the broken and for the poor ones—but you have to admit it, say you're overwhelmed. You can't handle it anymore. And then you ask, "God, would You please help me?" With those two postures, we can get through a lot of mess.

MAINTENANCE TO MISSION

Another topic we're exploring throughout this book is the difference between maintenance Christianity, just going to church on Sundays, versus mission-focused Christianity, living with the mission of Jesus. How can we implement this individually and organizationally?

On an individual level this is much easier because we live a pretty connected life nowadays. The probability that people already have social contact with others who believe something completely different is higher than any time in human history before. Young Christians are in situations to, as 1 Peter 3:15 says, "always be ready to give a defense to everyone who asks you a reason for the hope that is in you." They are constantly in that situation. They only need to be encouraged and to be given language, to be given models, of how they can live that out. Overall, this is rather easy.

The more difficult part, I would say, is finding places to connect people who are interested in faith that won't put them off. Then we speak about church planting or discipleship models, but we also have great opportunities in that direction. In the situation with COVID-19 and the effects on society, we see everyone is looking for answers. Everyone is looking for hope and people are very open. I personally do believe that openness to hear the Gospel will increase in the next years, even in Europe. That is my assumption.

Organizationally, there are very good models. In Europe I can point to the Anglican church in the UK. They are moving in a very good direction as it pertains to reshaping a church in the way of a missional church. In the Catholic church, I am part of a project called Mission Manifest, which is basically a call for the church to refocus on mission. There are initiatives taking place in other churches as well. There are fresh expressions like the Alpha Course. There are models that are easy to apply in the structural setting of a large church. I see good developments happening, but it can be a slow process.

EUROPE FOCUS

What do you see God doing in Europe in this generation?

I see three things. The first is that the level of unity is growing. Perhaps not as fast as we might hope, but it is definitely growing, which is very encouraging. The second is that the level of willingness to evangelize is pretty high, especially among young people. Most people want to see change and quite naturally share their faith in Jesus with others. I see that all over, and I see that as very positive. The third is that the level of prayer is rising, slightly. Connected to this is a fresh wave of worship and a shift in emphasis. Where twenty or thirty years ago many Christians would view their Christianity mainly based around regulations and what is necessary to believe in order to be saved, the young people in this "generation of worship," if you will, tend to be more to the other extremes. This has pros and cons of course. But the good thing about this shift is they believe we can and must experience God, and prayer and worship is a pathway into experiencing God. These are three positive trends I see in Europe.

In more of a political landscape, there is dialogue centering on questions like: What can be the sources for Europe? What are the spiritual wellsprings of our society? This dialogue is open again, and it is very important. It is answered in different ways in Eastern European nations than it is in Germany or France. Each country has its own perspectives. But I think that dialogue is about to gain momentum, and it is a very good discourse.

Are there specific countries you see God highlighting through Europe?

This might be my national view, of course, but I do believe Germany is a very decisive nation. Whenever Germans do something bad, they do it big time, right? If Germans start a war, it becomes a world war. If Germans start a theological innovation, it ends up a worldwide reformation. I feel Germany is a much fought-over nation, so it is not always easy, but it is also a decisive nation. God is doing something good in Germany. There are also bad things happening. My spiritual perspective is that the way Germany goes will always have an effect on the way Europe goes. Therefore, I am concerned, but also optimistic about Germany's path.

UNITY

How can we work toward more unity? How do we build unity when we have differences theologically?

I suggest two main things. The first is to go drink some coffee. Actually meet somebody. Sometimes we just write books or write blogs about other Christians. Do you know any personally? Go and look for Christians of other denominations in your city.

The second is to do something that you can do together. There is certainly something you can do together. If you have different understandings of the Eucharist, then don't take the Eucharist together. Maybe you can worship together or have a prayer time.

Maybe you can do something good in a social way. There are poor people in your city, and they don't care if you are Protestant or Catholic. They have real needs. There are women going through the question of abortion, perhaps children in foster care. Whatever area you choose, people in need do not need your theology as much as they need real answers.

The beauty of unity is that once we come together, we have visibility to the world. This is what Jesus speaks about in John 17, to paraphrase: "Make them one so that the world sees." This is what we are experiencing with the Germany Prays Together initiative. We would never have politicians and people from the public sphere getting behind an initiative like that if it was done by only one organization. They would not care. They would not want to be part of something polarizing. But if we stay together, this has a visibility. So I encourage you to drink some coffee, make some friends, and do together what you can do together. Start anywhere.

LIFE APPLICATION—THE BEAUTY OF INTENTIONALITY

In this interview, a major theme that stands out is intentionality. We have the opportunity to be intentional in every area of our lives, whether that pertains to pursuing our calling, working together, building unity among denominations, growing as a leader, or even overcoming disappointments. Another theme is prayer—its importance, its role, and the power it carries for all of us individually and corporately.

Let's look closer at intentionality. Johannes's calling as a leader in the prayer movement in Europe developed over time, but he also took intentional steps. Johannes remembers the monastery from his childhood, then the prayer meetings of his youth where Holy Spirit fell, followed by his personal interest in and study of prayer movements. This journey eventually led him to start the Augsburg House of Prayer. He was intentional in following this path and seeking God along the way. When he became a leader, he sought out coaching and learned needed skills. When positioning others, he works to help people find the right role based on their gifts and passions to create an environment of excellence.

Johannes intentionally works with Christians in other areas, such as evangelists. Prayer opens hearts for the Gospel and makes evangelism more effective. We are the body of Christ, and no part can succeed all alone. We need each other. Johannes is also intentional about unity. He gives easy, practical tips: have coffee with someone, do a social project with another denomination, bless your city together. It can be big or small, but be intentional about unity.

In terms of prayer, we are all called and invited to pray. Prayer is communication with God. Through prayer, we build our relationship with God, receive His comfort, sense His leadership in our decisions, and experience more of His kingdom. Both Jean-Luc and Johannes highlight prayer as a major key to experiencing Holy Spirit and awakening. There is great power in personal and corporate prayer. Please join us in praying for the harvest in Europe and in your nation!

Johannes gives advice about finding and pursuing our calling: find friends who share the same passion as you. Meet together regularly; again, be intentional. Keep the fire burning together. Do you have this in your life? If not, ask God to highlight people with similar callings. When we work together, we strengthen and encourage one another, and our ministry is much more effective.

Johannes also recommends following peace and getting wise counsel. Usually if God is speaking something, it will come from several directions, not just one time. As you look at your life, what makes you come alive? What are your giftings? What areas has God highlighted in several seasons and in different ways? Who can you run with? These questions will help lead you to your calling or to the initiatives God has for you. As you ponder and pray over this, I know God will guide you and help you find your place in the harvest.

3

Ben Fitzgerald

Organization: Awakening Europe
Position: Director
Location: Lörrach, Germany

Personal Background

What is your favorite thing to do on your day off?

I enjoy driving in my car, talking to God while I drive. I love being out in nature in beautiful places. I also enjoy playing golf. Even in that, I talk to God in the golf cart and ask Him what shot to hit. And when Dylan, one of my employees, beats me, that keeps me humble....

Who inspires you and why?

All of the biblical characters, but King David inspires me most because of his attentiveness to and his guarding of the presence of God in his personal life. In Psalm 16 he says, *"I won't even take the names of other gods on my lips."* The extremity of his conviction about how much he wanted to please the Lord constantly is powerful. David is a real hero to me.

My modern-day hero would be Reinhard Bonnke whose determination and simple obedience were unquestionable. I've never met another human being as possessed by one simple fivefold calling. He was absolutely possessed by evangelism, by the call to save souls. When I spent time with Reinhard, there wasn't any small talk. He was always sharing testimonies or vision. Billy Graham is also a real hero for me. Two other heroes are Heidi Baker and Basilea Schlink, a German nun who has gone home to be with the Lord. People like her, who fully devoted their lives to loving Jesus, inspire me.

Please tell us about yourself and how you came to faith.

I had run far away from God because my dad committed suicide when I was 10 years of age. After a mission trip to Africa, he suffered from schizophrenia. We prayed every night for his deliverance and truly believed he would be healed. We hadn't left our home overnight for several years, but finally my mother decided to take us kids on a fishing trip. I was so excited. Just before we left, my dad sat me down at the kitchen table and began to cry. He was very warm and said, "Ben, when you go away tonight, catch me a fish."

On the trip, I actually caught a little fish and couldn't wait to show my dad. When we got home, I ran inside holding my fish yelling, "Dad, Dad!" but he didn't answer. I ran into his bedroom and found him lying there, cold, dead. I took off running for hours. The police had to come find me. Everyone was broken and devastated, but in my heart, I couldn't believe he was really dead, and so I just ran. I was so affected. After the funeral, something inside me went dead, the grief hit me, and I just kept running. From that point on, I was gone. I was out.

By the age of 14, I was so rebellious that I was kicked out of school and left home. I wouldn't go anywhere near my mother, and I had turned my heart against God. I started dealing drugs, basically just to make money, and then by age 18, became addicted to prostitutes. My girlfriend and I lived with other drug users and dealers. I spent a lot of time in nightclubs and pool bars. I was using whatever I could to try to find value. I pretended I was tough, but inside, that little 10-year-old boy was still running.

Then one night, it was as though my eyes were opened. I remember the moment very clearly. I was in the dark corner of a nightclub, looking around at people dancing intimately, and I thought, *I'm not made for this. This is not how we were meant to be.* I felt something was really wrong—it all felt so fake. I had to get out of there. When I got home, I lit up a cigarette and sat down alone in the dark. No one was home, it was just me and the light of a cigarette. Then the Lord Jesus came into my lounge room.

My whole spirit began to tremble, and I felt something was there. I knew it was God. I heard His voice so loudly in my heart saying my name, "Ben." It went right through me. I was confused at how His voice could be inside me since I wasn't a Christian. Then He called me "Son," and His voice broke through all of my emptiness and all of my running. I was filled with overwhelming love and purpose. It was like the voice had known me my whole life, but I hadn't known Him. He spoke to me (in my thoughts) for about an hour about Paul the apostle, my life, forgiveness...heaps of stuff.

At that point, I didn't pray any special prayer, but I responded to Him talking to me. I woke up the next day with a hunger to go to church and read the Bible. I also wanted to speak to my mother again. Before that, I had never wanted to talk to her because she would tell me she was praying for me and that God told her I would be an evangelist. She honestly scared me. She was God's secret weapon: nothing can stand against a praying mother.

Everything changed the moment God spoke to me. I believe that's when I was born again—when I responded to His voice. A couple of weeks later, I got fully baptized by the Holy Spirit. I went to church and prayed to accept Jesus and got baptized. That was my conversion. My experience was like Paul's. He was thrown off his horse, became blind, then Ananias prayed for his sight, and straightaway he went and testified what had happened. That's kind of what happened to me. I began to testify to people about what Jesus did for me and what He was speaking. And I couldn't stop reading the Bible. I was reading about four to five hours a day. It caused chaos in the house after that, and it wasn't easy to live there. I wasn't fully sanctified yet. From there, it was still a bit of a journey.

MISSION, VISION, AND LESSONS LEARNED ALONG THE WAY

That is a powerful testimony. Praise God! And how did the vision for Awakening Europe begin?

I had been living in the United States for seven years. I was serving as a pastor at Bethel Church. Then, in 2014, my friend

Todd White and I were on a ministry trip in Germany. We were standing on a field in Nuremberg and God began to speak about what He wanted to do in the continent. He showed me a vision of different people coming from all over Europe, and they were crying out to God, "God, would You take back Europe?" In that moment, my whole life changed. Something changed in my heart toward Europe, and God began to call me toward the continent and to the European people. I feel in my blood, that's part of who I am now. Europe is part of my nature. I'm called and convicted to be there. I know that God is going to take back millions of people in the continent for His glory.

What do you see God doing through Awakening Europe?

Through Awakening Europe, God is doing exactly that— He is awakening European people. He is awakening His church to realize that He has given them a mandate to be exactly where they are. Where they were born, where they live, where God placed them in their daily life, is not by accident. They are not alive in Europe by coincidence. He has placed them there to shine. What good is it if a lamp is hidden under a basket? No one can see the light. God is awakening His people to shine. European people are becoming missionaries to Europe. God is turning their hearts back to their own families and friends who are not saved. God is awakening His bride to actually love the continent where they're living rather than look at the darkness or the increase of humanism and decide to become missionaries in foreign countries.

We are seeing people who have never before shared the Gospel, or who rarely ever shared their faith, go on the streets with 10,000 other people in European cities. It's historic to have that many people on the streets sharing the Gospel in Europe. God is bringing people together through Awakening Europe where there is no denominational boundary. They are coming together for the mission of exalting and proclaiming the name of Jesus in Europe and contending for their city. We've seen that as we've gone from Nuremberg to Stockholm, then to Prague, Riga, and Vienna. We've seen people from different denominations come together for their own country, and then begin to work sustainably and perpetually after that. People have started outreaches and haven't quit them in three years. We've seen a lot of things like that take place. Again, that's only by God's hand. When we pray and contend, "God, awaken Your people," He moves hearts back toward their purpose for living.

The second thing we've seen is thousands of people who've never met God turn to God. We've probably seen somewhere around 4,000 or 5,000 new believers turn to the Lord in Europe, which is amazing. That's thousands of people out of hell who were potentially headed to hell. That's just so, so huge. So when people say it is hard to see European people saved, we can say in a few years' time, we have seen a megachurch worth of people turn to Jesus. God is doing that, not just through us, He's doing that through many ministries. We are just one piece of the puzzle. It is shockingly amazing to me how God is saving people in Europe. He's taking back His people.

Why do you think God is moving powerfully here and now through Awakening, specifically?

It is hard to answer that about our own ministry, but I would say God is moving powerfully through Awakening because our team is really hungry. When we go into these events, we pray every day and ask God to touch that nation. We fast. We seek Him. I think it is the response to how much hungrier God is for the people of that country. I would say He's blessing Awakening because we're taking simple steps of faith when He speaks, and we're responding to His hunger with our own. When you put the hunger of man and the hunger of God together, it's like an explosion.

But let me be clear, when we see a crowd of 20,000 people crying out to God, and the worship goes an hour and a half over, and the crowd begins to lead the people, this one statement constantly comes to my heart and to our team: "It's God in the people." It's God drawing people. I believe it's successful because we're giving space, not just for us to tell them what to do, but for God to actually awaken His own people.

Rather than wanting God to follow our plans, we're trying to follow what He is doing. Some people think church is for people, or we need to cater to the five people who don't know God yet. But for us in Awakening Europe, everything we do as a ministry is first unto God. In worship or adoration, our posture is: "God, we're doing this for You. We want Your name to be glorified and Your presence to be honored in Europe." I believe that's why God pours out like He does in Awakening, people are drawn, and thousands get saved. We're not worried about the opinions of the minority. We minister to the Lord. Then He can take care of those few people who get offended.

A good example of this is Latvia. On the last night of Awakening Latvia, worship went on for nearly three hours. Then, in the five-minute altar call, more than one hundred people raised their hands. We heard the stories of people who brought a friend that night and the friend stayed through two hours and forty-five minutes of worship and was actually in awe, wondering what was going on. They didn't leave. God knows how to keep people. Our ministry is really, first and foremost, a ministry to Him. We focus on worshipping Him. Worship is always the marking point of Awakening.

EVANGELISM FOCUS

I know you are passionate about training people and ministries to grow in evangelism. Please share your heart behind this.

We want to help people get out of the place of just living their daily lives and move into a place of daily living with intention and bringing the Good News to people. We provide simple tools of how to start, even for those who have never shared their faith before. We go after the fear of human opinion, and then we also go after the disqualifying lies that tell people, "You're not good at this. You're not good at speaking," or, "It's not your role." We do evangelism training in person or online in many contexts as well as through video teachings. Through this training we equip people. We hear many testimonies of people stepping out and sharing their faith at work or on the streets. These are moms, people who work at an office, young people, older people…not just people you would see on a stage preaching. We love hearing these stories. It doesn't need to be big. We do big once or twice a year. Small obedience is big to God.

What advice do you give people who are nervous but want to start sharing their faith more? Where do you start? What are some tips we can apply to our lives?

You start by starting. There's no formula for that. I encourage people to go to a coffee shop or a supermarket every day or every couple of days. Then just tell someone about God when you feel a prompting toward them. Say something like, "Excuse me, my name is so-and-so." The worst thing that can happen is they say, "Do I know you?" Then you can just respond, "No, I don't know you yet, but I want to tell you, God knows you, and Jesus loves you." And often they'll say something like, "That's so crazy. Why would you say that? That's amazing. I had the worst day ever."

That often happens to me and to many people on our team. People respond, "I had a terrible day. I really needed to hear that message." We simply tell people, "Jesus cares about you, can I pray for you? God loves you." You'd be surprised what's on the other end of "excuse me" when you talk to someone. Start with just saying hi to someone and sharing the love of Jesus.

Maybe some reject you, but maybe they will be extremely touched as the love of God reaches through their walls making them feel seen and loved. It's important in our generation not to be moved by the fear of people, not to be pushed around by human opinion. After all, why should we really be concerned about a moment of human rejection when we've been fully accepted by God for the rest of eternity? Let's not put the opinions of people who don't understand who God is yet above God's desire to love them and reach them. When you feel the fear of rejection, just step forward in faith anyway.

There is also a strong connection between prayer and evangelism. We can share God's love with anyone and everyone, but we see that some people are more open and ready to receive the Gospel. We love to pray and ask God to lead us to those who are ready to receive. I also encourage making a list of three people in your life who are not saved yet and praying for them daily. Write their names on your mirror. Pray that God will open their hearts to His love and pray you will have opportunities to share with them. I have incredible testimonies from doing this simple act.

Please share a testimony from one of your events.

After one of our Awakening events, we did a mass baptism with over a hundred new believers coming to get baptized. A woman in her 40s came forward, and we asked if it was her first time giving her life to God or if she was rededicating. She shared that she accepted Jesus for the first time in her life at the last night of our Awakening event. We asked how she decided to come to the event. Then she said, "Yesterday, seven people gave me free tickets to the event, so I thought I should come." Those seven people who simply handed her a free ticket didn't necessarily know each other. They might not have even known she got saved or baptized. We can all be part of someone's story. Sometimes you are at the beginning, sometimes you are at the end. Paul said it like this: one sows, one waters, God brings the increase. You never know what part your small step of obedience is going to be in someone's life.

How can the person reading this personally enter into a mission-driven life rather than just maintaining his or her faith? What questions can each of us ask?

The best question you can ask is, "Is Jesus in this?" If you're doing something because you know you're supposed to or you are doing it out of habit or you are just going to church Sunday and Wednesday to maintain your Christian walk, is that the fullness Jesus has for you? When you ask yourself if Jesus is in it, if you feel like you're being robbed of the secret place, then no, Jesus is not in that. If you feel bound by fear and you can't stop someone on the street to share Jesus, would Jesus be in that? Is He in that fear? No.

An important question to ask: "Is this what Jesus would do? Is Jesus inside this?" Whenever it's Jesus, when it's about loving Him, when it's about obedience to Him and sharing Jesus with someone, you live with His mission. His heartbeat becomes part of your life. It's not maintaining, it's a relationship with Him, and that is way easier. It's actually much harder to maintain things than to live on a mission with a purpose.

Personal Freedom

Another thing I know you are passionate about is helping people get set free and live holy lives. What is your advice to people who want to experience this freedom?

It took me a while. Here's one piece of advice: the cleaner and quicker the cut, the better—even if it feels hard. For me, I sort of dragged it out a bit. I didn't want to move out of the house with my girlfriend, so I stumbled at times. I knew it was sin. I'd be grieved and run, weeping, to the altar of the Baptist church I was attending. They would pray for me, and they knew I was sorry. I was sorry. In hindsight, if I had broken off our relationship immediately, I wouldn't have had to drag her and others through the process. I wouldn't have been caught in the temptations. It might have hurt me initially. It might have even hurt her. But, if I could take it back, the first moment I was saved I would have moved out of that house, and I would have cut off everything that looked like sin.

I had good leaders though. They began to speak into that after a few months and helped me. I would say this to anyone who wants to be free—it's very, very difficult to thrive in a situation when you know God is saving you out of that place. The best thing to do is actually to get out of that situation for the time being and leave those temptations. Looking back on my life, I wish I had done that better in the beginning. But God was merciful, and I had good leaders. When I was water baptized, I really felt there was a change and difference in my heart. It was a further commitment. After that, I began to get more and more free over the years.

Is there anything that you persistently struggled with that was really hard to overcome?

Yeah, pornography. It took me years to get free from that. I was addicted from 8 years of age. I tried everything I could to get free. Then I had one clear experience in my bedroom with the Lord. That was it for me. The difference was this time I deeply felt and understood that I had hurt God. All of my repentance before that, I can honestly say, was about me. I said things like, "God, I'm sorry. God, help me. Pull me out of the pit. I'm in here. Look at poor me." I had said sorry a thousand times, but my heart wasn't changed yet. My prior repentance was based on Ben, not on knowing I had hurt God's heart. I grieved over the fact that all of that time, I had actually hurt God. God was grieving because He loves me more than I love myself. I realized every time I did that, it hurt Him. When I understood that, repentance hit my heart. Never again did I look at anything on the Internet. It was finished. One-day deliverance.

It was a night and day difference when I surrendered my sexuality to God. In one day, a 20-plus-year addiction was gone. I had tried everything before that. I'd fought hard, but it would never leave. I tried preaching myself into righteousness. It still wouldn't leave because I hadn't surrendered it. But I experienced what the Bible calls true repentance, where you grieve because you hurt

God. You don't grieve because you feel bad about your situation. That's not sorry.

Judas felt bad when he was caught with the money. He went and threw the money back. Whereas Peter bitterly wept because he knew he hurt the heart of God. So, only one of them wept unto repentance. Why didn't Judas run back to Jesus? Why did he run to the Pharisees to give back the money first? He was trying to fix it all, but it was still about him. Peter was bitterly weeping, "God, I'm sorry. I can't believe I broke Your heart like this."

If you are struggling with a sin, whether it's smoking or drinking or gambling or pornography, God can take it away in one day. But you have to ask the Lord and you have to ask yourself this question, *Have I really surrendered this to God? Or is this just about me?* It's similar with anything you know is wrong, you have thoughts like, *I know this is wrong. I should be in bed by now. I shouldn't be watching this dumb thing on TV.* You know it's wrong, but there's something keeping you there. There is a desire that you have to surrender and run to Jesus. When you stumble, maybe you feel badly, but that is still a focus on you. You need to focus on Jesus because He's the One who had to go to the cross for you. He's the One who hurts for us. I believe I could have been set free faster with that understanding. But, as my mentor Frank Clancy says, "Learn freely from my costly mistakes."

How do you respond when you make a mistake or feel like you've failed?

Some of my failures have been when I've responded too quickly to people. I've had an opinion or spoken too quickly when someone has shared something with me, or I've been defensive. Or I haven't judged a situation right. My intentions were good, but my discernment was off. When I realize that has happened, I think, *Man, I didn't represent You there, Jesus. I could have done better, I could have spoken kinder, I could have listened longer,* those kinds of things. The way I deal with that is to bring it all back to God and say, "God, I didn't represent You well there, but I still love You, and I know You love me. Help me to represent You better."

Then if I feel prompted in my heart, I go back to that person and apologize, saying, "I'm sorry I spoke so strongly," or, "So sorry I didn't hear your heart on that topic," or whatever it was. That brings great reconciliation and helps me understand the path of humility. God showed me the blessing in our lives comes from our ability to humble ourselves.

So how do I get over my failures? I humble myself and hit the failures headfirst. Instead of avoiding the person, I go right to him or her. That turns failure around and into a situation you can overcome and learn from. If you hide things or push your failures aside or deny them, if you don't have the guts to humble yourself, failures like that can quickly become condemnation in your thinking. So I overcome by bringing everything to God in prayer, obeying what God is saying, and hitting situations headfirst, not avoiding them.

Have you ever been discouraged or disappointed in your faith journey? What is your advice for someone who is feeling discouraged?

I honestly haven't been very discouraged in my faith journey. The only discouragement I've experienced is where I was personally struggling with sin and I wanted to get over it and break it. But that was me looking at myself more. My encouragement is to constantly keep coming to Jesus. If you look at Jesus and stay close to Him, discouragement vanishes because He's so encouraging. In His presence, there's fullness of joy, so when you come close to God, joy begins to manifest in your heart.

I haven't had many discouraging times when I felt let down by God. For me it was more that I let myself down. In that place I have to remember again God loves me more than I even love myself. If you look at the situation, it's easy to be discouraged; so instead, look at Jesus. Ask Him how He sees you and how He sees the situation you're going through.

EUROPE FOCUS

What do you see God doing in Europe in this generation?

He's raising up and returning the European church back to its identity. I'd say its identity was fractured after the war, and it went through ups and downs. There have been a few really amazing moves of God in Europe, but I'd say now people are coming to a solid conviction that they are sons and daughters and God placed them in Europe for a purpose. The church of Europe is determined to take back ground from the enemy and not sit still any longer. They are unwilling to let another twenty years go by and another 40 percent of Europe fall away from God and stop believing He exists.

The Lord is giving His church identity in the family sense of intimately loving God as Father, and at the same time He's commissioning an army. This army won't bow down to the little thoughts, feelings, and opinions that hit their hearts or cower at lies from the enemy. God is raising a company that is ferociously in love with Him and also on a mandate to share His Good News all across the continent of Europe.

It's a holy army, but it's also a family army of sons and daughters who know they were put on this earth with a God-ordained purpose. "I have a plan for you," says the Lord. "I formed you in your mother's womb," says the Lord. Now go forth and do something with what you've been given. I see that is happening in the European church. We do that in many ways such as serving people and loving people well. We do that by going into government, we do that by starting new businesses that represent the kingdom of God. We do that in all spheres. We do that by praying, contending, and by preaching the Gospel. It doesn't have to look a certain way, but it has to be intentional. We love God so much that we must shine in this continent. That's what I see Him doing in the church of Europe. He's waking them up and saying, "Arise and shine, your light is here. Now take it into the continent of Europe."

How can we have unity in this move of God? How can we get past our differences and see this continent saved?

Where does it say in the Bible that it's an option to have unity or not have unity? I don't see anything like that. The Word of God commands us clearly, *"By this all will know that you are My disciples, if you have love for one another"* (John 13:35). When we get to Heaven, we're all going to be in the same family and in the same Heaven. It's one massive church. We have to lay down all the secondary differences that are in our way of having unity and relating to each other as family.

If it's a pillar truth, for example, that a group doesn't believe Jesus is the only way and teaches there are many ways to God, I can't unify with that because that's false. If there is a difference that goes against Scripture, bending it, changing it, and making it say what they want, then we actually have to choose to not unify. That's another choice we have to make, to actually be strong enough to stay true to the Word of God.

However, when we are talking about Christians who have different preferences about how long worship should run or praying in tongues on the microphone, those are secondary differences. They still worship; they still love God; they still pray. We need to focus on their heart for the Lord, not those smaller differences. I've met many beautiful priests and people from more traditional denominations who have a solid and very reverent dedication to God, sometimes even more so than people I see in my own church. I don't look at the denomination, I look at the heart. That's the way I view the church. If I start to categorize people or generalize about denominations, I'm taking Heaven's mandate that we should be one out of the equation and looking at the church through the world's lenses.

My encouragement to you would be to ask if the difference is big enough to make a difference? Is the difference big enough to divide the family of God? If it's not, then you need to reconcile it or you need to learn to live with it. Unity doesn't mean uniformity; it doesn't mean everyone looks the same. But it does mean we believe the same truth, we believe the same Word of God, and we fight to keep that covenant with one another. Sadly, I see people fight more *against* each other than they fight *for* each other. I would love to see the church fighting for relationship instead of fighting to break it.

Are there any specific countries you see God highlighting?

The nation of Austria—He's highlighting that nation. God is also highlighting Russia. I really believe the Lord is going to do something great in Russia and the Ukraine also—I sense God highlighting that area strongly. Another one for me, obviously a big one, is Germany. And now people might think, "Well, that's one of the biggest or most powerful countries in Western Europe." It is, but I believe God is flipping its roots and the historic things that have happened. God is flipping it for His glory. I see God working in the hearts of the German-speaking people so, so much. God is raising up different sounds and songs in them, songs of praise coming out of the German church, songs in their own language. He is raising up a real cry in them. They had a cry for war that was used by the enemy, now it's a cry to be radical for the Lord. Germany is very much highlighted and dear to my heart.

But there are many nations in Europe that are highlighted— the Netherlands, Spain. I believe God is going to do something great in Spain. Over France, I almost feel God wants to shock Europe with what He does in France. I sense it will be enormously powerful. That's what I see in the future—there will be thousands and thousands, and tens of thousands of French people turning to the Lord. But I love all European nations. Anywhere the Lord calls me, every country I step into in Europe, I am filled with great hope.

How has all of this raised your hope for Europe?

If you don't have hope for what God is doing in Europe, then you might be watching too much TV. If you look at the unity movement that's happening in Europe, I believe it's historic. I believe it's the most profound movement on the earth at the moment. It's leading the way. People are laying down their egos and their logos for the sake of the Gospel being preached. We want to work together, and we are looking for relational connections, not just connection around conferences. We are connecting and working together and using each other's strengths. That kind of unity alone produces blessing, the oil that God pours out on the beard of Aaron when the people dwell in unity (Psalm 133).

The second thing is people's willingness to gather in mass as they are at events like Awakening and Holy Spirit Nights, gathering not just to worship the Lord, but to be used by God. There is a cry in the European church, "Use me, Lord, use my life." Because we are seeing thousands of people turn to the Lord, it's quite easy for me to have hope for thousands and millions more. We need to take up this call. It is an urgent hour; it's not an hour for playing games; it's not an hour for waiting. It is an urgent hour to respond to what He is saying.

Ask God to make you an arrow in His hand and go out into the battle. If we look at the media and what some are saying about Europe regarding the increase of communistic mindsets and atheistic mindsets, or the rampant sin, we could easily become discouraged. Instead, look at how God uses your daily life to reach a neighbor or to reach a friend, and then think about millions of Christians around Europe doing that. That's very hopeful.

I personally believe we've stepped into a moment when the Lord is answering all the prayers of generations, at least a hundred years of prayer from little grandmas on their knees for days and days on end asking God to take back Europe; and now in one generation, He is saying yes. I believe we are in that time right now. I don't believe it's the time to come, I believe we're in it. That's very, very hopeful for me. I encourage everyone who reads this to take your place, your spiritual place that God has given you. Whether you're living in Europe, whether you have a heart for it, there's a reason why you're reading this book. I believe the reason is because God has placed a mandate and something special in you that you need to bring to this harvest field, that you need to bring to this point of destiny for the continent of Europe. That destiny wouldn't be fulfilled and complete without your part of the picture. As you read this, please know that there is a reason why you are alive and a reason why your heart is called to Europe.

LIFE APPLICATION—NOTHING IS IMPOSSIBLE WITH GOD

When I reflect on Ben's story, I am reminded of Matthew 19:26, *"With men this is impossible, but with God all things are possible."* After his father committed suicide, Ben suffered deep pain. He tried to fill the void with drugs and women. His life became very dark. But Jesus! No one is beyond the reckless love of God. Jesus radically saved him and transformed his life. Ben wishes that he had cut ties with his old life sooner after getting saved. He recommends making a clean break from things in your life that are drawing you into sin or temptation. If you are trapped in any cycle of sin, ask God for true repentance. Jesus paid the highest price to set you free, look to Him, feel His heart of love for you. Freedom is possible, and it is so sweet.

Let Ben's radical encounter and total life turnaround give you hope for anyone in your life who is running from

God. They are not out of reach. If God can do it for Ben, He can do it for your friend or family member too. Keep praying and keep believing just like Ben's mom did. Share Jesus with people you know and people you don't know yet. Ben encourages us to start by going to a grocery store or coffee shop, stopping people and telling them about Jesus. As he said, many times they will be grateful for your love. Don't let fear hold you back. Start small, but start somewhere.

We see the "nothing is impossible" theme again with Ben's dream to start Awakening Europe. When he first set foot in the stadium in Germany and had a vision for God to fill stadiums in Europe, many people told him it was not possible. He knew the truth: our God can do anything! The stadiums are filled, the streets are flooded with the Gospel, Jesus's name is lifted high, and many are receiving salvation. Nothing, nothing, nothing is impossible with God! What is your dream? What did God put on your heart? Where can you start?

Ben shared that many in Europe are being called to be missionaries to their own nations, maybe that is you too. Every sphere of society needs Jesus. Maybe you are called to be a teacher and reach students and parents. Maybe you are in the business world prophesying into companies or praying for coworkers as you do your daily job. Wherever you are, look at it as part of the harvest field. Know that you are an important and valuable member of the family army God is raising up.

As you take your place, remember the importance of unity. It is not optional. If someone has a different style than you or you disagree on certain points, don't let that divide you. Lay down those secondary differences for the sake of the Gospel. Join together with other Christians and reach your city and your nation. The fields are white, are you ready?

4

Selma Uamusse

Organization: Independent Artist
Position: Singer, Musician
Location: Lisbon, Portugal

Personal Background

What is one of your favorite Bible passages?

There are so many, but lately I have been reading a beautiful section from Ecclesiastes 3:

> *To everything there is a season, a time for every purpose under heaven: A time to be born, and a time to die; a time to plant, and a time to pluck what is planted; a time to kill, and a time to heal; a time to break down, and a time to build up; a time to weep, and a time to laugh; a time to mourn, and a time to dance....*

This is revealing. Sometimes we are so concerned about why things are happening or why other things are not happening. God tells us many times about His time, doing things in His time and using every opportunity to work toward the things He has for us. This passage gives me peace when I feel agitated or anxious. It helps me remember there is a time for everything, and most of the time, my time is not the time of God. We have to be very conscious about that. We can get concerned about doing things, even nice things for God, but they are not always in line with God's plans or timing.

What is your favorite thing to do on your day off?

I really love spending time with people because I love people. Actually, the other day I asked my two daughters what Mommy likes to do. They said, "You like to pray, go to church, and stay with your friends and talk, talk, talk." They described me well. I'm a very social person, so I like to bond with people. I use my free time to spend quality time with people. I could use it to rest or go to the beach or see nature or travel, and I do like those things, but I like to do them with my family and friends. I also enjoy meeting new people whom I might reach with my love.

If you could have lunch with someone who inspires you, whom would you choose and why?

I am going to choose a controversial person, a person I am very curious to talk with, Kanye West. He released an album titled *Jesus Is King.* He had a very controversial past, then had a huge revelation of who Jesus is and experienced Him doing things in his own life. He has faced judgment from Christians and from non-Christians. I would want to ask him about his journey and how he stays engaged with his purpose and doesn't give up. I believe that can only happen when someone really has a deep revelation of what God is going to do through his life. I would love to have lunch with Kanye West and hear about his inspiration.

Please tell us about your ministry.

My main ministry is actually my job. I am a singer. I have a solo project that is Christian inspired. Through my work I try to get people to feel curious about the energy and love that is inside me. I have lots of opportunities to talk about Jesus after my shows. I have a music career, and I use it to reach people. It's actually not an organization, it's my calling. I was an engineer before, but I realized the world I wanted to change as an engineer could be reached much more through music. I could reach more hearts. I see music as my main mission.

I also lead and sing in a Gospel choir that I started with two friends. I personally received Jesus while singing in a Gospel choir, so I want to reach others just like I was reached. Our vision is to help many people meet God through Gospel music.

That is powerful. Please share your background and how you met Jesus.

I was born in non-Christian family. My father and my mother are Mozambican and were both born in 1958. By the time they went to university and were married, a revolution was taking place in Mozambique. They were part of the movements of freedom and the emancipation of women. My grandparents were Catholics, but my parents stepped away from that and we didn't attend church. I was raised in an intellectual, not anti-God, but very independent family. They were focused on their role in the development of Mozambique as a new and independent country. When I was 4 years old, my father received a scholarship to study in Germany. Then when the Berlin wall fell, he moved to Portugal. Our family joined him there when I was 6. My mom earned her Master's degree in African History and Arts, then worked in the arts. Their goal was to return to Mozambique.

When I was 12, I felt God was talking to me. I told my mother and asked her why she never taught me about God. She thought it was strange, but I was raised in a very free-thinking environment, so my parents allowed me to learn more about God. My friends were Catholics, so I attended Catechism classes with them and was baptized at age 13. My parents were there supporting me. Then I began a life with God. I was very interested in the New Testament and the teachings of Jesus. Shortly after that, my parents moved our family back to Mozambique, but I didn't adapt. I really wanted to keep studying in Portugal with my friends, and I convinced my parents to let me go back. I had a good school and community to return to in Portugal.

I lived with my godmother from the Catholic church, but she had a nervous breakdown and left me to live alone at age 14. My parents wanted me to return to Mozambique, but I was very stubborn. They couldn't support me, so I started working. Although I had a good community, that period was very difficult. I was depressed. Sometimes I didn't have money, but there was always a way that God showed me He was with me. Eventually, I felt the Catholic community I was part of was not really following Jesus. I was very disappointed and detached from the church. I still believed in God, but on my own.

Then something incredibly special happened. I always spent the summer holidays with my cousin. We loved to go out dancing at discos. Then she met this guy who started telling her about Jesus. We mocked him over the phone and thought he was crazy. But the next summer, she didn't want to go out anymore. She was no longer mocking that guy; in fact, they were friends. At the end of her birthday party, he asked if he could pray for my cousin. It was just her, her mother, me, and him.

As we held hands and prayed, something amazing happened. We started singing, and I started singing, and then this beautiful presence of the Holy Spirit came upon us. I start crying, crying, crying, and praying, *"Oh God, what's happening with me?"*

The guy invited me to join a Gospel choir (this was in September 1999). It was open for anyone to join, not just Christians. I was scared and not sure if I would go, but I wanted to try new things. I always said yes to challenges, so there I went. I found the rehearsal very strange because it lasted for four hours, but for the first two hours, we didn't do vocal exercises, warmups, music techniques, or even learn new songs. We prayed. People were laughing and crying on the floor. I thought it was really weird; but in my heart, I felt it was honest and sincere. When we sang after praying for two hours, it was very powerful. It felt like fire was on us, and I could not deny that God was there.

Week after week I thought I would not go back with those crazy people; but every week I went. Many people invited me to their churches, but I politely told them it wasn't my thing. Then one day a friend told me, "You've been coming to this and there's fire in you, you need to make a decision. Do you want Jesus in your life?" I told her I wanted Jesus but not institutions, because of my negative personal experiences. For the first time, I prayed a profound prayer, the salvation prayer. I felt it was the beginning of my new life with Christ. At the time, I was 20 years old.

After that, we sang at a church called Logos Comunhão Cristã (Logos Christian Fellowship) several times. I had always wanted to be part of a community where I could share and learn more about God's love, but I never identified with the groups I experienced. Then the minute I went inside this church—full of flags and the beautiful Holy Spirit presence, and people with tattoos and purple hair—I knew it was the place for me. I have been part of that church ever since. I am also a worship leader there. The church was started by a missionary, so there are always missionary people coming and going and sharing various experiences. I really fell in love with this beautiful community of people.

MISSION, VISION, AND LESSONS LEARNED ALONG THE WAY

Now, as a singer and musician, how did you end up studying engineering?

I always sang and knew I could sing well. All my friends wanted me to enter contests or become a professional singer. But for me, as a Mozambican, singing and dancing were part of my culture and national identity. In Mozambique there are so many people singing well and dancing well, so I didn't think it was a skill. Although I started singing in 1999, I only decided to become a professional singer in 2012. For me, it was just part of my identity, I didn't need to be a professional. I didn't need a stage or fame. I just liked to sing, and being part of the Gospel choir was a way of being close to God.

I wanted to become an engineer as my profession. Mozambique had been through a civil war and gained independence in the early 1990s, so there was a lot to rebuild. Throughout my life, I always felt connected to Mozambique. I often went there for several months at a time to be with my parents and younger brother. My mother was very intentional in our communications. She called me almost every day, wrote to me, and sent me articles keeping me updated on the politics, cultural life, and current events in Mozambique. I wanted to be part of the reconstruction and rebuilding of my nation.

After successfully completing my studies, I worked as an engineer at the university. During graduate school, while studying civil engineering, I chose a parallel study of jazz music. I also formed a band called Selma Uamusse New Jazz Ensemble. That was the moment that I started to understand music was really powerful as a missionary weapon. I realized I could use all this joy I felt in the Gospel choir toward my goal to help rebuild my nation. I started to understand there was something more important than buildings—our very own souls. A shift happened where I stopped caring about material things and started caring about people's souls. I gave up on being a missionary of constructions to become a missionary of building hearts.

Your calling as a singer seems to have come about in a very organic way. What is your advice for people still searching for their calling and purpose?

Well, it seems organic now, but at the time, it was not so evident. I went through a lot and had to make many choices from then until now. I don't think callings are ever fully evident from day one. Of course, I do think God confirms by putting His grace on the things we do. If you feel that something is easy for you, maybe that is a clue about what God has for you. For example, I always found it easy to communicate and talk with people, so I thought my purpose could be to become a speaker. I do speak after I sing, but people feel more impacted when I sing than when I just speak.

God gives us talents and gifts. They don't have to be spectacular for God to use them. Maybe people think being a singer or being an international missionary are incredible callings. I think if your calling is to reach your neighbors, and if you have grace whenever you talk with people or help them with practical things, that is just as significant. Never underestimate small things. Recognize what feels easy and natural for you, but also touches other people's hearts.

I used to sing in a very well-known rock and roll band, and we traveled around the world and throughout Europe. People were impressed by my energy, my singing, or my appearance—but those things don't reach hearts. You can have a talent that doesn't reach other people. That is not a way of showing Jesus's love. We need to focus on when we have His grace. When God is in what we are doing, that is what touches people.

For example, I have a very good friend who is a musician, and he has so much grace to love the homeless. Sometimes we will be walking down the street on our way to do something, and he stops to see the people who are often not seen. He really stops for the one. Even when he just looks at people, they feel the love of God. That is powerful. Sometimes we are concerned about our shows, our missions, or our goals, which are good things—but I believe our purpose is revealed when we stop to do something inspired by God. Then we feel His grace, and we share His love.

That is beautiful, Selma. You said your journey to singing professionally wasn't so evident at the time. Please share more about that journey.

It started in that first Gospel Choir I joined in 1999, when I grew closer to God. At one point, our maestro (choir conductor) moved to London. The new maestro organized the Hundred Voices Choir, and I was chosen to lead the soprano group. That position gave me more technical responsibility and more spiritual responsibility. I had also started getting more involved with my church. Later, challenging circumstances caused the choir to end, so my friend and I started a new Gospel choir with an evangelistic vision to reach people with God's love.

Through the Hundred Voices Choir, we had a lot of shows. That was when our evangelistic ministry increased. There was a wave of Gospel music across Portugal when American movies like *Sister Act* popularized the genre. Everyone wanted to have a Gospel choir at their wedding or event. We also created an album with a popular rock and roll band and did several concerts with them. One day the drummer called and invited me to go on tour with them. I wasn't sure, but I have always been an adventurous girl, so I accepted the challenge.

The band members had no Christian experience at all, so I grabbed that opportunity as a mission. I always had my Bible with me. My ground rules were that no one could drink, smoke, or curse in the car with me, and I would be allowed to read my Bible and quietly pray. They were laughing but accepted my requirements.

Touring is really exhausting, and by the end, everyone wanted to ride in the car with me because it was clean, safe, and quiet.

During that tour I got a lot of experience with the music industry. We played at concerts with 100,000 people, met influential people, and performed at famous places. There were also backstage areas with tables of drugs. It was an interesting time because when trouble or challenges came, people asked me for advice. They respected me and noticed I was often praying.

Throughout my life, I always understood that my mission is to be light in the dark, not just to sing at church or evangelistic circuits. But in the beginning, I was not prepared for all the bad things going on around me. I never struggled with drugs, but I found the environments very challenging. I made some mistakes along the way, but God continued to speak to me and tell me, "This is the place where I want you."

Touring with that rock and roll band opened doors for me as a singer. The band was very famous, and one of the few Portuguese bands traveling internationally, so singing with them gave me visibility. I started to receive many more singing invitations. I got to know and sing with people from jazz music, rock, funk, soul, and other genres. My demand is always the same, that I can control the message of what I'm singing, and that people respect me for my beliefs and who I am. I always strive to bring the love of God. I feel God chose me to be in some circuits that are not easy to reach or to get into. He opens the doors, just like He brings other people where they are called. Sometimes it is heavy, but I know my mission is to be in places where people don't feel any connection with God to bring His light and His fire. I want to bring awareness and love and cause curiosity.

In the artistic environment, people struggle with temptations of sex and drugs. They are very resistant to the Gospel because they don't want to be dependent on anything, they want to be free. It's really challenging because the minute people know that I'm a Christian, they watch what I'm doing to see if I live out what I say. It is also hard because I don't just struggle with people outside the church, I also encounter Christians who don't know how far the Gospel can go. Maybe that's why I would like to have lunch with Kanye West. From a very small perspective, I do feel I understand the judgment on Christian artists, even from Christians. Despite challenges, I'm sure that it is my call and that God is in all of it.

Please share about your current connection to Mozambique.

"When I started to develop my solo project as singer, "Selma Uamusse," I knew I wanted to have Christian inspiration in my music. I also knew that if my original goal before becoming a singer was to help my nation, then my singing should continue toward that same goal. As a musician, I want to always be engaged with this mission. I want to help give Mozambique a new "label." Mozambique has been known for years as one of the poorest countries in the world, known for floods, droughts, and war. I believe God wants to give Mozambique a new name, a new identity. That is why it was very easy to fall in love with Iris Global, a Christian interdenominational missionary and humanitarian organization based in Mozambique.

I knew about Heidi Baker, cofounder of Iris Global, but became more familiar with the ministry in 2019 when Mozambique was devastated with two cyclones and floods. I decided to perform at a public event to support Mozambique and to support Christian organizations that provided healthcare, education, and childcare in a spiritual way. I worked with two Christian organizations to host a big fundraising event. A friend showed me a video of Heidi talking about what was happening, and I was touched by what she said. I sensed something special about her and connected with Iris Global. Two of their leaders came to our event. They were so honest and pure, beautiful from the inside out in the way they carried the love of God. They didn't force anyone to do anything, but the fire and evidence of God's love was inside them, and they were unstoppable. The event was very successful, and we divided the funds to support eight organizations.

After that, I personally wanted to go to Mozambique to see the impact of our support. I visited Iris and spent time with Heidi and her team. Heidi is an incredibly special person. Two things she did really touched my heart and showed me who she is. It was our last day, and I was having a meal at the hotel with my agent Felicia, who is not a Christian. Heidi personally came to say goodbye. She and her entire crew (of mostly kids) gathered around us in the restaurant. Heidi shared powerfully and personally with Felicia that God truly loved her. Then she prayed and used our leftover bread and wine from the table to share a communion meal together. God's presence came strongly, and we were laughing as she prayed for us. It was symbolic of her humility, ignoring the spotlight, and coming to people naturally. It communicated the message that she wasn't trying to convince us of anything. She was just being herself, full of Jesus's love, and loving us. Felicia was greatly impacted by this experience.

Then I went with Heidi to a farewell party for the military and firefighter volunteers from Brazil who had been helping with disaster relief. Because Heidi had spent so much time with us at the hotel, she was late. She said she is often late, but it is because she stops for the one. That time, she stopped for my friend, and it was really special.

Everyone at the party was waiting for her. She apologized for being late and told them I would share something. I didn't know if the Brazilian volunteers were Christians or not, and I didn't really want to share, but God has His purposes. I had a moment of adoration for Him and then shared some things on my heart.

After I shared, Heidi did not share. She told me that when God speaks, she doesn't need to add more. God spoke through me, and people received, so she didn't need to share. What an example of humility and of God's love. I am very enthusiastic about this self-explained love that Iris develops in their missions—love that speaks for itself. I also had the opportunity to visit Iris bases in Brazil when I was touring there, and I felt the same bold love for the lost. It is the essence of Jesus's love. I really admire the work of Iris not only as a mission, but the way they carry God's love without barriers or being narrowminded, just self-explanatory love.

PURITY IN PROMOTION

I don't know if you've experienced this, but some people who are in the spotlight or who are famous, whether that's through music or preaching, face challenges over what people think of them or over their identity. Did you experience that?

Yes, of course. It would be a lie to say the opposite. If you work in a bank or a grocery store, you can be nice and talk to people, and share Jesus at work, but there is a separation between your work life and your Christian life. Of course, we all live our faith all the time, but it is different when you are in the spotlight. You have to be who God wants you to be 24/7. It's hard because people place expectations on you.

That is why I kind of fell one or two times, as I mentioned at the beginning of the interview. It wasn't about wanting to be famous, it was about being convinced God was with me all the time, to the point that I let my guard down. There were some areas of my life where I wasn't really living out my values. When you are in the spotlight, you really, really have to clothe yourself with righteousness and holiness hour by hour. I know how lucifer fell, and I know how easy it is to be vain or think people are coming to shows because of me. During some concerts, I felt such a strong spiritual struggle. I would pray and ask God to take care of every situation, whatever was going on.

Now, one of my demands as an artist is to bring my personal assistant with me. She is also my intercessor. Nobody really understands, but it is especially important to have her close to me. She has authority in my life to tell me if I am being vain or not doing things right. She prays for me and calls my attention to any areas, professionally and spiritually, that I need to pay attention to. I am very aware that I can't make it by myself. I really need someone close to me and aware of the spiritual environment, particularly when I sing in really dark places.

We are never alone with God, but we should also keep our lives guarded and have believers around us. Sometimes she's very tough with me, calling me out. Sometimes I get angry, but then I understand it is God talking with me. It's important to have people surrounding you who are authorities in your life, who you know are with you and are strong in God.

Do you ever feel like people just want to be close to you because of your fame?

Yes, I don't find it strange. There is a kind of natural attraction toward someone who is on stage. One thing I do during my concerts is to always get off stage and go into the audience, whether there are 100 people or 3,000 or 10,000, whatever. I do that not for the show, but so people realize I'm just like them. I'm not superior. I'm not any different. I sweat; my makeup gets messy; I cry. People are often surprised that I am shorter than they thought, which is the perception from seeing someone you admire on stage. There is a lot of admiration, so I do this exercise to keep myself grounded too. I want to demonstrate that I am just like everyone else, perhaps even shorter, physically and/or spiritually speaking.

Of course, sometimes people want to be close because of who I am. I often feel pressured because followers on social media ask me to share things or join events on a daily basis. Every chance I get, I try to connect with social work addressing poverty, education, health, and other needs. Almost every day I receive letters from organizations that want me to be their ambassador, that want me to represent them. That can be tiring, but it is part of my calling, and I can't say no to my mission.

Part of getting favor is also having pressure, but I choose not to feel bothered by this. I can decide if I feel honored because people want to be with me, even if it's for the wrong reasons. I try to take advantage of situations where people want to get to know me and use that as a way to tell them about Jesus. If they really want to spend time with me, I'm going to tell them about who I am and who is inside me. I like to shift the perspective, taking circumstances as opportunities, not as threats.

How do you keep your own personal relationship with God strong and how do you balance your time with many commitments?

I've learned the hard way that being busier with other things than with God is not good. Keeping the balance requires discipline. My husband helps me a lot with that area. My main trick is that I wake up early and have my "me and God time" before the children wake up and before talking with my husband. I try to take an hour every day in the morning with the Word because I know it will get busy after that. I often have concerts at night and my children need me in the afternoon. So, I try to be very disciplined with my morning time when there's silence and I can talk with God.

I also try to keep my journal pretty alive with what God is speaking to me and the things I am praying about for myself and others. Life can be really busy, and it's really hard to have discipline, but the moment I lose it, it's like a snowball and it seems I can never catch up with what God was doing. If I have a chaotic day ahead, it's even more important to start with God. Then He can help me do all the tasks, and I can be more productive.

In these past few years, I've been trying to be very disciplined and not ashamed of who I am in Christ. I don't try to shock people, but I also don't want God to be shocked with me. I'm never embarrassed about praying in front of other people or sharing who God is when I think it makes sense. I'm not perfect, not at all, but these are things that are very important for me. I also highly value being part of a church community with friends who will help me think about my lifestyle and point out areas to pay attention to.

You shared earlier that you had some challenges. Would you be comfortable telling us more about what you went through and what you learned?

Okay, I got divorced. When people are very busy, we can lose our focus. I had so many tasks. I became a mother and that is a big revolution in terms of hormones, body, mind, everything. It is tiring, but you still think you have energy for everything, for your babies, for work, for church activities, but something gets left behind.

During that period of my life, my relationship with God was left behind in a way. If my relationship with God had been strong, my marriage would not have suffered in the same way. It was really hard to see that my busy life and connection with other people and working and babies were more important than my relationship with God. It became about giving thanks and asking for things, not intimacy and spending real quality time and letting Him touch my heart. We need to have those deep moments when we stop and leave time for Him to speak. I was just talking with God and not really listening.

I was doing all the "right" things, all the activities, going from one to another. I did crazy things, like when touring, I had concerts on Friday and Saturday, and then traveled through the night to get to church on Sunday morning to do intercession and lead worship. I was all over everything, but I wasn't having actual intimacy with God—something was left behind. I really learned that lesson the hard way. I don't blame my ex-husband, it takes two people to leave a relationship; but as a couple, we misjudged the importance of having a daily and intimate relationship with God. I learned it is really important to take time not only to read, not only to pray for other people, not only to ask for things, but just to listen. What is God telling you to do right now? What is He saying? What level of intimacy are you having with God right now?

Wow, Selma, thank you for sharing so deeply. I know many others have gone through divorce or other challenging situations. Sometimes those experience cause shame or cause people to draw away from God or people. What would be your advice for someone who is in a situation like that right now? How did you get through that season?

It took me a long time. It is a challenge of maturity. If you don't admit to yourself and God that you are far from God, it is difficult to move forward. Good community is really important in this process. I know some people have communities that are judgmental toward them, and that is not easy. In my case, people were very supportive, but my whole world fell apart. I had two baby girls, and I was very young. I did not have enough money. It was really awful. It was a desert of shame and crying.

It is really difficult to go through these phases of life. First, you have to admit you failed; you can't just blame the other person. Be honest about your part. Honesty with yourself, honesty with God, and staying close to people who will lift you up are key in getting through those times. We need people who raise us up and support us. Some people say they don't need to go to church or be in community, but that is really sad to me. We actually do need other people, people who are honest with us and lead us to the cross with them.

If you go through a tough time, take small steps, take very small steps. Cry as much as you need to, but don't just stay there in the awful sadness—see the hope. See the hope because God shows His love in so many ways. Sometimes we read and know all the stories and experiences in the Bible, but we don't feel personally connected. We think those stories were from many years ago and not for us. The exact opposite is true. There is a moment when we have to feel like the prodigal child coming home from the pigsty, coming from all the shame—and then seeing our Father running to embrace us. He is very happy when we return to Him, to His place (Luke 15:11-32).

EUROPE FOCUS

What do you see God doing in Europe right now?

I am part of the Europe Shall Be Saved movement; and through that, I joined a group from the Lausanne Movement. This is a very interesting group of people reflecting together on how God is moving in Europe. They give us articles with reflection questions, and we all give our opinions on what we see God doing. For me, it is interesting reading articles from Sweden or Denmark or Germany and finding out that the reflections of people from other countries are so close to what we are feeling here in Portugal. It is really an exciting time to be in Europe.

Europe was one of the first and most affected places in the world by COVID-19. I believe this became an opportunity for Europe to open to God and really depend on Him. This old continent, as we call it, is where Christianity spread to the most and from where Christianity was spread around the world. Then over so many years, Christianity in Europe became religious and institutional rather than a personal relationship with God. This continent is full of privileges. People have healthcare, money, government support; but suddenly, all these material things don't matter as much when people realized they could die at any time from the pandemic. God is calling Europe to the place of repentance. It is wonderful to see how we are responding as a continent to God's call and to see Catholic churches gather with Protestant churches and people from different denominations.

During quarantine, I was part of many movements and worship groups with people from different places and from different countries and from different churches. This is the essence of God's love, that we're a body. We're not just this church or that church or this person or that person. We are a full body preparing for Him, and it's really beautiful. This is a time of repentance and forgiveness. Europe needs to ask for forgiveness from God for all the apathy and for all the coldness. I see the fire is being prepared. It's easy to see all the revival movements in Brazil and in Africa, in America and Asia and then compare them to Europe and find Europe boring. But people are getting fiery. People are getting hungry for God's presence, and we want more! I feel really privileged to be part of this movement. I feel great joy in my heart. I didn't know how much God was doing across the continent, and it is beautiful to see!

How do you think we can continue to build unity when people have different beliefs or styles of worship?

My husband and I lead a sharing group online. We gathered a group of our friends without any connection to any church. Sometimes it is challenging to talk with people who have other beliefs, but I always felt God calling me, and now my husband and I as a couple, to challenging terrains. People are open-minded about spirituality, mindfulness, or meditation. People are even comfortable talking about God because God is very mystical and esoteric. It is a bigger challenge to talk about Jesus and call Him by name. But I do believe that the name of Jesus is really powerful, especially when we talk not only about His name or His sacrifice, but when we talk about His example and lifestyle.

Jesus is the ultimate example of divine love through a human body. That is a really powerful truth, and it doesn't have to do with denomination. It has to do with the person of Jesus. Talking about Jesus and His life, His sacrifice, and His resurrection is fundamental. It doesn't have anything to do with any specific church or with any specific denomination. The secret to unity is the truth of who Jesus is. It is simpler than we think. It is the person of Jesus and the revelation of the Father's love through Him.

LIFE APPLICATION—GOD WRITES THE BEST STORIES

God writes the best stories with our lives. Looking back, we truly see how He works all things for our good, even things that felt painful and confusing as we walked through them. He sees every minute detail of our lives and does not miss a beat. We also have choices along the way. We have choices about how we spend our time, who we make time for, and how we will react to promotion.

Selma was always a very talented singer. This led her into the music world, touring. She was in dark places where she had battles to face. People had different lifestyles and didn't always understand her faith. Sometimes we underestimate the spiritual battles or the temptations we will face. We can also overestimate our own capacity and strength spiritually. Selma shares how in the beginning, she let her guard down and went through tough times. Then, she adopted a vital strategy: she brings her assistant/friend/intercessor to all her events. She doesn't try to go it alone anymore. This woman has a voice in her life. She is not afraid to tell Selma the hard things or point out areas that need attention.

When you are promoted, in a Christian or secular environment, people will want to be around you. Some will use you for your followers. Others will just tell you what you want to hear and never confront you. That can be because they want to stay on your good side or because they see you as a leader, which affects their perception of you. I love how Selma jumps off the stage at all her events to show the crowd she is a real woman—even shorter than they expected. It is crucial to stay grounded in God and stay connected with people who know and love you, flaws and all. Cultivate these relationships in every season, especially when promotion comes. Don't let pride or any other temptation take ground in your life.

I also love what Selma shares about connection with God. For her, life became so busy with good things. She was singing on the worship team and professionally ministering through her music. She was a wife and mom. She was in all the church groups. Her life was full of great things; but she was so busy, there wasn't time for deep, intimate connection with God. There weren't enough moments of staying still and listening for His voice. She didn't see it clearly until her marriage collapsed and her world fell apart. Now Selma is doing amazingly. She is married again and still a mom, singer, and worship leader—but she truly knows how much she needs God. She wakes up early every morning to put her quality time with Him first. On the busiest, chaotic days, she makes it top priority so God can be in every moment and every meeting.

There are so many more lessons we can pull out of this personal and beautiful interview. But I will leave it at that and ask you: How intimate are you with the Lord? Who is speaking into your life? Do you have strong support from God and community to hold you up through the highs and lows, the promotions and the challenges?

5

BISHOP DOMINIQUE REY

Organization: Roman Catholic Diocese of Var
Position: Bishop
Location: Toulon, France

PERSONAL BACKGROUND

What is your favorite Bible verse and why?

I would quote Matthew 6:22-23, *"The lamp of the body is the eye. If therefore your eye is good, your whole body will be full of light. But if your eye is bad, your whole body will be full of darkness. If therefore the light that is in you is darkness, how great is that darkness!"*

The conversion of the heart, to which the Christian is called, passes through the conversion of the gaze. That is to say, seeing the gifts from God rather than what the world says about itself. This challenge is essential for the fruitfulness of the mission.

What do you like to do when you have a day off?

Faith goes through the heart, the intelligence, but also through the feet. The few occasions of free time that have been granted to me usually result in walking, not only as a physical exercise, but also as a spiritual exercise of regular swaying of the body from one foot to the other. The direction of my course leads to experiencing an advancement toward God through the always fragile balances between His grace and my nature.

If you could choose, with whom would you like to have a meal?

With Saint Joseph, this just and silent man who would allow my mouth to be occupied with tasting rather than chatting. In a world of chatter and turmoil, silence is not silent. This happens when you have nothing to say. Silence is essential when you have too much to say.

What would you like to tell us about yourself?

In a few words, I am a bishop in charge of the Diocese of Var, which is in the south of France on the Côte d'Azur. Our region includes cities such as Saint-Tropez, Saint-Raphaël, and Sanary. There is a total population of a little over 1,100,000 inhabitants. I have been a bishop for almost twenty years.

I have always had a great desire to be a witness of my faith and to develop a missionary church. This is my DNA, my mission. This mission includes the leadership of the community in a missionary spirit. I am careful to read and understand what is happening in our society on different levels. I am committed to teach relevant words that aim deep into what I can see in the contemporary world, through its fractures, its failures, but at the same time, through the hope we can find in the Lord. He works this world much like yeast leavens dough. My role is to bring life to the community and guide the community. For this role, it is necessary to be both communal and prophetic in order to be missional.

MISSION, VISION, AND LESSONS LEARNED ALONG THE WAY

What is happening in your diocese?

I have four pillars in my diocese, which are for me the four audiences of Jesus. The first audience Jesus met was the family. He was born into a human family, and I believe all evangelization begins with the family. The family is the first place not only to build society, but also to pass down our faith.

Then Jesus lived his childhood. He spent his childhood in Bethlehem and Nazareth. Jesus always had a special relationship with children. *"Assuredly, I say to you, unless you are converted and become as little children, you will by no means enter the kingdom of heaven"* (Matthew 18:3). Jesus blessed the children. I believe the child is the image of what we must one day become and reclaim. Georges Bernanos put it this way, "When I present myself before God, it is the child I was that will go before me." We must reestablish this spirit of childhood, wonder, and acceptance of our dependence on God. Then we have hope because we are looking to the future.

The third audience that Jesus met was the apostles. He made His disciples into apostles. Our concern should not only be for family and education of children, but also for training leaders.

This includes lay people and priests. Evangelism begins with the transformation of leadership.

Finally, Jesus's fourth audience was the poor. He ministered to the lowest in society, those who had lost their inheritance, the abandoned ones everyone had forgotten, the disheartened ones. All of their poverty came together and put itself in front of Him on His way. This poverty was physical, material, and emotional. Jesus responded with compassion, healing, and salvation.

The diocese I lead is oriented around these four pillars: family, childhood, the formation of leaders, and also the care of the poor and forgotten. If we hold these four audiences together, I believe that we embrace the entire Gospel. For each of these categories there is a specific program. For example, we are working on the Christian educational curriculum within the Catholic schools in our diocese. We are trying to improve the presentation of faith within the education and to teach about healthy sexuality and relationships. This is critical during a time when there is a break-down in the family structure. We have also organized universities for young people.

To address the audience of family, we created several family homes to accommodate all these fractured family situations we find today in our society. We help families to take on their educational and missional positions. We also educate and train priests and lay leaders. Fortunately, we have a seminary, as well as a training center for lay people in leadership. For people at risk and those who are suffering, we have a hospital for the homeless and other initiatives. We also have programs for solidarity. All these areas are the foci of our efforts and especially our prayers.

One of the missions of the Europe Shall Be Saved movement is to reach the lost for Jesus. We want to see Europe enter a new era of evangelism. What can you share about the Catholic church in regard to this mission?

It seems to me that it is very important to consider the way we should look at the world. Before acting, it is necessary to take the attitude of a watchman. Before launching into action, we consider the world with the viewpoint that comes from God, not a worldly viewpoint, not a view that is linked to the superficiality of media conditions. We must see things from God's perspective to realistically see both the wavering world that needs God's salvation now more than ever, and at the same time to see sources of hope. I am struck by what could be considered a collapse of our society on a number of anthropological and ethical points. These points are related to the loss of the sense of God that leads to the loss of the sense of humanity. At the same time, I consider that at the bottom of our societies there are expectations, new initiatives on the part of creative and prophetic minorities, that are a real source of hope for me.

Please give us one or two concrete examples?

What immediately comes to my mind is an experience I had with a group of young people. They came up to me and said they would like to participate in the World Youth Days with the Holy Father. I encouraged them to register and begin to organize things in order to participate. They told me they wanted to do things differently. I was interested and asked them what they proposed to do. They had the idea to join with a large group of young people and drive to Rome in old cars. This is exactly what they did. It began as an individual initiative, but by attraction and influence, many others wanted to join. In the end, there were more than 200 young people who joined with old cars. The intuition and creative idea of one young person spread. Today people are developing proposals that are off the beaten track. These are signs of hope for me.

As I lead the church, I am very attentive to what can flow and what can be born. I also learn from other countries through my travels. Notably, in Brazil I visited a small community called Caminho, "The Way." The sisters in this community live and serve in the favelas in the district of São Paulo. Favelas are poor urban communities in Brazil. There is a huge problem with gun violence and drug abuse. The sisters work there and live among the poor. They pick people up, take care of them, and share Christ with people in their worst moments of distress.

I brought the sisters to Europe. They came to France and shared with my diocese about the extraordinary work they do. Despite the challenging conditions they live in and the situations they face, they are full of joy. They have the joy of faith, and it touches many people. Their insight was that the moral distress and incredible loneliness that many experience in Europe is more challenging than material lack.

If we sow small seeds like that in God's garden, it makes an incredibly beautiful garden where everyone brings their own color, charisma, and dynamism. In that context, the church can flourish again.

One of the topics we are exploring in this book is the shift from maintenance to mission in the church. In the past, churches have been focused on maintenance, creating structures that last. Now, many sense that we must move into a much more missionary and prophetic time. How does this concept manifest in the Catholic church?

It is beginning to manifest itself. In the Catholic church, there are many traditions and rituals. I believe today there is a renewal of rituality. There is also a temptation toward consumer Christianity. When I arrived in the diocese, I was told that there were many Catholics but few Christians. The challenge we face is to reach people who think they are Christians but who are not really Christians yet. This mission begins with the pastors. We need to experience the spiritual conversion of pastors.

We need a conversion where Christians try to live up to their baptism and live out their faith. This is through the inner radiance of the soul; the radiance of a holy life. That is what will affect and touch many people. The greatest evangelists in the history of the church have been saints. There is strength in community, helping one another to live out this holiness through the access to God's grace. This will make the church and our communities profoundly missional.

Thank you for sharing these insights. We also see that we can learn from our failures. Is there any advice you can share with us about what didn't work out well, but taught you something along the way?

Yes, we can certainly learn from our failures as well as our successes. We also know that today's successes might be tomorrow's failures and vice versa. You have to keep a long-term vision so as to not just focus on short-term success.

We know that all Christian fruitfulness is sacrificial, it passes on the gift of oneself. We must follow in the footsteps of Christ who saved us through the cross. He invites us to imitate Him and bear our crosses to bear fruit. We must not sink into a willingness to suffer in order to suffer. It is about being associated with Christ, completing in our flesh what is lacking in Christ's Passion. Colossians 1:24 says, *"I now rejoice in my sufferings for you, and fill up in my flesh what is lacking in the afflictions of Christ, for the sake of His body, which is the church."*

I believe we should not be afraid of the resistance and even the rejections that we may experience in our lives. We all experience many misunderstandings. I see some people who do not want to change. I also notice some areas of resistance. There are dark spots, but we are making progress with that. I like the story in the Gospel when Jesus tells the paralytic to take up his mat and walk. He doesn't tell him to leave his mat behind, he tells him to take his mat, the reminder of his problem. Moving on in the midst of our problem is real deliverance.

There are parts of our "old self" that we will have to carry to the end. Even the apostle Paul speaks about this. He prayed and desired for the thorn that crucified his flesh to be taken away from him, but it remained. It is through our weaknesses that God speaks, acts, and spreads His power. I observe this in myself through my own limitations as well.

I see the reluctance when we talk about missional transformation. We encounter dubious and skeptical attitudes from people who do not want things to change too much. We realize it is not that easy. At the same time, we also have signs of hope that make us believe we must move forward.

EUROPE FOCUS

Last but not least, what would you like to say about Europe's destiny, from your own point of view?

Europe must return to its Christian roots. Originally, Europe was built on the message of faith. Christians have not always lived up to this message, but this contribution of Christianity has been the root that made Europe. Europe can only understand itself from the Gospel. If we want Europe to be established, in light of the social fragmentation we encounter today, it is only on the basis of the message of the Gospel that it will be reestablished.

We are witnessing a very strong affinity for individualism, with social fragmentation, corporatism, or pure affinity groups. We observe a kind of dispersion of the social bond, which will only be recovered by the proclamation of faith, which must be the common denominator. Only through the central precept of the Gospel, to love one another, can we have the ability to coexist and live with people who are fundamentally different from us. For evangelism to succeed, the church in Europe needs to rediscover this fundamental foundation, its roots, which are part of its history, its memory, and its heritage. It is not just a question of looking back, but of drawing sap to build the future.

LIFE APPLICATION—BRINGING HOPE TO A FRACTURED WORLD

The way Bishop Rey communicates is full of poetry, beauty, and wisdom. He sees the fractures and failures but also the hope in this world. As a leader, he takes time to read about and be informed on what is going on in society. That allows him to address these topics in a relevant way and help his congregation do the same. This is a missional perspective. He lives out his faith with a goal to bring life and guidance to his community, not to stay in a Christian bubble, hidden from the world, and also not to condemn or judge. Our mission is to bring Jesus to a lost and broken world. Jesus is the hope, the resurrection power.

This concept carries down to the four pillars Bishop Rey shared: family, children, apostles, and the poor. In each area, as we follow Jesus and live as He did, we become carriers of hope and God gives us capacity to bring transformation. We are all called to love the poor and the broken. This is fundamental in the teachings of Jesus. We respond with prayer, hope, and practical solutions. In order to do this, we must see the world from God's perspective. This is not superficially through the media's often negative or hopeless viewpoint, but instead realistically and full of hope and possibilities. We see the real problems, but we don't become discouraged or hopeless, we remember that we have the Living Hope within us.

Another point that Bishop Rey addresses is the need for Christians to be truly converted. Some say they are Christians, but what evidence is there in their lives? Are they "living up to their baptism" and "living out their faith"? A mark of this is living a holy life and calling our Christian brothers and sisters to do the same. This will make us profoundly missional.

Paul explains this concept in Hebrews 12:1-2: *"Therefore we also, since we are surrounded by so great a cloud of witnesses, let us lay aside every weight, and the sin which so easily ensnares us, and let us run with endurance the race that is set before us, looking unto Jesus, the author and finisher of our faith, who for the joy that was set before Him endured the cross, despising the shame, and has sat down at the right hand of the throne of God."*

We cast off sin and run our race with endurance. We do this by looking right at Jesus. He overcame death and the grave. Now we live in the hope and glorious power of His resurrection. We have the strength we need to finish our race because Christ already finished His. When we feel weak in this, we can remember that it is through our weaknesses, God's power is revealed. Do you feel hopeless or hopeful? When you see the brokenness of society or even in your personal life, do you truly know that Jesus already won the victory? He is the hope, and He has a solution for every need. In fact, He is the solution, He is the Way, the Truth, and the Life. Fix your eyes on Him and then transform this world for His glory.

6

Shapoor Ahmadi

Organization: Operation Promises
Position: Founder and Director
Location: Liverpool, England

Personal Background

What is your favorite thing to do on your day off?

I like watching football and playing football. I also like watching movies, especially funny ones.

If you could have lunch with one person, whom would you choose?

Heidi Baker. When I see her, I become hungry for God and thirsty for prayer. She makes me think about going lower and slower and learning to be humble. My heart beats for Jesus, and for poor and broken people when I hear her share. She always gives me more vision about what it means to serve.

What would you like to tell us about yourself and how you came to faith?

I was born in northern Iran. I grew up in a Muslim family. My dad took me to the mosque when I was 8 to learn about the beauty of Islam. I began doing all of the duties required by Islam, including reading and memorizing the Quran, praying five times a day, going to the mosque and fasting forty days per year for Ramadan. I was a top student at memorizing the Quran, so my school asked me to recite scriptures and lead prayer every morning. I did this for five years in front of all 400 students. I was recognized as a leader, although it was in the wrong place with the wrong belief.

I was a diligent and successful student. I earned my university degree in Survey Engineering and got a good job at an oil company in southern Iran. I had a high salary and bought a house, a car, and everything I wanted. I was trying to obey the law of Islam. That was my background until I was 21 years old. My life is kind of like Moses' life. For the first forty years, Moses thinks he's somebody. In his second forty years, he realizes he's a nobody. And in his last forty years he understands what God can do with someone who has come to the point of realizing he is a nobody. My life can also be broken into these three parts.

In the first part of my life, I thought I was a somebody because I had a house, a car, good morals, and obeyed the Quran. My family was proud of me. I became a role model in my family and community, but I didn't have peace inside. I was taught that if I did good things, God would bless me, but if I did bad things, He would punish me. Pleasing God was such hard work, from childhood on. I obeyed God because I didn't want to go to hell, disappoint my father, or make God angry. When I messed up, I would try harder with more fasting and prayer. It was not a relationship.

In Islam, God spoke to the prophets because they were blameless, and everyone else follows the prophets. There is not a two-way relationship or the concept of God as a father. Intimate relationship with a loving God was beyond my imagination at that time. In Islamic beliefs, you stand before God on judgment day, and He judges you according to your good and bad deeds. Imagine how I had to work to try and keep that scale right. I didn't really enjoy my life.

That is my background. Then I was suddenly and unexpectedly forced to leave Iran, which was very unusual at that time. The oil company I worked for became very famous, which made it suspicious to the Iranian government. They were constantly searching us and watching everything we did. As survey engineers, we needed to map out areas, so the secret police were constantly questioning us. Then people told me that even though I was just a normal, innocent person doing my job, the Iranian government didn't trust anyone who might have important information. They said I was not safe and I should leave Iran. I went through a month of pressure, stress, anxiety, fear, and torment. I couldn't sleep. I couldn't survive. During the day I was literally terrified. This is when I went from being a "hundred" to being a "zero."

I had no idea where to go or what to do. I couldn't even share with my family because it could put them at risk. I read the Quran all day and asked God why this was happening to me. I tried to figure out what bad thing I could have done to deserve this punishment. I had to leave quickly and could only say goodbye to my father, no one else. He was shocked and didn't know what to say.

Someone connected me with agents who help get people out of Iran. We had to go on a long, difficult journey through the mountains to escape. I could almost hear the sound of wolves and the shouts of government officials trying to catch us. It was terrifying. All of this happened so suddenly and was a huge shock for me. One minute I was signing papers at my desk, just doing my job—the next minute, I was being forced to leave my own country at just 21 years old.

The day we tried to cross the mountains, we had to walk for nine hours. It was winter and there was very deep snow. Both my legs froze, so I couldn't walk anymore. The agents wanted to leave me there because otherwise everyone would be caught by the government. They had a big argument over what to do. Finally, they called one of the other smugglers to bring a horse and carry me back. When I got back, I was terrified of getting caught and of losing my legs. Thankfully the doctor miraculously saved my legs. That was a tough, tough journey. After that, they found another way to help me escape to Turkey with a fake passport. They said to stay there until they could bring me into Europe. Then, some men tricked me and stole my (fake) passport and all my money. I was so upset. I had already lost my family, my career, my country, now what? For two days, I didn't have anything to eat. It was unbelievable. Finally, a friend sent me money. Then, eventually, we found people to get us to Greece.

That was my desert experience, like how Moses went to the desert or Abraham went to an unknown land. Where are you going? I don't know. Who are you going to? I don't know. Where are you heading? I don't know. What is your plan? I don't know. Do you know anybody who can help you? No. I was just crying out to God. I started drinking and smoking, trying to forget my pain. It wasn't helping me. I went to concerts, clubs, and bars. On the outside everyone was pretending they were okay, but literally nobody was okay. That was my second "40 years": pain, agony and stress. I had relief from the government but struggles within myself. I was wondering what the answer was. I started thinking a lot. Who is God? Why am I here? Why are people here? Is it for suffering, for dying? For what?

Then the third part of my life began when I went to a refugee camp in England. I was still struggling with stress and anxiety. I couldn't sleep. I was scared. My mom was worried that she would never see me again and would call me weeping. I was trying to be strong. I told my family everything would be okay, even though I wasn't sure if that was true. I never told them the full story of what happened to me. Even today, they only know about 10 percent of what I went through.

In the refugee camp hostel, there was an outreach group. I remember one of the men always had a giant smile on his face and invited me to church. I thought they were crazy religious people and politely declined. He kept coming to see me, and the group prayed and fasted for us refugees. I noticed the ways they were helping people in the camp with practical things they needed. They asked if they could help me with anything or if I wanted to have a meal with them. They said they were there to love us. I didn't show it on the outside, but their unconditional love, prayer, and fasting touched me. At the same time, I was very firm in my own beliefs.

At the end of 2007, they prepared a Christmas gathering for all of the refugees, especially since most were separated from family. One of my friends invited me. I didn't want to go, but he kept bothering me, and finally I agreed to go for five minutes. I did not want to spend much time with the Christians because I was a devout Muslim. When we arrived, I saw people worshipping in the front. I thought the dancing was disrespectful and not religious. It was very different from how we pray in Islam. I just wanted to leave.

Then during that worship time, the song lyrics "Jesus, Prince of Peace" on the screen caught my attention. Holy Spirit began to show me everything from my past. I was very religious, but I didn't have peace. I had a good job and family, but I didn't have peace. I had to drink a lot to sleep because of all the trauma. I would wake up in the night, scared of being arrested by the Iranian government. I closed my eyes and wondered, *God, would You give me peace?*

Suddenly, I felt water like rain falling on my head. I literally thought my friend threw water on me. I opened my eyes, and everyone was worshipping. I looked at the roof, but it wasn't leaking. I was scared. I said, "God, if this is You, show me again because I'm confused." The presence of God came like fire and my whole body started shaking. I was on my knees crying and weeping like a baby. I prayed, "God, if You don't leave me, I will serve You all my days." Even the words I was saying were outside of my control. I didn't know why I was saying that. I had this sense of a hole inside me that could only be filled by God. I felt surrounded by God's presence. People prayed and asked if I wanted to give my life to Jesus, but I wasn't ready for that yet.

On the way out, I heard the audible voice of God say, "Matthew 6:33," but I had no clue what that meant. At the same time, someone gave me a free Bible. I asked if he knew what Matthew 6:33 was. He showed me the verse, *"But seek first the kingdom of God and His righteousness, and all these things shall be added to you."* As I heard that, I was instantly set free from all my worries about the future. I didn't know the terms of the verse, but I somehow understood that my needs would be met. I didn't understand what I had experienced that night, but I knew it was good. That night I had the best sleep in my whole life—no anxiety, no panic, nothing. The next afternoon, I tried to smoke and drink, but I literally couldn't. I was smiling. People asked what had happened to me and said I looked happy and different. I couldn't explain it either.

I started reading the Bible and going to church, but I was wrestling over what was really true. I knew the peace I received was something I never had before, but why were there two billion Muslims in the world if it was wrong? I spent about seven months carefully studying and comparing the Bible and the Quran. I especially focused on the teachings of Jesus. In the Bible, Jesus says to love your enemy. The Quran says to hate your enemy. Jesus says what you eat or drink does not make you unclean. He speaks about having a pure heart. Islam has many rules about food, drink, and outward things. There's no salvation in Islam. Jesus says He came to give eternal life to everyone who believes in Him. I began to realize that Christianity is the exact opposite of Islam. I couldn't comprehend why people say all religions are the same. I didn't find any similarity, even in prayer and fasting.

I came to the point of wanting to follow Jesus and His teachings, but I was still wrestling with the topic of the Trinity. Saying Jesus is God makes you an infidel in Islam. This topic of the Trinity and Jesus as the Son of God is challenging and confusing for many Muslims. Then I had a powerful dream where I was dead in a coffin. I heard a voice say, "You were dead, but now you are alive." A giant cross full of fire and light came toward me and pushed me out of the coffin and into church. I said, "Now I know Jesus Christ is the Lord and Savior." These were the words I was struggling to say in real life as I wrestled with the divinity of Christ.

In the morning, I went to a conference. I completely forgot my dream. The speaker preached about how many Muslims struggle with the Trinity. He said if you know you are a sinner, if you know Jesus as the Savior, but you have a problem with the Trinity, then God wants to come to you. He will teach you. It is not information; it is revelation. You can't know Jesus without the Holy Spirit. I listened and realized that this was me. If that was true, nothing was stopping me from accepting Jesus. I was the first person to run forward for the altar call. I had a powerful encounter with God and my dream replayed in front of my eyes. I was crying, weeping, giving my life to Jesus, and getting touched by the Holy Spirit.

Many people at church were part of my process, showing so much love, patience, and hospitality. That was in 2008. My whole life was transformed. Imagine, God brought me all the way to England to meet me. I didn't search for Him. No one in my family was a Christian. None of us had ever heard the Gospel, no one evangelized to us, we had never held a Bible in our hands or heard a worship song or heard Christian radio. Then God chose me and gave me a new life and a purpose.

MISSION, VISION, AND LESSONS LEARNED ALONG THE WAY

What happened after that? Please tell us about your ministry, Operation Promises.

After I became a Christian in England, I saw that there were a lot of people like me. They never knew Jesus as the Savior and what He'd done on the cross. They only knew Him as a prophet. My heart started responding to the Lord's call to share about Jesus the Savior with those who don't know Him yet. My ministry is based upon God's grace for my life. There are a lot of refugees and Muslims here who have never heard the Gospel. I recognized the need for a place or a connection point specifically for these groups and those who want to serve them. We desire to help people meet Jesus, find their calling, and become who God created them to be.

We reach out to refugees and Muslims around the world, especially focusing on Europe. We have two main areas—evangelism to reach those who are not saved and equipping and training those who are saved. We also build connections with people who have a heart to reach these groups; we connect them together through this ministry. We take teams on trips to the Middle East and Europe where we do conferences, seminars, and all types of trainings.

You are also a pastor of an Iranian church in Liverpool. How did that happen?

The church I am part of, the same one where I was saved, was pastored by an English couple, my spiritual parents. After a few years of reaching the refugees, I became a small group leader. The church had a heart to work with refugees from all nations. The church grew with many Iranians, and we became the majority in the congregation. Our pastors felt led to give the church to Iranian leaders. I was one of the main leaders at that time, so they released the church over to me and a friend of mine. They mentored us and still pour into our lives.

FAITH IN ACTION

When you were saved, you started sharing your faith boldly. Some people struggle with this. What is your advice for people to step out in a greater way and share their faith?

Christ said, *"...without Me, you can do nothing"* (John 15:5). The best thing is to stick with Christ. Stay close to Him. Abide in His Word. If we have intimate relationship with the Lover of our soul, He will guide us. His heart is to spend time with us every day. Read His Word and pray. He is the Source. If we lose that Source, no matter how many ministry or outreach programs we have, they won't endure. The first step is to keep that intimate relationship. Have fellowship with the One who loves us, the One who came to lay down His life for us.

The second thing is that we have the anointing for what we were saved from. For example, if someone was addicted, and God redeemed them, then they have an anointing to break that captivity. If someone comes from broken relationships, they have the heart for and the anointing over that area. When you personally know what someone has been through, you have compassion, and you want to do something to help. Ministry is not just being a machine; we need to have compassion to love people. Stepping out means loving people. We can most easily love people who have the same pain we've been through. We know how awful it was. God redeemed us, so now we have the answer, which is Jesus.

For me, I was freed from the pain of being a refugee, the pain of not knowing the future, the confusion, the fear, and the anxiety. I didn't know the term "evangelism" for two years, but in that time, I invited more than 300 people to Christ. I didn't know what evangelism meant, but it is what I did. I reached out to lonely people. I brought food when I saw people were hungry. There was compassion in me. I helped other refugees at the camp, just like others had reached out to me. When they asked me why, I told them it was because Jesus loved me first, and I freely give what I received.

Just start by helping people struggling with the things Jesus set you free from. You can also show others the same love that was shown to you. If someone invited you to their house, invite others to your house. If somebody prayed over you, start praying for people. That reminds you that what God did for you, He can do for other people too. This simple way sets you free from fear or pressure.

Also, don't try to become like someone else. Just because someone else is preaching on the streets, doesn't mean you need to. Start with what you're comfortable with. Follow your heart, be yourself. God could change the whole world in one hour. He is not looking for workers to work hard and be religious. He wants to change the inside of us. We are children of God who follow the steps of Jesus and love other people.

Third, we are not created to work alone. Join a team and work together. Participate in a ministry trip or go to an evangelism outreach. Learn from other people and stay connected with the body of Christ. Be part of whatever your church is doing in missions or outreach. If you have a heart to cook, then cook. Everything can be used for sharing the Gospel.

That is so great Shapoor! Will you share a testimony of someone's life getting transformed by Jesus?

There are thousands of testimonies. By God's grace, over the past ten years since I was saved, we've seen more than 3,000

Muslims come to Christ all around the world. And 2,000 of those salvations were in Europe. We have seen many people with cancer healed, including my cousin in Iran. She was healed of throat cancer through prayer. The doctors didn't know what happened. They said there was miraculous restoration in her throat. We know refugees who were told by the doctor they were going to die, but they were miraculously healed.

One testimony that is special to me is when my sister got saved. I shared the Gospel with her for seven years. (It was over the phone because she was in Iran, and I am not allowed to go back there.) I asked someone to give her a Bible, but she didn't want it. I invited her to a home group, but she didn't want to join. Then Jesus appeared to her and said, "I am the way, the truth and the life. I am eternal Life. No one comes to Father except through Me." My sister was on her face crying and weeping. In the morning, she called me crying and said, "Jesus is the truth." I said, "I was trying to tell you for the last seven years!" So, that encounter with Christ was just phenomenal. What God did for my sister is a testimony. At that time many of my family members were against me. They didn't want to become Christian. Now, 98 percent of my family members are Christians: aunties, uncles, cousins, and others. Keep praying for your family!

I will share another beautiful testimony about a man in our church. He was a car mechanic in Iran, but one day he was opening a battery and acid sprayed into his eye. He became about 95 percent blind in his left eye. He had several unsuccessful surgeries in Iran, then came to England to explore other options, but nothing helped. One day, he asked me to pray for his eye. I honestly was not in the mood to pray, and I did not have faith for his eye to be healed. I prayed a simple prayer, "Jesus, by Your stripes, he is healed in Your name. Amen." I was feeling discouraged and didn't have anything to give. Nothing happened, and I did not expect it to. We went to go drink some tea.

The next morning, he called me crying. I thought something terrible happened, maybe with his family in Iran. But then he said, "I can see! I can see!" I said, "Are you sure?! Are you just looking through your good eye?" He said he tested reading something far away, and truly, his left eye was totally restored. His wife checked it too. I was shocked. I told him to come to my home because I needed to see it for myself. I saw it; he was 100 percent healed. We took him to the doctors and they didn't know what happened. They said that the vision of his left eye was better than the right eye. He has had perfect eyes now for last six years. He is still part of our church. Before his healing, he was coming to church sometimes, but had not given his life to Jesus. After he was radically healed, he became 100 percent Christian. Now he's on fire for Christ.

WALKING THROUGH DISAPPOINTMENT

Have you ever been disappointed or discouraged in your faith journey? What is your advice for people walking through discouragement?

I have been discouraged many times. The first thing is to go back to Christ. Get intimate. Many times, our serving, evangelism, or whatever else becomes our walk with God. Ministry can actually get so busy that it distances us from Christ. Spend quality time with Him, shut the door. This is first and the best. Abide in His Word—this is very, very important. Read the Psalms.

I read the entire book of Psalms maybe twice a month when I was discouraged.

The second piece of advice is to learn to cry. Learn to be honest. Learn to show your true emotions to the Lord and to close people. When you feel lonely, be honest. Don't try to be a hero. I have personally learned the value of brokenness. Many think "disappointment" is a negative word, but for me it is not negative. It leads me to brokenness. God can break anything in me, my heart and my ego and my thinking, to bring the fragrance of Christ. I don't ask God to give me disappointment; but when it comes, I bring my pain to God and surrender again. Let everything bring God more glory. We need to understand the value of brokenness, the value of crying, and the value of dependency on Him. It is beautiful.

Someone wrote that if you never felt the loneliness of Christ on the cross, then you are not a Christian. That is huge. We need to remember the suffering of Jesus in Gethsemane and on the cross. Many Christians know God understands them, but few Christians understand God. Many Christians know God feels how they feel, but few of them feel how God felt. Christ felt loneliness. Christ felt pain. None of us would want to go through that. His closest friends betrayed Him. None of us want to go through challenges, but if we can try to understand one part of what Jesus felt, it is worth it. Somehow those lonely places and low places help us understand Christ and make us like Him, so embrace them.

The last advice is to read about people in the Bible who experienced disappointment and overcame it. Learn from them. Then spend time with people. Don't go through disappointment alone. Find people you can trust and be yourself with. We need to be understood, listened to, accepted, and embraced as we walk through disappointment. We need someone to tell us they went through difficulty too, but they got through it. My pastors invited me into their home many times, and they reassured me. We all want to give up sometimes, we all go through disappointment. It is part of the journey. That is advice I can give for when you are in a low place.

Did you ever feel as if you made a mistake or failed in some way? How did you get through that?

Many times. For me, my biggest sin was not staying close to Christ. Many people don't think that is sin. I think neglecting Him and allowing the world or ministry to become your everything is sin. Several times I've neglected that close relationship with Christ. And what I did to overcome that was to become empty, zero, nothing again—and make Christ my all and everything. We have to go back, and go back, and go back.

Second, I was disobedient to my pastors and leaders. I had only been a believer for two or three years, and I had so much passion, but I was rebellious. I did not like being under authority and was thinking they didn't know things, or they were too traditional. I thought they didn't have big ideas or big vision. I compared them to other leaders and talked about my negative opinions with other people. I didn't want to be under discipleship. It was rebellion and pride. Then I experienced the mercy of God and the mercy of my leaders. They were patient with my arrogance. Time after time they'd come to me and help me and bring me back. God is so faithful and always teaches us His ways. He brings other people to help us. Just keep going back to Him again and again.

EUROPE FOCUS

What do you see God doing in Europe in this generation?

I see God giving Europe the way to bring awakening and salvation. Literally, Europe shall be saved; I believe that. But I believe the way He chooses is not always the way we are thinking. I believe God brought the refugees. There is an answer for Europe through the refugees. God's people should see that. The refugees are broken and don't have anything, so God becomes everything for them. Europe needs to come to that brokenness if they want to see revival. God is giving Europe chance after chance, in a good way. He is pursing Europe with mercy and love. He has an amazing plan for people to get saved and have their lives transformed. He has plans for the kingdom of Heaven to invade Europe, in social places, workplaces...everywhere. The kingdom of the Lord is coming.

God is also using Europe in a mighty way. First, many refugees are coming to Christ through Europe. Many of them will go to the Middle East and bring salvation to those nations. God is using the openness of Europe. I also see that the awakening happening with the refugees is bringing awakening to the church. Some churches have not had many new people or salvations. When refugees meet Jesus and start attending church, the church leaders have to think about how to involve them. When they see people come in and receive salvation, they get excited. It's like a well opening. In Nehemiah it says to restore the walls and the gates. The gates are being restored in Europe. This is what I see.

Amazing opportunities are happening—awakening, salvations, and lives transformed. How are we going to respond to the new believers in the European nations? There are more Muslims who have come to Christ in the last ten years than during the thirteenth century (the beginning of Islam) until a decade ago. That shows us what age we are living in. There are massive opportunities to lead Muslims to Christ.

What was sown in the nations is now being reaped. England and Germany and others sent missionaries around the world for years and years. Now they are reaping the people. Now, people are coming into their nations and becoming evangelists there. God remembers what they did. The missionaries are returning, but not necessarily as official missionaries through an organization. God's ways are higher than our ways. Refugees encounter Jesus and then God puts it on their hearts to share the Gospel with the German people, the English people, the European people. This is a time for Europe to see that there is a huge need for Christ and God.

Are there any specific countries you see God highlighting in Europe?

I could easily say the Netherlands, Germany, and England. With these three, there's something deep happening. And maybe Greece? These three or four countries are going to see big, big things happening.

And what about unity? How do we build unity in the church when people have different perspectives and styles?

If we only understood one prayer that Jesus prayed for us, and we answered His prayer—it is John 17. Jesus prays for us that we may be one like He and the Father are one. When we are united, we are answering Jesus's prayer. If we understand how important that is, we will work to find many ways to fulfill that. We also need to allow God's ways to change our ways.

A key for unity is coming to God and saying, "Your ways are higher than my ways, and Your thoughts are different from my thoughts." This is a huge truth. If we want to become more united, sometimes we need to let go of our traditional ways. Sometimes people just continue in what they are doing and ignore the fresh things God brings. That can look like being flexible or recognizing another culture. We need to give space for diversity of ideas about how to do ministry. Some people want to do massive evangelism, and some want one by one. That type of diversity is the beauty of coming together.

Another way to help with unity is supporting each other. If people pay attention to other ministries and what God is calling them to do, people will feel more valued. Help other ministries, pray for them, give financially, do administration for them, join groups, share ideas, teach in schools, attend events. Come alongside people and encourage them. We can ask people, "What is your vision? What has God put on your heart? How can I help you? You can send people to their event, you can rent your building to them, introduce them to someone, preach in their church or event, etc. And, of course, pray for each other. Many people are supporting each other already. It is beautiful how we can help each other.

It will also help if we have more creativity by welcoming new evangelists, young people, the people God is bringing in now. Maybe they're not known, but ask them, "What is your vision? What has God put in your heart, and how can I help you?" That's bringing the network together.

That's great! And so through all of this, are you hopeful for what God is doing in Europe?

Yes, 100 percent. I could not be more hopeful than now. I believe God brought me to Europe and God is bringing thousands of people to Europe. Sometimes when people watch the media and see so many refugees coming, they are shocked. This is human thinking, not God's way of thinking. God is not surprised or concerned about this! Isaiah 46:10 says God knows the end from the beginning. If God allows things to happen, He knows what He is doing. And I think it is massive.

I love Europe with all my heart. I love the freedom that we have to go and share the Gospel. I love the people; they are coming together. God is calling many people, bringing many people to Europe to come and be part of what He is doing. We are living in an extremely exciting time in Europe.

LIFE APPLICATION—THE RECKLESS LOVE OF GOD

I love Shapoor's testimony. His life demonstrates the relentless love of God and the radical power of the Gospel. Shapoor was the top Muslim student, chosen to recite the Quran daily. Then he almost died fleeing for his life. He went through dark times, but in his hardest season, God broke through. Everything changed. The Gospel is real. The fields are white for harvest among refugee communities. What some have deemed the "refugee crisis" is actually a powerful opportunity for the Gospel. The enemy wants to use terrorism to bring fear and hate, but

God wants to bring love and salvation. Let's recognize the times we are living in and receive refugees with the love of Christ.

I also deeply appreciate Shapoor's perspective on discouragement. All of us have walked through pain, challenges, and disappointments. How we respond is important to God and to our own journey. Shapoor reminds us to go back to Jesus. If ministry makes us so busy that we don't have time to abide, it's time for a shift back to the secret place. From there, let your pain out. It's okay to not be okay, but don't suffer alone. Invite God in and talk and pray with people in your life. Finally, Shapoor describes this beautiful process of letting our brokenness draw us closer to Jesus. Surrender everything to Him over and over again and be dependent on Him. Fellowship with Jesus in His sufferings. He knows the lonely places. He also brings us through and into the power of His resurrection.

When it comes to ministry, Shapoor presents an interesting concept. We have authority over whatever we were saved from because we understand the pain firsthand, and we have experienced the victory. That is powerful. Jesus healed the sick with compassion. We can have the most authentic compassion for those suffering because of things we ourselves have been through. From where did Jesus rescue you? From what pain, brokenness, or darkness were you set free? Oftentimes God uses us in the very areas that used to trap us. This can be another clue to help you find your calling.

Shapoor encourages us not to copy anyone else. If you are not loud, you don't have to become loud. Just be yourself. If you love to cook, cook for Jesus and share your food with the hungry. If you love to paint nails, have a spa day and invite friends who don't know Jesus. Join in with your church and go as a team. Sometimes we put pressure on ourselves to minister in a certain way or compare ourselves to someone we see on the platform or on social media. The great news is, God created you to be you! You don't have to model your life after someone else. The pressure is off. Search for what makes you come alive. Search for the people groups that move your heart. Everyone everywhere needs God's love. There are desperate and broken people in every city and every nation. That means the opportunities are vast for you to share His love wherever you feel drawn. You get to shine as your beautiful, wonderful self. Go for it!

7

Matthias Kuhn (Kuno)

Organization: G-Movement
Position: Senior Leader
Location: Thun, Switzerland

Personal Background

What is your favorite thing to do on your day off?

I like spending quality time with my wife or with my family. Only one of our children is still living at home, the other three have moved out. When the children still lived at home, I always spent a lot of time with them. We all like sports—tennis in the summer and skiing in the winter.

If you could have lunch with one person, whom would you choose?

I think this is a boring answer, but the most important person next to Jesus is my wife. She is really my best friend, so I like to spend a lot of time with her. Otherwise, I like to spend time with other people in general. They all have great stories of Jesus. I can learn something from every person, and I like to hear people's stories.

Please tell us about yourself and how you came to faith.

I have been married for thirty years, and we have four children. Three are already married. I grew up in the countryside in Emmental, Switzerland; this is where the Emmental cheese comes from. I was born into a Christian family, but my parents attended a more traditional church. They did live really passionately and ran a discipleship program, working with people with alcohol addiction. My father brought many people into our home who were sick or struggling. I saw faith in the life of my parents. It was so nice to see that Jesus really lived at our home.

When I was a young man, 14 years old, I attended a more Spirit-filled church. I started going regularly and later stepped into leadership. For the past twenty years, I have been leading a church and now a movement. Ten years ago, we planted a discipleship school. We invite people to come for one year and live together, and we help train them in the lifestyle of Jesus.

MISSION, VISION, AND LESSONS LEARNED ALONG THE WAY

Please tell us about G-Movement.

We initially planted the church about 20 years ago, and now it has developed into the G-Movement, a church planting network.

I will start with the story of how the church began. I was working with three other churches running outreaches in a skate park in our area. Through the skate park outreaches, many young people came to Jesus, but then I felt that the churches were not ready to welcome all of these young people. They liked me, but they didn't seem to like my organization of young people. Then God put it on my heart to plant a new church and gave me vision for this. That was the start: me and these young people from the skate park.

During the first leadership and mission meeting, God spoke one sentence to me. I heard Him say, "Plant a church, not to build an institution, but plant a church to give your life to a lost generation, a lost world." This is one of the most important things for us, not to build something big and have big events, but to keep our focus on the lost world. When I spoke about this vision for the first time, the Holy Spirit came so strongly in the room. It was amazing. We knew this was our vision, and we were called to begin this movement. We knew we weren't called to plant a church for new things or new events, but to plant a church for the lost world.

How do you as a movement keep your focus on this mission and what God called you to?

I think that the most important thing for any church or organization is not to gather people and make them happy. We do gather together and have fellowship together and experience new dimensions in God, but the most important thing is to *send* people, not to *gather* people. I like to bring the Gospel to the people, not bring the people to the church. This is the most important focus in my mindset: we don't build a church for the neighborhood and focus on bringing neighbors to church; instead, we build a church to train disciples to take the Gospel into the neighborhoods.

This mindset shift was crucial for me. Before, I worked at a church where we spent so much time empowering people to invite people to the church. In my opinion, that is not the right way because Jesus sent His disciples *out*. He gathered them to empower them, and then He sent them out again. As a church family, we send our people out every morning to share the Gospel at their school or at their workplace. It's a different strategy, not to gather the power and all the gifts from the people to the church; that's one way, but we have to go both ways. I like to see people take responsibility in their neighborhood, not only in the church.

Wow, that is a shift of mindset. How have you been able to teach people in this way and carry out your vision?

One of the most important parts of the strategy is that we only gather as a larger church once a month. When we first began the church, many people wanted to join, but we did not want them to spend all their energy on coming to church each week and get too tired to take the Gospel to their communities. We told our church to begin small groups with other Christians in their neighborhoods, so they could be salt and light. These house churches are more like families, and people can invite others to the small groups. In the groups, we read the Bible and pray with other people in our community. So we model church, not with a lot of events, but with a clear lifestyle. Then once a month we all gather together for a larger service.

Who are the leaders of the small groups, and what type of training and input do they receive?

The most important time is our monthly small group leader's meeting. There, I spend time with our small group leaders, bringing them into the vision and sharing my heart with them. For me, as a church planter, this meeting is even more important than Sunday services because the small group leaders bring the vision to the people and carry out our heart. It's important that they understand my heart and are empowered to bring this to their groups.

That is the first point. The second point is that Jesus did not tell us to make believers, He told us to make disciples. We don't just see the small group leaders once a month at a meeting, we spend time together regularly. I am their friend and a spiritual father. Then they are spiritual fathers to the next leaders.

Church is a family; and when new babies come into our family, we spend the time to empower them and send them out. We invite people, and then we train them. The goal is not to keep them there for life; the vision is to send them out to build new families. So we invite people, train them, and send them out to plant new families. When we have monthly church gatherings, all these families come together as a community of relatives. Each family has their own unique style. The larger gathering is like a gathering of relatives, not the closest circle, but still part of the same family.

Have you seen a lot of growth and people coming to Christ through this model?

We see two things through our model. First, a lot of people grow in Jesus because they take responsibility for their lives, their families, and their neighborhoods. When people take responsibility, together with Jesus, they grow up. Many people in our movement have become very mature in Christ through this process of taking responsibility for their communities.

The second thing is that some people have a real heart for evangelism and bring many to Jesus. There is a very social area in our city, but a lot of dark things go on there. About sixty or so people from our church decided to move into that area and live together right in the middle of it. They spend a lot of time with their neighbors, inviting them to the small groups, helping them in their normal lives, and sharing the Gospel. Some people have come to Jesus, other people are on the way to come to Jesus. Overall, we see a lot of people grow up and take responsibility and share the Gospel.

The most important impact we've had is in the youth movement. We have a youth event every month here in the area with about a thousand young people. This is where we see the most fruit through evangelism. Evangelism is also our lifestyle. All of us spend time with our nonbelieving friends with the desire to share Jesus. This is our focus.

Why do you think God is moving powerfully through you and your movement? What can we learn from your experiences and your model?

We all need the grace of God—that is the most important thing! Jesus gives grace to us in our weakness. In our model, people can't delegate responsibility to the church. They have to take the lead, and in that place of weakness, they need the grace of God. God loves these moments when we stand in our weakness and ask for His grace. We don't have a big Sunday service each week. I love Sunday services, and I preach at churches most weeks, but there is more power there. This is a key: we help people come to the place of weakness, so they have to cry out to Jesus to help them, and God answers with His grace.

You have a unique model of small groups and once-a-month corporate service. Many people who will read this book go to church on a weekly basis. What can they learn from your model that also applies to their context?

I do not believe only in our model. I have a call to make disciples. This is the Great Commission that Jesus gave His followers, to make disciples, not to make believers or church centers. It is not about following our model, but every person should ask themselves, "Where are my disciples?" Our model might not be possible in a bigger church, but this is a personal question, not a question about structure. Every person should be making disciples, bringing their neighbors to Jesus, training them, then helping them to bring other people to Jesus too. This is most important and can function in different ways and contexts. Our model is not the point, our heart is the point—to make disciples.

What advice do you have for people who are searching for their calling and how do you help people find their calling?

Sometimes people come and ask me to give them a ministry or a platform. I tell them I can be a friend to them and help them take the Gospel to their neighbors. I think it starts with little steps. Some people don't like this, they just want to be on the big stage. That is not the way in my opinion. The way of the kingdom of God is to start with the little things, and then the little things lead to the bigger things—not the other way around. My desire is to be a father who helps people take the little steps to obey and share the Gospel and invite the people around them, and then to do it again and again and again until their breakthrough arrives.

SHARING YOUR FAITH

Please share a testimony of stepping out in faith and seeing a good result.

Every week I walk around in my city, spending time with God and praying for hearts to be prepared. I also look for opportunities to share the Gospel wherever I am. About three years ago, I went to get my hair cut, and at the salon, I was standing at the counter sharing the Gospel with the man next to me. A hairdresser heard me and said, "You are a crazy man. You like Jesus, what is this?" In Luke 10:6, Jesus teaches His disciples about finding a "man of peace." This is someone who will welcome them into the area and help them share the Gospel there. I felt in my spirit that this hairdresser would become a person of peace.

I started going to the salon every week to share more with her. The woman and I started a friendship, and she was open to the Gospel. Now, whenever I go to the salon, she tells all of her many customers that I am a pastor and asks them if they have any prayer requests.

So today I went to get my hair cut, and a Chinese man was sitting there. As usual, she told him I was a pastor. She said I don't really look like one, but that I am a believer in Jesus. Each time I go, she opens the door for me to share the Gospel, so I get to pray with many people in the hair salon! Today I was there for an hour talking to several people about God. It is a great networking place, and it all started with a small conversation. I like that God shows us people of peace. She is one of them. Ask God to lead you to people of peace who will give you access to and credibility with groups of people you might not otherwise meet. This is one strategy Jesus teaches us for sharing the Gospel.

Another story: I was flying through Caucasus, a mountainous area between the Black Sea and the Caspian Sea on the border of Asia and Europe, a special place with a lot of Muslim people. It is actually about 99 percent Muslim and an "unreached place" for the Gospel. The plane was crowded, my seat felt very small, and it was right next to the bathroom—not the best place! Then God spoke to me, "Look toward the right side." On the other side of the aisle, there was a Russian woman around 60 years old. God gave me a word of knowledge for her, but she didn't speak German. Actually, forty years ago, she learned a small amount of German, but hadn't used it since then. Then I spoke to her, and she understood everything!

She felt it was such a miracle that she could understand my German, and she replied with a few words. I prayed with her about the word of knowledge, and she was completely healed. She asked me to meet her at the baggage claim to pray for her two friends who also had sickness and pain. It was so special because I got to share and pray with them right in the middle of all the Muslim people! Both of the friends were completely healed. After three days, I called them; and because they were all completely healed, they repented and gave their lives to Jesus. Those are two God stories that are lifestyle stories, not the big event. I like events too, but everyday miracles are more common than we realize.

That is so encouraging! Many people are afraid to share their faith, don't know what to say; or they have even tried sharing, but their experience was not as fruitful as the stories you shared. What is your advice?

Part of our challenge is that sometimes the devil wants to kill our fruit or stop us from sharing the Gospel. That said, I frequently put it like this: I love my wife, so I talk about her. The most important thing is to love Jesus; because when you love Jesus, you will want to share Him with other people. My goal is to share with someone every day using the name of Jesus because His name is powerful.

When I mentor people, I encourage them to take time with Jesus and fall in love with Him—that is the start. Begin there so that you can share something from your heart, not something you were trained to say or something you're saying because you are trying to be a good Christian. People today are looking for authenticity. They can tell right away if you are being real or fake or following a manual. The most important thing is to really fall in love with Jesus and spend time with Him. Then pray for God to give you situations where you can speak about Jesus. Look for those moments.

What might that moment look like? How do you start a conversation?

Here is one tip I've learned: normally, we ask people how they are doing. When they reply "Good," ask them to tell you more. People are normally shocked, and they will start talking to you because they feel you like them and want to hear their heart. When we spend time with people and give them honor, they will tell us more about themselves and also give us honor, opening the door for us to share more too. Then we can start talking about Jesus.

NAVIGATING DISAPPOINTMENT

That's great advice! The next question is about facing disappointment. We all go through challenging times. What is your advice for people who are feeling discouraged or disappointed?

The important point here is that we all need community, and not just a community where you go when you're happy, but the type of community where you can say, "I'm disappointed." To me, this is a small group. I'm reminded of the story of Elijah in First Kings 18 and 19. Elijah, a devoted prophet of God, takes a stand against 450 prophets of Baal and 400 prophets of Asherah. God did a mighty miracle and showed Himself when Elijah asked Him to come. It was so powerful, yet shortly after Elijah was extremely disappointed, even asking God to take his life. The bigger enemy is not 850 opponents, but the solitude of being all by himself.

You have to spend time with other people. This is our secure place in which God empowers us afresh. For me, I can share my disappointments with my people around me, because they know me. They know my failures; they see my failures. They do not only see my Sunday face. They see how I live, so I don't have a problem sharing my problems with them because we know each other, which is the point.

But when I am only a pastor, then I have a problem because the pastor always has to have a smile on his face. I think of myself as a father rather than as a pastor, and a father can be angry sometimes or disappointed. It's not a problem for my children because they know me.

Have you ever started a new program or tried a new idea, but it didn't go very well? What did you do?

Yes, it's always a challenge to start new things in the kingdom of God because we have an enemy. Here's an example of a "failure." Sometimes when I go to the streets or shops, I feel I have a word of knowledge, so I approach the person. I might ask if he has a problem with his back and then he may say, "No, what's your problem?!" Then I have to remind myself that it is okay because I am still a child of God. I can have failures. We say in our community that we have a culture of risk, and a failure is not the end. It is part of life. When I take a risk, it is possible that it ends in a failure. When I risk nothing, I never fail but I also never see anything good happen. When we are willing to take risks, we will get to experience the incredible things God has for our lives.

Of course, there were times when we had a vision and started it, and it didn't go as we hoped. We planned an Alpha course, for example, and no one came. We shook the dust off our feet and moved forward. Jesus said we will have dust sometimes (Luke 10:11). If we only sit alone in the secret place, it would not be very interesting or productive. We would have no failures, but we would also have no wonderful experiences with God.

EUROPE FOCUS

What do you see God doing in Europe in this generation?

I sense this generation is so disappointed because they see no fathers. I feel they have a hunger for real relationship. When I look around the world, every revival is an answer to the biggest needs of that generation. The biggest need of this generation is for relationship. Now we stand at this point where people are crying out for real relationship, and the church has an answer for this need. I'm so hopeful!

The second thing is that Jesus said the first will be the last, and the last will be the first. When we see the history of the church, Europe was the first continent to be reached with the Gospel. And now I feel Europe is the last continent to come back to Jesus. So, it's time for Europe!

And are there any special countries you feel God is really highlighting?

Of course, I think Switzerland and my town. I also feel Iran, but it is not in Europe. God is calling the Muslim people to His heart even in Europe. Iran has the biggest Christian growth right now, but they are mostly underground. I think we can all learn from the underground churches around Europe.

Then for Europe, one year ago I went to Austria, and I had been there many times before. In the past, I never really heard of people coming to Jesus in Austria. But now, a lot of people are coming to Jesus and churches are growing quickly. I feel Austria is a country God is highlighting in Europe, but still not on the level of Iran or other Middle Eastern nations.

How do you think we can work toward building more unity among churches and Christians?

We need a unity view or a unity vision. Sometimes we all come together because we all love each other and enjoy being together, but this is not real unity. We need a unity calling for the harvest. When we gather, we can't just gather because we love each other. I love people and being together too, but that is not building long-term unity together. What we need is a clear view toward Jesus and His harvest because His passion is to bring the harvest to the Father. I think this is real unity—when we have a view and a vision together.

What does that look like if people or churches have different beliefs or different styles?

When I see that people love Jesus and have a vision for the harvest, the other things do not matter. It doesn't matter if their church has a different culture than mine. Actually, we need those different cultures coming together, not just one style of worship that I enjoy, that is not the point. The point is when I see Jesus in people, and they also have vision for the harvest, those are the most important points to come together over, not our culture or style.

LIFE APPLICATION—WHERE ARE YOUR DISCIPLES?

Kuno has a burning passion for lost people to meet Jesus. His ministry, his friendships, even his trips to the hairdresser center on this one thing. And where does this start? It starts with falling more in love with Jesus. It's not about a manual or a checklist, it's about loving Jesus and loving people. His advice is simply to start by asking someone how they are doing. When they tell you the standard, "Good," ask for more details. People long for connection. They long to be seen and known. They long for authenticity.

Kuno took this a step further, and it led him into his ministry model. It began with skater youth who met Jesus but didn't fit in at church and the churches didn't seem comfortable receiving them. So, he started a church where they were embraced. Based on his experiences, he found church could take a lot of time and energy, then people were asked to bring friends to church. This isn't a bad thing, but he found it was even more effective to flip the model and bring the Gospel to the neighborhood. The focus is on sharing Jesus and making disciples. Jesus gave the Great Commission to disciple nations, baptize, and teach people His ways. Whatever model we choose, Jesus's Commission should be our core mission. Kuno asks this question, "Where are your disciples?" Are people meeting Jesus, learning more about His ways, and reaching others?

The last point I want to highlight is that church is family. We share about Jesus because we love Him, and we want others to love Him too. We bring people into the family of God. We bring them into relationship with God and with the people of God. In this family context, no one is alone. We support one another, and we live life together. We encourage one another to follow God and take risks. Then if things go badly, or we get discouraged, there will be someone close by to help us out. We all need each other. Even Elijah, after defeating hundreds of false prophets, got so lonely he wanted to die. That is extreme! So, if you feel lonely, you're not the only one. Reach out; talk to someone. And if you see lonely people, invite them to coffee.

The way we build solid relationships is through honesty and vulnerability. We've seen highly respected leaders fall with devastating repercussions for their families and for those following them. The way we prevent this in our own lives is by having people who know us inside and out. Share the little struggles along the way so they don't become bigger and bigger. Family allows us to be imperfect and that creates a safe place for everyone. Kuno puts it this way: he is not just a pastor who has to have a smile on his face all the time, he is a father who is allowed to be angry or disappointed. Please take this to heart. If you are struggling with something big or small, don't let shame keep you hidden. Find a safe person and share it. When we confess, we get free. When we allow ourselves to be real, on the good days and the tough ones, we find ourselves truly known—and that's family.

8

Paulina Zoetebier

Organization: House of Heroes Church
Position: Co-Leader of the Worship Team, Church Elder
Location: Harderwijk, The Netherlands

Personal Background

What is your favorite thing to do on your day off?

I love to go out with my family, to take our girls and jump into the car and go anywhere. We like going for walks, renting a boat, or going to the zoo. We love to be outdoors. I also love to motorcycle ride with my husband.

What is your favorite Bible verse?

Psalm 40, it is a testimony of my life.

> *I waited patiently for the Lord;*
> *And He inclined to me,*

And heard my cry.
He also brought me up out of a horrible pit,
Out of the miry clay,
And set my feet upon a rock,
And established my steps.
He has put a new song in my mouth—
Praise to our God;
Many will see it and fear,
And will trust in the Lord
(Psalm 40:1-3).

If you could have lunch with one person, whom would you choose?

My husband, of course. And if it is a possible answer, I would also choose Jesus.

Please tell us about yourself and in what areas you minister.

My husband and I co-lead the worship team and serve as elders in House of Heroes Church, led by Mattheus van der Steen. We have a team of about forty-five people including the band, media, sound, and prayer teams. I also lead a choir for Gospel Music Festival. We travel and minister around the world and see God move in powerful ways. This group is more like a family, and our rehearsals are like services full of God's presence.

I coach worship teams from many different types of churches and am a personal worship coach for people from all over. People see me at a worship conference and God speaks, or they get inspired and reach out to me. I really love it. I didn't think I was a teacher, but I just stepped in, and now it's my passion. God is really working, especially through the one-on-one coaching. My heart is to encourage people and raise up healthy sons and daughters who know who they are—beloved children of the Most High King. I teach about how to live close to Jesus every day, stepping into intimacy through worship and prayer, and never leaving this place.

When we live from the intimacy of God's presence, we learn about Him, and we learn about ourselves as well. We learn who we truly are. After people understand this revelation of intimacy, then I teach about taking our authority. The Book of Revelation says the devil is accusing us 24/7. We need to learn how to step into our position as sons and daughters of God and open our mouths declaring from our authority. I also disciple in making good choices and obeying God. Through the coaching, all of these areas come together.

I also speak and teach in different contexts. I spoke at a Dutch event called Opwekking, "Revival." This is a large event where many Christians from different denominations come together. Their main event draws about 25,000 people. I spoke at a pre-event, sharing about worship, intimacy, identity, and authority. It was an honor that I was invited as a charismatic worship leader. There is a desire in our nation to go deeper and experience something real. People are surrendering their hearts to Jesus in a new way; they want to see more. God is doing something special because I am receiving invitations into these streams, which traditionally have a different style but are now opening up more for Holy Spirit to move through worship.

I absolutely love everything I do!

How did you come to faith? Please share your testimony with us.

I grew up in a Christian family and Jesus was part of my life since my childhood. I couldn't imagine a life without God. Unfortunately, our family was somewhat dysfunctional. My father was a powerful, inspiring evangelist and singer. My three sisters and I grew up singing. My father taught us to harmonize and sing together. We sang while he played the organ—a bit like the Von Trapp family from *The Sound of Music* movie. This helped me so much because singing and harmonizing now come as easily as breathing for me. Sadly, my father suffered from depression and mental health issues. He started drinking and became an alcoholic, so it was unsafe in the house. The atmosphere was very tense and lonely. When I was 11 or 12, my sisters had all moved out to marry or study. My guitar became my best friend, and I began writing songs about birds, the sky, anything—music was a comfort.

In the midst of all this, God was very important to me. I was baptized when I was 17. Unfortunately, my view of God was mixed with the realities of how my natural father was, so I never really felt accepted or loved. My impression of God was that He was a father you had to work for in order to receive grace. Growing up, our home had a challenging spiritual atmosphere that wasn't peaceful. I was always very prophetic, and I sensed spiritual battles when I closed my eyes. In order to sleep, I had to imagine green hills and flowers to try to find peace.

When I was about 28, I took time to recover and receive restoration from God for my brokenness. God used many people and spoke to me personally to heal me. Someone gave me the exact right book, someone said just the thing I needed to hear, in that way many people came alongside me. This healing recovery process went on for about two and a half or three years, where God did so much restoration over my identity. I really started to understand I am a daughter of God and made after His own image. He put everything in me.

God led me through processes of breaking off past hurts and helping me to see Him as He truly is, instead of through a broken mirror. Throughout the journey, God was always faithful and always with me. Rene, my husband, also went through a lot because he came from a broken background and didn't grow up Christian. We didn't have friends who could relate or help us. It was just us and Jesus, and He really did a miracle in our lives. Our lives are a testimony.

Although it was a process, there was one distinct moment that felt like a "reset" moment for me. We had friends over, and one friend pointed out something hurtful I had said to Rene. I defended myself saying I hadn't meant it that way. I felt very angry, but at the same time I knew she was right. She put her finger on something in me that was part of the old religious mindset, not loving or gracious. I felt exposed, but I decided to let God into that moment. I asked Him to break off all my religious mindsets and give me a new perspective of who He really is. I was brought up in a religious church that taught us that all other churches were the anti-Christ and taught false beliefs. Letting go of all I was taught and the way of thinking I grew up with felt scary, but I knew I needed to do that.

I didn't really know who I was or how loved I was by God. When I gave God permission to change my mindset, I felt like I would fully lose control or even lose my mind. But when I did, everything changed. When I read the Bible before, I didn't understand it; but now, the words began to touch my heart. I would cry as I read. God also connected us with spiritual mothers and fathers who loved us unconditionally. Our natural parents weren't able to give us that model of love, but now we began to receive through the people God put in our lives. This was a massive turning point for us. God fully changed my perspective on everything—who He is, who Jesus is, how He loves me.

In the past I also struggled with fear. One time when I was in the house alone, I got very scared. My house felt full of darkness, and I could barely breathe because I was so afraid. At first, I went back to my old system of praying, with intense, battling-type prayer. Then I reminded myself I needed to pray from my new understanding of God. I prayed the Lord's Prayer, but it didn't help; I felt the darkness come closer and closer. I thought I would choke.

Then I went upstairs and decided I would not do anything, but just fall back into God. The darkness felt so heavy I thought I would die, but then God came. It was like a thick, white cloud in my bedroom. I saw a rider on a horse with a torch in His right hand, and I heard the audible voice of God saying, "I win for you." In that moment, peace, light, and rest flooded into the room, and I immediately felt better.

That moment changed my life, and I thank God for it over and over. I knew in a new way that Jesus really exists, and He will show up when I need Him. Even in our worst moments, He will show up. I didn't even know how to pray because I knew it wasn't my old system from growing up, but from knowing Him in a new way. Even when I woke up that night, I felt His rest and light still in the room. He changed everything in a moment.

Those encounters mark you forever. When I go through storms now or challenging times, I thank God for all He did in my life. I thank Him for those encounters. I thank Him for rescuing my marriage and being with my children and changing my life. So that is my testimony!

MISSION, VISION, AND LESSONS LEARNED ALONG THE WAY

Please tell us about House of Heroes and the Gospel Choir. What is your mission and how do you live out that mission?

Our heart is really after souls. When you have a heart for souls, everything else changes as well. Your worship changes. The heart of our church is apostolic: equipping people and sending them out into their destinies to see nations changed. We want to help people utilize the talents they have whether that is in business or any other area. In House of Heroes, our heart is to equip, help, encourage, and set people free. There is a world out there that needs Jesus, so our goal is to go beyond the four walls of the church and reach the lost. As a choir, we love to sing out on the streets and assemble flash mobs. We love to use our worship for evangelism.

Worship and the presence of God is central. God is enthroned on the praises of His people; and when we open our mouths to worship and live lifestyles of worship, He comes in a powerful way. We love the presence. Jesus is everything. In the choir, we teach people Jesus needs to come first and be in the center of everything we do personally and as a group. As we worship, words of glory, love, healing, deliverance, revelation, and prophecy are released and birthed from His presence. Our mission is to glorify Him because

He's worthy, and our goal is to bring people together into the place of witnessing His glory and experiencing how Holy Spirit works.

Please share a testimony of seeing God move in a powerful way through your ministry.

We were invited to France to sing in a Gospel Music Festival. The organizers felt a Gospel singing event would be a great way to reach people. The event was held at a nightclub, where anyone was welcome to attend. Another Gospel choir sang first, then left right after. When it was our turn, our choir worshipped God as we always do. Then Mattheus preached the Gospel. It was clear that many people there were not used to this type of worship or preaching. The club owner thought the event was just Gospel singing and seemed uncomfortable during the preaching. The sound technician actually seemed irritated. I knew God was going to move in their lives though, and I was excited to see that. When we realized the event was different from what we expected, we asked God for a new strategy.

The second day, we went on the streets and did flash mobs and worship in the market, with permission from the mayor. We shared the Gospel and gave out fliers for the event. It was strong and powerful. Our team was well connected, and we experienced healings in the streets that afternoon. Then the time came for the evening meeting. I felt God wanted to use our choir, but we needed to connect to the audience in a different way, especially those who weren't Christians. We made it really fun, inviting people to clap, dance, and sing along. We even sang some songs in French—God gave me the grace for that! People responded really well and opened their hearts. Then I shared that God heals people and wanted to heal people that night.

God healed a woman in the choir earlier that day, so I invited her to share her testimony. She showed them how, before, she could not bend over because of strong back pain, but then Jesus healed her when people prayed for her. She demonstrated that she could now bend down and pick up a water bottle. You could feel Holy Spirit come in as she shared, and it felt like faith was stirred. We sang "Alpha and Omega" in French, and the presence of God came.

Mattheus wanted to honor the owner, but we also knew God would touch people that night, so he got up and preached the Gospel with passion. It was the right decision because forty people gave their lives to Jesus, including the owner of the dance club, the sound technician, a dancer from the club, and many others! It was a very powerful God experience.

The club owner even decided to start having Gospel nights on a regular basis from then on! We saw clearly that God has a strategy for each place even if there is resistance at the beginning. The presence of God came, and love filled the room. Everyone was part of it. Our choir was a huge part of it. They are not just singers. They are sons and daughters who know who they are and what they carry. They see people who are broken and they pour out love. They are a ministry team, not just a worship team.

STEPPING INTO CALLING

You shared that you loved singing from a very young age, but when did you start to step into your calling as a worship leader? How did it begin for you?

When I was in my 30s, I was asked to lead a worship night for a youth camp for refugees. I was surprised that they asked me because I wasn't leading worship yet. I can remember when I was preparing for the evening. I was sitting in my backyard, and I felt so much compassion for the youth. I chose some songs I thought would be good. When I got to the camp, there were a few men making trouble there. It was also so hot—we were all sweating. But when we started the program, I just took my guitar and started singing. As we were singing, the atmosphere changed immediately. I was amazed at what was happening.

All the leaders of the youth camp were from much more traditional backgrounds, mostly Dutch Reformed and Baptist. I was the only evangelical. I led some songs, then I led a practical exercise. I had all of the youth make up their own rap, song, or dance about who God is for them. Everyone came up to present, and everyone was crying. There was so much presence of God. It was incredibly touching. By the end, everyone had their hands up in worship. I could no longer tell who was from which denomination. We were all together in unity. We all carried so much love for the refugees. We were together for one goal, that was Jesus and seeing Him work in the refugees.

All walls just fell away, and worship connected us. It was really strong. That was the point when I knew God was calling me to lead worship. I could feel everything come together—souls, love, taking care of people, being one, not being divided. When these things come together, God comes. I didn't understand then whatI didn't understand then what I understand now, that it was the beginning of something new in my life. That was the start of me understanding what it meant to be a worship leader.

Now you are having a huge impact, but how was the journey for you? Please share more about your story.

It's a journey. You make a choice. You just grab Jesus, hold on tight, close your eyes, and say, "Take me anywhere You want me to go." That's how it is. When we stepped in, God led us clearly to Mattheus van der Steen's ministry. At the time, we were part of a church in our local village. God also spoke to us about reaching the lost, so we started a ministry where we prayed for the city, helped refugees in practical ways, and provided food for the hungry. We also joined Arch, a training and equipping program led by Mattheus on Sunday afternoons. At one point, our local pastor asked Rene to become an elder and asked me to lead the worship team. We knew we would have to stop being part of Arch and be fully committed to our church if we stepped into the church leadership. We asked God to speak clearly that weekend and help us choose which direction to take.

That afternoon, we were at an Arch service and Mattheus announced that there would be a meeting for people who have a heart for music and worship after the service. They wanted to make a team for worship and ministry at Arch events. We were not expecting that, but we loved Arch. We were just eating up everything taught there. The speakers came from all around the world, and they were doing the type of ministry we had a passion for out in the harvest field.

At the end of the service, Rene and I looked at each other, and we just knew God wanted us to be at that meeting. Nobody really knew us there. Mattheus didn't know us. But we went to the meeting, and when we came out, we were head coordinators over the music team! I'm not exaggerating, that's exactly how it went.

It was a "suddenly" of God. It was a clear confirmation that God wanted us to be there.

At that time life was like a roller coaster. Mattheus started the House of Heroes church. We helped him with it from the start. We went through the process of defining our vision and DNA, both of the church and of the worship team. I also remember reading Mattheus's book, *Dare to Dream,* before I knew him personally. As I read the words God spoke to him, they were familiar because they were so similar to what God had spoken to me. I recognized the voice. We came together as we realized we had the same heart and the same DNA.

Then we were invited to a big campaign in Myanmar with Mattheus and a team. We had taken local vacations in our caravan but had never even been on an airplane! That trip changed us. During the trip, we got to know the heart of the ministry. We did outreaches in the slums. We saw the Holy Spirit work powerfully. We really saw blind eyes open, deaf ears hear, children crying out for the Holy Spirit touched by the Holy Spirit. We were overwhelmed. The heart and vision Mattheus carried were exactly the same as ours. That first trip marked us and changed us. We knew this was what God was calling us into.

Of course, our other ministry was also foundational and great preparation. I cried so much for our city and for lost souls. I remember having times when I felt such a burden to knock on doors, run up to people, and share with them about Jesus. I felt God's heart for people. I could see and sense how serious it was that many people around me were lost souls. We prayed for the lost and did ministry in our city. So, our hearts were similar to Mattheus's heart for the lost. The fact that we came together was really appointed by Heaven; it was God's will. From that time, my husband and I have had a covenant friendship with Mattheus. We helped build his church and the worship team. We have gone through many things together.

Please share your hearts as leaders of the worship team. What is your focus?

Rene and I personally love the culture of family. We are like a father and mother for many people on our team. That is who we are. I love honesty and being real; I hate masks. We love encouraging our worship family to grow in a healthy lifestyle of knowing who they are, knowing how much God loves them, and obeying God from that place. The main thing for us is to help people become who they are in God and walk into their calling and destiny. Of course, we also help them vocally and train them in their gifting.

Because the DNA and vision are very clear, people want to join and step in. It is important to have a clear vision. People who join have the same heart for reaching the lost and taking care of the poor and the needy. That is what we love. Worship with our voices and with our lives. I believe worship has to be connected to taking care of the broken and those in need. I get irritated when worship sets just feel like performances, because it shows they've missed the heart of it. Worship has to be for God. Also, we are in a battle and worship is our weapon. When we worship with that mindset, we take in the land. We don't get distracted.

That's why it's so important to start at the beginning. You have to know who you are and how much God loves you. It is about being connected, being loved, breathing Him in and breathing

Him out. That's the best place to be, and that's where you get your identity. That has to be solid because otherwise your performance becomes your identity, and then it's not about Jesus, it's about you. You don't want that! It's so much better and more fulfilling the other way around. When people know their identity as a son or a daughter, not an orphan, they immediately feel it in their worship. This difference is a key to true worship.

Our identity in God comes from intimacy with Him and rest in Him. Take time to meet Him, worship Him, and fill yourself with water from Heaven. Let God show you how truly loved you are. Then everything you do will flow from rest and true identity. This affects the choices we make and how we relate to those around us. It keeps our thoughts and mindset focused on Him. Stay connected to God and let everything flow from there. This is the most fulfilling way to live. This is how we lead our teams, and it is my advice for all of us.

All of us go through personal challenges or difficulties with other people. What is your advice for how to love well and stay close to God through those situations?

We often want to justify ourselves and prove we are right when we go through challenges with others, but I have learned that does not work in the kingdom. Just stay quiet, stay at peace. In spite of everything, love. That's really what God has taught me through the interpersonal challenges I have gone through. You have to see there's a spiritual battle going on, then you don't take the situation as personally. That's very important because then it's way easier.

Of course, sometimes there are moments when someone hurts you. It's especially hard when something happens that you didn't expect, and it takes you by surprise. When that happens to me, I talk with God as my Dad sitting with me at the table. I just tell Him how I feel, like a daughter, even with tears. I say things like, "I don't like this, Father; this really hurts me." I am really honest. I love that. I am so thankful God showed me this is also okay. You have to be real with what you're feeling. I can cry in this time and express everything I think and feel about the situation. Then I listen for His voice in the midst of it.

You have to know who you are because when you have restored identity, God can also teach you things, and you won't feel rejected. We can all learn and grow. Sometimes He shows you that your reaction came from an old wound or something got torn open in you. Then you sit and talk with God about it. He brings comfort, but I find He also leads me to honesty and humility. This is recognizing our part in situations and apologizing when we hurt someone. It is honest and open communication.

I also remember there was a period of time when I recognized there was a spiritual attack on communication in our team. I don't like to blame things on demonic spirits, but sometimes that is really what is going on. In this case, I learned a lot about it and understood what was happening. For example, I would have a good conversation with someone, and even have another person there hearing it all. Then I would find out the person heard something completely different from what I said. The words got completely twisted. It caused clashes in relationships. Then I began to see it was spiritual, and I learned how to react to it. Love is the answer. Always be loving and always be honest. Speak out honestly, but also keep your love on.

Staying in this love is really a weapon. Always remember there's a battle going on in the spiritual world. It's not about flesh. We are all on the same side, brothers and sisters in the Lord's family. That is how unity comes. Unity is the knock-out against the enemy, especially when we walk in unity in a nation. We've seen that in Myanmar, and we see it happening now in Holland. There's a lot more connection and unity building. It's beautiful to see.

EUROPE FOCUS

What do you see God doing across Europe right now?

Hunger. God is stirring up hunger. I see it happening. I also see the world is groaning, it is waiting for sons and daughters (Romans 8:19-22). People want the real thing. They have had enough of religion. I can feel it all over the place. It's time. A lot of churches are hungry for more, and they want to connect. They want something real. We're living in a wonderful time. It's also a time to really keep our focus. Stay very close to Jesus, but also step forward, because it is a time where we have to arise and shine. You hear it a lot, but it is the truth. We have to stand up and reach out. I feel that in Europe. It's really the time.

Do you see specific countries in Europe where God is moving powerfully?

Holland! I actually see God is moving all over Europe. There are people who did the preparation time and sowed into Europe. Now when He lets His fire fall, it's like oil on fire. You can see it. There are people ready to launch and ready to be used on the front line. When I was in Sweden on holiday, I went to a prayer meeting with all kinds of Christians and leaders together, and there was so much presence of God. God appointed this meeting for us, it was really special. I cannot really say just one nation. There are a lot of places. It feels like God is searching for all the places where people have already prepared themselves in their own time for this time. That is what I sense. It is Europe's time.

LIFE APPLICATION—TRUE IDENTITY AND TRUE WORSHIP

Paulina shared very openly and vulnerably about some of the challenging circumstances she walked through in life and how they affected her. All of us have parts of our history that are painful or broken. Those areas can deeply affect us and carry through to our present mindsets and emotions if we don't address them together with God. Paulina's father was an alcoholic, which made their home unsafe. Her sisters were older, so she was the only one left at home from a young age. The spiritual climate was also intense, and she struggled with fear at times. All of this affected her views of God and of herself. It later carried into her relationship with her husband.

Thankfully, God brought her into a beautiful process of healing and restoration. She notes that it took nearly three years. Often, we want a quick fix, but for deep wounds from our past, there is often a process (or multiple processes) to walk through with God. The main focus was on identity, God's true identity and her own identity as His daughter. It is so important to know God as He truly is and allow Him to heal every broken place in our hearts that doesn't believe He is a good Father. When we really know who we are as unconditionally loved children of the Most High God, everything changes. Everything changes.

Paulina and her husband both went on this journey. They were honest with God, friends, and each other. Now they are spiritual parents for many. When we overcome with God, we have the great privilege to help others on their similar journeys. This is the beauty of kingdom family. Paulina and Rene help people know their identity, know how much God loves them, and then obey God as He leads them into calling and destiny. Paulina also trains others vocally, sharing her giftings as a worship leader.

Paulina is an amazing worship leader. She has natural talent and grew up singing, but that is definitely not the most important thing. I believe the journey of healing and identity she allowed the Lord to lead her through is a key to her anointing in worship. The more you know God, the more you can truly worship. Worship is for Him. You can give an offering to the worthy, beautiful, holy King of kings. Worship also changes our hearts. It draws us even closer into His presence and His love for us.

After identity, Paulina teaches on authority. That is the next step of knowing who we are in God. He gives us authority to trample snakes and scorpions and tear down strongholds. There is a real battle going on, and we need to take our place as sons and daughters of victory. Worship is warfare. It shifts the atmosphere.

Whether you are a worship leader or not, you can be a worshipper. You are also a son or a daughter, and you have the very best Father. If you are still struggling with identity or with issues from your past, take the time to heal. Seek wise counsel and mentors. Spend that time resting in Him, filling your home with His presence and letting Him speak to your heart. Let everything you do in life flow from that place of healed identity.

9

Maximilian Oettingen

Organization: Loretto Community
Position: Leader
Location: Vienna, Austria

PERSONAL BACKGROUND

What is your favorite thing to do on your day off?

I like to work in my garden and go hunting with my boys.

If you could have lunch with one person, whom would you choose?

I would want to have lunch with the Pope John Paul II. From reading his books and from what he spoke about, I can tell that he was a very inspiring person. He had a prophetic edge to him, and

I like to hang out with prophetic people because it is normally very encouraging.

Please tell us about yourself and how you came to faith.

I encountered God when I was around 11 years old at a pilgrimage site. It was the first time I ever really prayed. After that, I found myself searching for God from the time I was 11 to 17 years old. By the time I was 17, I had become skeptical, with many questions that are common to youth. I grew up in Germany and heard about Loretto prayer groups and knew a few people who attended. At that time, there were only two prayer groups in the Loretto movement—one in Vienna and one in Salzburg. (Today, we have about forty-three prayer groups with about 1,000 to 2,000 people attending every week.) What caught my attention the most was that they seemed to be very normal people. They acted normal, looked normal, and there were even a ton of good-looking girls who were involved.

At that time, I was in a life crisis because I questioned whether following Jesus would mean that I would have to live in such a way that contradicted what I had in my heart or not. Basically, I didn't trust God. However, I knew that if I would go to one of these prayer groups in Vienna or Salzburg for a few years, while I studied, I would have a context to be around young people with some of the same questions and perhaps mature. That was the reason I went to Vienna in 1995—because of that prayer group. I began to pray with other young people on a regular basis, and that is what got me back on track.

MISSION, VISION, AND LESSONS LEARNED ALONG THE WAY

Please share with us about the Loretto Movement.

Loretto is a movement mainly in Austria, but also in southern Germany, western Hungary, northern Italy, and Switzerland. It is spreading among young people. It's not a normal congregation, a parish, or a monastery; it's a movement. There are about 600 people who meet on a regular basis in small groups. Twice a year, we have larger gatherings where all 600 meet together, they are the core. For the core members who meet regularly, there are prayer groups that meet night and day throughout the week. There are prayer houses, worship schools, and different formats of teaching and discipleship. We also have a huge festival at Pentecost when we host 10,000 young people. There are also smaller festivals in Vienna.

Our main desire is that from the core group, a prayerful discipleship and missionary movement spills out that makes space for young people to encounter God. The core members are a bit older, anywhere from 18 through their mid-40s, and they do the work for the younger generation. They create space so the younger ones can encounter God. The basic idea is that there is a huge hunger for the presence of God and not many formats where people can experience His presence. We want to fill in that gap. Young people who are hungry can just drop by and see what happens. They don't have to do anything. So that is what we do, create space for people to encounter God and His presence.

Is Loretto only for Catholics or can anyone attend and join?

Anyone can come, and there are people from different backgrounds who do. To be honest, we don't know exactly who attends our groups because we don't count them. They don't sign up; they just come. We have featured people coming from different places, and we work together with ministries like YWAM, HTB Church, Pete Greig (UK, 24/7 Prayer Movement), and Augsburg House of Prayer. It is very nice because sometimes they wouldn't expect Catholics to be so normal. There is a lot of collaboration.

How does it spread? Is it through word of mouth or do you intentionally work to reach people?

The main method is through word of mouth, but we also have a social media platform that lets people know when we gather, especially when we have a festival. However, word of mouth is what we focus on, and we see that it is what works best. With the prayer groups, we let people know that there is about forty-five minutes to an hour of worship time. Then there is teaching and a time of adoration. After that is food and fellowship. It is very simple. We also encourage people attending the groups to bring their friends.

Please share a specific testimony of a person whose life was transformed through being part of your movement.

There was a 28-year-old man who came to one of our Pentecost festivals in Salzburg who told us about how he encountered Jesus during the time of worship. When it came time for an altar call, he looked back in his mind and saw darkness and death. When he looked forward, he saw light and joy. He went to the front to accept Jesus and was filled with Holy Spirit. He immediately stopped using drugs and stopped smoking marijuana. He began to live a sober life and began to study. Now he's on one of our fellowship programs teams—a wonderful guy.

Why do you think God is moving powerfully through you and your movement? What can we learn from your experiences and your model?

I don't know why God is using us. Thank goodness He's not *only* using us. The concept of church has a few questions that come with it. However, I think people are looking for something, especially among young Catholics. I can see that there is a huge hunger for God. We have managed to have a package where the content is still the same—it is always Jesus, of course—but the package is just a bit different, it may answer a few questions that people have. If it doesn't fulfill every bad cliché people have about "church," people are interested.

I heard Nicky Gumbel share at a conference a couple of years ago. He said, "The content of church must stay the same, but the packaging must be different." Many people try to work within formats, and this has become problematic, especially among Catholics. At Loretto, we do a lot of midweek stuff. That way we don't go in and reinvent mass or try to do things differently. We simply have prayer groups that don't look or feel very "churchy." Young people who are searching can come and experience something different. That's one of the reasons it works.

We are also creating a culture of discipleship, which is attractive because many people struggle with knowing their true identity. If you go into that subject a bit, you really touch the nerve of our time. People want to know who they are, where they are from, and where they are going. We give biblical answers through discipleship, and they really get interested. We also manage to have a culture of mission in the sense that we like to send people out so they know they live with a purpose, whether they go to a business, work in politics, art, or anywhere else. This is very attractive especially to young people.

These are the three big focuses of Loretto. The first is a *culture of encounter* that surprises people. People come to a prayer group and don't expect much, but then they encounter God and it really touches them. The second thing is *discipleship,* which is all about identity, as I just shared. The third is moving into the question of *vision and mission.* People begin to ask, "What is God's vision for my life?" We allow people to ask these questions and help them figure out the answers. These are the three main areas we focus on, and it's attractive to many.

How do you do discipleship in Loretto?

We know there are numerous circles. We have a huge circle that might be around 20,000 to 30,000 people who come to the different events we do every year. Then there are smaller circles with people who are taking their journey with God more seriously. We encourage these people in the smaller circles to take steps toward discipleship. We have various programs where they can go for discipleship training courses for nine months or three weeks. We encourage people who want to move on with Christ and want to have a fruitful life to take a step in that direction. If people are looking for fellowship, we encourage them to attend our house communities and invest in relationships there. It is also possible for people to come less regularly. We don't require a commitment, we simply offer the next step of discipleship. It's up to them whether they decide to take it.

What is your advice for people who are feeling discouraged or disappointed in their calling?

That's a tough question. It is important that you have people around you with whom you can be totally normal. It's important that you have a mature believer with whom you can talk, scream, and cry. You need relationships in which you can be totally normal on a human level; because the truth is, life is hard when you are discouraged or disappointed. The journey is long, and you have to keep the pace. Often, it's just not easy.

For example, when I stepped into leadership in 1995, when I was maybe 22 or 23, I didn't know all these things. I wasn't educated in ministry or how to do any of this. I did a short Discipleship Training School, but I, and many of us in my generation, didn't go to some kind of incredible ministry school. We didn't have many good role models. I was discouraged quite often, actually. That's why it's important to have somebody with whom you can be normal. It also helps if they are a bit older and have been in ministry a bit longer.

What would your advice be to someone who wants to start something like Loretto? How do they begin?

I would normally encourage people to look at their natural talents and ask Holy Spirit if they also have a supernatural gifting in that area. That is a good place to start. If you know that there is something that fascinates you, like a specific model, and you notice yourself looking into it a lot, you can ask Holy Spirit if that is a model for you to follow.

For example, you may have been looking at Holy Trinity Brompton (HTB) church, in London, for the last few years and reading their website. Or maybe you attended their leadership conference and you notice that you think about it often. It's obvious that something about this church fascinates you. You can ask yourself if this is a model that you want to copy. If you can answer "yes" to that question, then the next step would be to get people who are very good at the practical side or administration and/or organization and begin to copy the model together. I would also involve a couple of theologians to review the plans to ensure it is theologically sound.

To sum it up, I would look at the following before I begin: First I would check my giftings. Then I would look around at ministries that fascinate me in His kingdom. Is there a model I especially like? From there I would copy it in a practical way, with friends and make sure that it is theologically sound.

CULTURE SHIFTS

Many churches and ministries are looking at how they can shift from a culture of maintenance to a real sense of mission and purpose. Please share your thoughts on this issue.

That is definitely a huge issue, which is similar in any traditional or state church; for example, Anglicans in England, Calvinists in Switzerland, and Catholics in Austria. In the large Catholic Archdioceses of Vienna, there are about 640 different parishes, which is quite a lot. They were established that way in the late 1800s, with structures of that time. During that time period, there was a perspective that nearly everyone was a Christian. The faith was passed on and the churches were full. In the early 20th century, in Vienna especially when the city grew, huge churches were built because they were full, not because they were empty, of course.

However in the past fifty years, we have tried to keep up the whole structure and keep the whole thing working as if we would have the same number of people who went to church as fifty or sixty years ago, but this is not the case.

For example, in Austria in 1990, there were 1.3 million Roman Catholics attending mass every Sunday. Then by 2013, there were about 650,000 attending mass—half the number. Yet the number of parishes, as well as the way of the whole system, have stayed the same. So what to do? Do you keep the system as is, or do you find new ways to attract those who are not in church? At least 90 percent, if not more, of the population are now "unchurched" (do not attend church anymore). So how do we reach them? How do we set things up so that they can be reached?

This does not mean, from my perspective, that we have to change the DNA of Christianity, but we do have to change perspective. We have to look outward; and once we do, Holy Spirit can tell us how to reach people. Then things begin to change. I think these three steps are very important: encounter (or prayer), discipleship, and mission. If we establish a culture where these three things can occur, things begin to work.

Ministries should be set up with the understanding that many of the people who attend church do not know a lot about Christianity and have not met Jesus yet. Maybe they are not saved yet, even if they are baptized. Once they do meet Jesus, everything changes. Once they have the security of knowing Christ, being loved by the Father, and being anointed by the Holy Spirit, they begin to move easily, even among a traditional parish structure. They know how to handle it. They would then be inclined to go to Sunday mass without having a problem that it looks old. I'm not saying parishes shouldn't be mission-focused, but once people realize they can meet Jesus there, it kind of works.

How does establishing a culture work, based on encounter/ prayer, discipleship, and mission work?

Our prayer groups that I later became part of began in 1987 with three teenagers who simply prayed the rosary for twenty minutes. Afterward they ate a sandwich for fifteen minutes and went home. That was the beginning. So that's really simple. They didn't do anything else for about one or two years. One of the things we always say is that if it's a kingdom thing, it has to begin small. Everything in the kingdom begins small. Jesus began small; church began small; everything begins small. A mustard seed is small; it is nothing. It doesn't need to stress you out.

There are a few lessons we can pull out about what is needed: natural giftedness, a model, friends to do it with, and theology. Maybe it begins small, but it's best to enjoy it in these stages. You should enjoy whatever you are doing. If you want to run Alpha in your congregation or you think you need to run a small group, but yet you don't like leading small groups, just don't do it. It has to be enjoyable.

EUROPE FOCUS

What do you see God doing in Europe in this generation?

God is reestablishing identity. It's all about learning what it means to be a son or daughter of God and being royalty, that we have dignity and we have a purpose. This is one of the main keys. Especially in the German-speaking world, there is the huge Nazi question where the whole question of authority was broken. There is an important reestablishment of living under the authority of a father. This is being reestablished very strongly.

And are there any countries you believe God is highlighting?

England, Germany, and Austria. I don't know what is happening in every country. I am basing my opinion on what I see among churches and leaders I have relationships with, but I would specifically say these three countries. In England there is a very strong move. There is something very natural and sweet that is appearing. I think it has to do with the Celtic spirituality. To a certain extent, the church in England is finding its spiritual Celtic roots again. They are learning that they are allowed to be wild again.

In Germany, what is happening in parts of the church is beginning to spread through the whole nation. Germany is a very large nation strong in literature, art, and science. The German Christians are daring to think big again. They are daring to lead, which is very nice to see.

In Austria there is a very strong anointing on worship and prayer. If you look at the natural culture of Austria, it is full of music, which is being reestablished very strongly. In the Austrian Catholic church, in regard to culture and music, what we are seeing in a very broad way is that many people are engaging in worship. It is very beautiful and very simple. They just love to worship.

What are some keys for unity? How do you think we can work toward building more unity among churches and Christians?

The main key regarding unity is to go for the friendships. The whole unity question is all about friendship. Specifically, work on friendships with people who are not from your denomination. Jesus states in John 17:21, *"that they all may be one, as You, Father, are in Me, and I in You...."* The question: How were the Father and the Son one? They were one through the Holy Spirit, which is love. And so the key to loving one another is in friendship—that is the whole thing.

If you become friends with someone from a different denomination and you have love, no matter what happens, you can stay friends. I think the division of the churches of the East and the West, and also within the West specifically, has to do with sin, not theology. The division came up around theology but because of sin. Thankfully sin is covered up by love. Look for friendship and begin to love one another, which actually helps unity emerge.

Please share more about this concept that division in the church came from sin, not because of differences in theology.

Historically, around 1060, the division between the church of the East and of the West was the result of the way people acted toward one another, and especially the way the heads of the church acted toward one another. They were not loving; in fact, they were insulting and disrespectful to one another. Between the Orthodox and the Catholics, East and West, there were always a few cultural differences. One group spoke Greek, the other Latin. They had a strong perception of Holy Spirit. We had a strong perception of Christ. They had a strong perspective on the glorifying work of the Holy Spirit, the Holy Spirit making us like Jesus. The Church in the West had a strong perspective on the sanctifying work of the Spirit so that we become justified through Christ.

Essentially, there were always differences, but they were always complementary. What broke things apart was people acting in a sinful way toward one another. When that happened, what was created to complement was used to contradict. It's the same in the West. I don't know all of the details, but from speaking to Protestants and Catholics, it was the same way. There are always great reformers and good people who had groundbreaking ideas, but we have to work with them. We need to accompany those people.

I haven't read too much about who accompanied Martin Luther, but I highly doubt that he was accompanied well. I wonder what would have happened if someone had sat down with him for a year and talked through biblical issues with him. What if someone said, "Oh, you're an Augustinian Monk, so you've read a lot of Saint Augustine's writings...." During that time in the fourth century, people talked a lot about the same things that Martin Luther spoke on, so it wouldn't be all that complicated to put it into context.

In 1999, there was a Joint Declaration between the Roman Catholic Church and the World Alliance of Protestant Churches on the topic of justification. In theological terms, on that level, we are already one. There is no question about this anymore. That issue has been resolved. To be honest, it was never really a question. The thing is, sometimes people just see things differently, and it can be complicated to make them complement one another.

But when sin comes in, they begin to contradict one another and there is no more common ground. That is what I mean.

For us, today, it is important to approach one another without thinking about what's wrong with the other person. Instead, we should ask ourselves what we can learn from one another. Then, we can approach them as a friend and say, "I want to learn from you." This opens the door for us because they are flattered and disarmed. That is the beginning of an honest friendship where we get to learn together. From there comes love.

The theological questions will come up, but then you can see that the questions really are not that difficult after all, even if you don't end up agreeing. There is a famous quote from John Paul II from a long letter that he wrote called Ut Unum Sint, "May they be One," from John 17. He made a very simple point that what unifies us is much greater than what separates us, so we must look for that which unifies us.

Overall, are you hopeful about what God is doing in Europe?

Yes, of course I feel hopeful. I have the impression that in all of this, the church, in general, is finding its role again, in the sense of being a creative minority. We are beginning to understand that we are no longer a state church. The state church is more of a "nanny" of the king or the country. Instead, we are understanding that we are actually a mustard seed. From the perspective of being a creative minority, but by having a high profile, we can be very explosive. It's a movement that is, in a way, much smaller, but having a much higher profile. The movement is almost contradictory.

When you look at the church, you might say, "My goodness, we are losing influence, power, and property. We are losing

everything." Sometimes, it's true, sometimes we already lost everything and don't have anything anymore. However, I think we are
actually growing into our intended role, which is a creative minority that has the power to transform a society. So yes, I am hopeful.

LIFE APPLICATION—MUSTARD SEEDS MOVE MOUNTAINS

I love this concept of a mustard seed that comes up a few
times in Maximilian's interview. Loretto started with
three teenagers praying for twenty minutes and eating
a sandwich for fifteen minutes. Now there are tens of
thousands engaging from multiple nations. Maximilian
got involved by simply showing up to the prayer group.
It impacted his life, and he wanted to help other people
meet God in this same authentic, life-changing way.
Throughout the book, most of the people I interviewed
began with something small and watched it grow way
beyond their expectations. It was usually connected to
something that touched their life first. This is often what
happens in the kingdom of God as you follow Jesus and
follow your passions.

Maximilian breaks things down very practically. He suggests looking at what fascinates you in the kingdom. Is
there a church, a model, or a ministry reaching a people
group that is on your heart, or some other expression
that sparks excitement in you? Maybe it is a person who
really inspires you, perhaps a business leader who shares
the Gospel to clients and coworkers, or a mom who helps

other young moms meet Jesus. From there, he suggests looking at natural giftedness, the model, friends to start something with, and theology. Then look for these fruits: Are people encountering Jesus? Are they learning how to follow Him? Are you all finding purpose and mission in Him?

Another point I want to highlight here is unity. It starts with friendship. Many divisions in church history came through misunderstandings or a lack of love. We will never agree with everyone about every single thing. That is just normal. Sometimes the points we disagree on feel so important that we want to fight for our opinions to be heard. We want to prove ourselves right. But are we walking in love? Can we somehow be friends? I don't think Jesus would have prayed His John 17 prayer asking that we would be one with each other if it was impossible. If it is possible, then let's go after it. Jesus even told us to love our enemies. Again, if He said it, it must be possible.

Paul brings this perspective, *"Therefore let us, as many as are mature, have this mind; and if in anything you think otherwise, God will reveal even this to you. Nevertheless, to the degree that we have already attained, let us walk by the same rule, let us be of the same mind"* (Philippians 3:15-16). We can actually trust God to reveal truth to people. Our job is to walk in everything we have already learned. When we are building friendships, especially with people who think differently, the starting point of, "I want to learn from you" is a fantastic stance. As Maximilian says, it flatters and disarms people. It opens the door to great conversations. That, plus the commitment to love each other, will already take us very far on the path to unity.

10

Rodrigo and Saara Campos

Organization: Northwind Church
Position: Leading and Founding Pastors
Location: Helsinki, Finland

Personal Background

What is your favorite thing to do on your day off?

What are you talking about? What is a day off? Just kidding. We really love family time. We enjoy movies that we can get some sort of prophetic insight from. Superhero movies usually have an encouraging, prophetic message in disguise. We love hanging out with friends and family, enjoying quality time. We love cooking food together, sharing a meal, and living life together. The kids love simple, family life. We like that too.

If you could have lunch with anyone, whom would you choose?

Rodrigo: I would love to have a double date with Brian and Jenn Johnson because they inspire us a lot. That's what came to my mind first.

Saara: That is a hard one. Since I have already had lunch with Heidi Baker, I will say Bill Johnson. He just gets me every time. The fatherhood he carries blows my mind and my heart. He carries it in such a strong and beautiful way. To me that speaks loudest, the fatherhood and the motherhood. It speaks volumes to me. That is why I would choose him.

Please tell us a little bit about yourselves.

I am Saara Campos from Finland, and I am 36 years old. I'm a wife and a mom of three beautiful daughters, Bella, Vivi, and Celine. That is who I feel I am: God called me to be a mother. What I do in church and in our ministry is just that, I'm mothering people. I carry our nation and Europe in my heart as a mom. It all comes from this place of motherhood that God taught me about. It's really organic and really natural and effortless since it comes from this heart. I just think it's simple. It's loving God and loving people. It is laying our lives down for the sake of Jesus and what He has done. So that's it, simple.

I am Rodrigo. I'm 36 years old, and I'm Brazilian. Fifteen years ago, God called me to Finland. I was just a young man who didn't have much, but I had a heart and a yes to Jesus. Saara and I married and live here together. We have been leading worship and writing songs together. The church we have now is the fruit of our lives, it started very organically. People started running with us and became family. Then, we started giving birth to this vision. All of a sudden there were sixty of us in our living room. We understood we needed to take a step of faith, and we started the church. We are a very young church at the moment, about four years old, but we have almost 300 people gathering every Sunday in the center of Helsinki. We have countless testimonies of God's power, healing, and salvations. We see people being saved every week. We have baptized about sixty-five people already. Even in the wintertime, they want to be baptized in the ice-cold lake!

Saara: One woman had never been baptized before, but she was in such a hurry. She got saved out of a New Age background and wanted to get baptized right away. She and her friend were happy to jump in the lake, through a hole in the ice, so we just dipped them in the water! They just went for it. Crazy lovers of Jesus!

I love it! And how did you two meet Jesus?

Saara: I grew up in a Christian family, but my parents both came from really broken backgrounds, especially my dad. That made it hard for me to see God as a loving father. I walked away from God until I was 19 years old. Then I got radically saved. It is a longer story, but the very short summary is that I heard God's voice audibly. He spoke to me. He showed me that I was at a crossroad point where I needed to choose the direction of my life. I got radically saved, and in the same day God also restored my relationship with my father. I saw him cry for the first time in nineteen years. Jesus was all I wanted after that.

What was your life like before that?

Saara: I was away from God. I left home when I was 15 years old and moved to a studio apartment in another city. Most of my classmates still lived with their families, so my apartment became the party center. I partied a lot and had a boyfriend. We were actually engaged. I was very lost and broken. At the point when God took hold of my life, I was depressed and had no future. I couldn't see anything; there were no colors in my life, just darkness and depression. Then everything changed in one day, it was really crazy. I was delivered that day.

Were you baptized in the icy lake?

Saara: Actually, I was baptized at the beach in Brazil. Shortly after I was saved, I went to Brazil to spend time with Rodrigo's family. (I already knew them.) Then we started our relationship, but that is another story...

What about you, Rodrigo? How did you meet Jesus?

Rodrigo: I was born into a Christian family. My parents were both pastors. I grew up in the church, so I really cannot tell you the moment when I got saved. In my early teenage years, I learned more about what it means to have a relationship with Jesus. That was a journey for me. I was baptized and filled with Holy Spirit. I also learned more about identity versus religion. Growing up in the church is a different reality, so for me there was a journey in my youth of deepening my personal relationship with Jesus. At this time, there was a huge revival going on in Brazil. My father was a pastor and worship leader who was very involved in the revival, so I got to see everything from very close. I also started worship leading there. That was really special, and it marked my life. I had no idea what God had in store for me back then. I was so wrecked by the presence of God and by revival that I was ready to say yes to whatever Jesus had. I was completely willing to lay down my life.

Later on, I discovered His plan for me was moving to Finland. I didn't know anything about Finland, I imagined a land of penguins and igloos. I really had no idea about the country, but God knew. The craziest thing is I'm from São Paulo, South America's largest city, with 20 million people. Then God called me to a tiny Finnish village with 3,000 people. When I share Jesus with Finnish people, I tell them God loves them so much that He took me from a megacity, made me move to a completely different nation, made me fall in love with a culture that is completely different from my own, learn this crazy language, one of the hardest languages in the world, just to say that He loves them. That is my testimony.

Mission, Vision, and Lessons Learned Along the Way

Please tell us what is happening in your church. What is your mission and vision?

Rodrigo: We are really passionate about the whole Great Commission. Many people focus on the first part and teach about going to all the earth to preach the Gospel. Yes, we do that, but we are really passionate about the second part, making disciples. We see our mission as the whole package, preaching the Gospel, making disciples, healing the sick, baptizing people, and everything Jesus teaches us to do. We stress this aspect of living a missionary lifestyle in our own nation. We don't need to go to Africa to do missions. We share the Gospel everywhere we go— on the bus, in the store, anywhere we are.

Then when people come to the church, we are also responsible for discipling them—helping them grow and inviting them into the family. That is the culture we live out daily. These are the testimonies that come out of our church, the little, normal, day-to-day stories: "I went to the store and prayed for someone." "I was on the bus and had a conversation with someone, and he gave his life to Jesus." This is how we live on a daily basis.

Saara and Rodrigo: Our main goal is to activate every church member to lead a Gospel lifestyle. Another characteristic of our family is that we encourage everyone to really be family. This is how we do discipleship. If your neighbor gets saved, you don't come to church to try and find a small group for them. You lead the person and share with them. You invite them to your home to eat a meal with your family. It is organic, not programs and institutions. It is about being family, simplicity, opening our homes and our hearts and our families to live daily life together. Discipleship happens there. We are really passionate about this, so this is what we teach and live in our church.

We also take teams on short-term mission trips internationally or send people from our church on short-term trips. We have taken teams or sent people to Brazil, Mozambique, South Africa, India, Estonia, Sweden, the USA, and other places. In the future we might have longer term projects in other nations, but we are still a younger church. We are passionate for the nations and love going on mission trips.

I really love your hearts for family and for living a Gospel life. Earlier, you said that the church was birthed out of sixty people in your living room. Please share how that happened.

Saara and Rodrigo: It was a family thing. We didn't start a church, Holy Spirit started it. We were ambushed. We were leading a worship team first. We traveled around Finland leading worship and making worship albums.

Actually, before that, we lived in Brazil for a season. We were part of Ana Paula's worship band and ministry. This is a very well-known ministry in Brazil. Their church had more than 60,000 members at the time we were hired as pastors. Rodrigo was the worship pastor. The worship team alone had 1,000 members. We loved being there, and they loved us. It was a beautiful season, and we learned so much. There were also difficult parts, but ministry-wise especially, it was a wonderful time for us.

Saara: Then God called us back to Finland. We had nothing there. We wondered what we were doing there, and why God asked us to come back. In Brazil, the doors were completely open for us, and we could have stayed. Ministry-wise, it seemed like the fulfillment of all our dreams with wonderful leaders, a wonderful church, open doors, everything. But God called us back to Finland to start from scratch. Everything started really organically.

Before we left Brazil, I had a vision of people knocking on our door in Finland, begging us to let them in. And then that started happening...people just appeared at our house. We were leading worship and traveling Finland, but it was mainly just the two of us and a few musician friends. People began coming to us and asking us to be a mom and dad for them. It just happened; really, we had no plans. It just happened.

There was a big event here in Finland with Heidi Baker that we helped coordinate. God moved powerfully. It was crazy. We were laying on the floor in the hallway, a feast in the hallway. Heidi was there. Laura was there too. We led worship with our team, so they were all part of it.

It's true, I was there too. There was so much power and presence of God that we were all laying on the floor praying for hours... that was a very special time.

Rodrigo: The next day we asked everyone on our team to come to our home. We planned to have a short debrief about what God did and what He had spoken to each of us. It turned out, we stayed there for six hours, opening our hearts, crying, praying. I remember telling Saara, "I feel like something new was born today. I feel like our church was born today." That was exactly what happened. After that, we began taking steps toward starting the church, but it was very organic, very natural. It was a work of the Holy Spirit. Most of us are very young, in our 20s and 30s, a bunch of young people, but we have hearts for our nation. We want to see God's kingdom established here.

Why do you think God is moving in such a powerful way through your ministry specifically?

Rodrigo: There is hunger here. In Finland right now, I sense there is hunger. It is something that has been building up since I moved here. I can clearly see it. Things are different from how they were ten years ago. People are hungry for truth, authenticity, and power. People are tired of traditions and systems and religion. The time is ripe. It has been building, and it is our moment. The hunger is spreading, and we can see that happening. Nothing else satisfies. People are coming to the point where even though they have so many things like welfare, well-being, and material possessions, none of it fills them. They are still empty inside. They need something real.

There are so many people who are willing to lay down their lives for Jesus. They are full of passion and ready to give everything. When you see that happening with one, two, three people, then a whole group of people, that is good news.

That is powerful. Amen. As people read this, I hope hunger is being stirred up in their hearts too. What would you tell people who want to start living fully for God?

Saara: The first thing is to get to know the heart of the Father. When you get to know the heart of the Father, you let His heart heal you and speak to you about your identity. You experience His unconditional love for you. Then when you continue to press into His heart, you naturally start to feel what He feels for His children. As you grow up and mature in your faith, it is no longer just about you, you, you—it is about other people. You pray and ask God about what you can give and what you can do. These types of prayers rise up in you. You feel compassion for people and for the lost. I think it is simple—you just press in to know the Father. If we really know the heart of the Father, our hearts change, and it is not just about us anymore.

You are worship leaders, and you've led worship teams in Brazil and Finland. Now you are pastors as well. How do the two sides fit together?

Rodrigo: That was an interesting journey, because at first I felt unqualified to lead a church. I thought, *I'm just a worship leader.* That was something God had to break in me, those wrong concepts I built in my mind. God spoke to me about David. He was a leader and a king, and he also started as a worship leader. That never changed in his life, he just got upgraded, got new territories and responsibilities, but his heart for worship never died. He built a beautiful legacy of worship that we are still eating and drinking from today. We understand that God uses our hearts of worship as we lead the church. Many times, I pastor through the gift of worship and worship leading.

Saara: Even though we are a very young church and our finances are still building up, we have already produced two albums. The church financed these albums because a big part of our calling as a church is to fill Finland and Europe with worship. There is also more to come. We are not done yet. There are many worshippers in our church. We love to raise them up and pour into them. It is also beautiful because God has brought people to run with us who have other giftings and can help with other areas of church life.

I do believe we are doing everything God has called us to do with no compromise. We get to focus on building a church, but we are also doing things for the entire nation. We are a local church, but we want to bless the entire nation of Finland with everything God has given us. Worship is one of those things.

Rodrigo: One characteristic of our church is that we have many artists who are crazy talented. We have very talented people. We have been able to reach people in the music and entertainment industry as well. Some have been saved and are attending our church, so we are touching that ground too. We feel called to reach these people. Arts, music, and culture are hugely influential for the nation and culture overall. We feel we carry that piece. We are focusing on this area. God has been opening doors in these fields.

We have had the opportunity to share the Gospel with people who we wouldn't normally bump into through street evangelism. God is opening the doors for us to share with people in high positions in the music and entertainment areas.

Please share a testimony of God opening the doors for you in this area.

Rodrigo: This is not a complete testimony because we are still praying for the complete breakthrough, but God is moving. One particular artist watched one of our music videos and was very impacted. The person said, "I have never heard anything this authentic and powerful. These people are so talented that they could be doing whatever they want, but they decided to sing about the truth." Now, she has been to our home, and we prayed for her. She came to our services a few times and even raised her hand in the altar call. She hasn't fully given her life to Jesus yet, but we are sowing seeds in her life. We believe God is calling her, and we are very intentionally praying for her. We have been very straight forward in sharing the Gospel and also loving her in practical ways. She told us she is being ambushed by Jesus everywhere she goes. It's hard because we can't share the full story yet, but it's coming.

Saara: God is opening doors for us to go to events and spend time backstage with some of the top artists. We can love on them and share Jesus with them. Some of them are coming to church and rededicating their lives to Jesus or hearing the Gospel for the first time. This is an area where we are gaining ground. This happens all the time. We are advancing in this area because the door is open. God is making the connections for us to share with these people, and we are praying for them.

Rodrigo: Last summer, we had some gigs at big music festivals with our friend. She is a singer, and we had the opportunity to sing background vocals together. We only accepted these invitations because we knew we could be missionaries in this field. We had opportunities to pray for so many people and love on them. These people really, really need Jesus, and I don't know how else they would hear about Jesus. It was very, very precious for us to go to those places, like secret agents. When we were in there, it was full on Jesus. It was very fun.

WORSHIP AND LEADERSHIP FOCUS

What advice would you give people who feel called to worship or worship leading, or another creative area? Where do they start? What can people do to pursue that type of calling?

Saara: Fall in love with Jesus more and more and more because He is the Source. I think many times we try to impress the world, on the world's terms. It is never going to happen. We will never be able to impress the world or the industry with their own tricks. It's God and being connected to the real Source of all creativeness. He is the true Source of it all, and we should be brave enough to pursue Him as our Source.

Rodrigo: Also, sometimes people who grew up in the church have a tendency to think the world has something better to offer or is more professional, better quality, or whatever, but dispelling that mindset can be very eye-opening. For example, one of our worship leaders came from that background, high up in the music industry. She was on her way to becoming the next pop star, with a contract from the biggest record label. When Jesus came into her life and she started attending our worship events, she felt she needed to cancel her contract. She was very deep in that world, and she says it is a horrible environment and nothing there can satisfy. She can't understand why anyone who knows Jesus would want to trade that for the nonsense the world has to offer. Jesus is so much better.

Fall in love with Jesus. That is our encouragement. Get rid of all religiosity and lies of the devil that try to make you believe there is something better out there—when in reality you are connected to the very Source of everything. When you learn to fall in love with Him, when you learn to gaze into His eyes, be in His presence and love His presence like David did, that's where all life will flow. That's where your art, your music, and your worship will bear fruit. Then, you will have something to offer. It's actually my only encouragement. I really don't think there is anything else. Yes, we did study music, we did do other things, but it is all nothing if we don't have Jesus. Without Jesus, it's just music—just sounds and melodies. With Jesus, He is the life behind it all.

Have you gone through any discouragements or disappointments? What is your advice about navigating through those seasons?

Saara: I remember one particular thing that happened when we were starting the church. We were really insecure when God spoke to us about starting a church. We felt unqualified and wondered if God could really be asking this from us. We thought maybe it would be better if other people would lead. We could just bring all the people who had come to join us, and another person could take the leadership position. We thought we were not qualified for what God was asking from us. Out of that, we made a mistake. We met other people who also wanted to start a church and seemed to carry the same things, so we jumped in and decided to begin something together.

We joined them because of fear and insecurity. We did not really ask God or spend enough time praying over this. We were just so relieved that someone else would carry the responsibility, and we wouldn't have to carry it alone. It felt so frightening to do something this big. We didn't take God seriously in what He asked us to do. We didn't pray enough about this before we started. Because of this mistake, we went through several very challenging months. We began to realize we were not actually carrying the same vision as the other leaders. We went through fire. It was painful. We were ready to give up on everything—the vision and everything God had spoken to us. We started to doubt everything. We even questioned if we had really heard God or if we made it all up in our heads.

But I think we needed to go through that fire, because in the end God used it to strengthen us and clarify the vision of what He had given us to carry. Because we made a wrong call in the beginning, we went through a really hard time. People got hurt in the process. After realizing for several months that we had a different vision and calling than the other leaders, we decided we needed to leave the group. It was painful and challenging. We knew we needed to have the courage to jump. We knew if we stayed in that situation, we would not be choosing God's best for us. We would consciously be choosing not to follow His plan A for our lives, to follow the vision He showed us. So we took a huge leap of faith and started again, from zero, trusting God had asked us to do this. And here we are, but it was a mess in the beginning. That question of, "Could God ask us to do this?" was overwhelming. But He had asked us, we just didn't believe Him in the beginning.

EUROPE FOCUS

What do you see God doing in this generation in Europe?

Saara: I see an army. I see an army of people, not one or two great, powerful men and women of God. I see an army. I have seen that army since 2005, and it is rising up. People are really believing their calling and identity in God. It's not a movement of some known women and men of God. It's an army of God.

Rodrigo: I see God restoring things that were broken. I see God, once and for all, breaking the curse of orphanhood and all the pain the wars have caused. I see God restoring family in Europe. Fathers and mothers are rising up, and spiritual orphanhood is being completely erased. I see unity for the body of Christ.

Saara: Erasing the spiritual orphanhood will also lead to the end of physical orphanhood. Children will be adopted into families. Church will be a family.

Do you feel God is highlighting specific countries?

Rodrigo: Finland! I also feel God has been highlighting Russia to me. I feel it strongly in my spirit. I sense God is going to blow across Russia. Another country is Portugal.

Saara: Yes, Portugal is very highlighted. And of course, many times God has something specific for us in the countries He is highlighting to us, but I really feel Portugal is significant. He has been talking to me about Portugal.

Rodrigo: We see God moving through all of the Nordic countries. There is something very unique that God wants to do in the Nordic countries. They are even presented in the mass media: Nordic trends, Finnish education, Swedish style, etc. These countries are highlighted in the global sense. I feel God is raising up the Nordic countries to bring revival. Finnish and Swedish people are known for being reserved or introverted naturally, so their turning to Jesus speaks loudly when they are completely on fire for Him. This makes a big impact. People see that and think this really must be God because these people are not normally like that. It's one thing to see Brazilians shouting and jumping or Africans dancing because it's their culture, but when you see that happening in Nordic nations, it speaks even louder.

Are you hopeful that Europe shall be saved?

Saara: Oh yes! We are filled with so much hope for Europe!

LIFE APPLICATION—PURSUING THE SOURCE OF ALL CREATIVITY

I love what Rodrigo and Saara shared about encouraging each member of their church to lead a Gospel lifestyle. This means walking out the Great Commission, sharing the Gospel and making disciples in your normal life, not just on a mission trip. Ben Fitzgerald brought up a similar point: many Europeans are being called to be missionaries in their own nations. We live this out when we intentionally love and reach out to our friends, family, neighbors, and coworkers.

As they shared, it starts with simple conversations at the store or on the bus, and it can be amazing how people respond. From there, we welcome people into family. Each one of us can share what we know about Jesus, that is already discipleship. We don't have to be theology experts. Sometimes we feel like we aren't qualified, and we need a pastor to help, but actually, we all have so much to give. Every lesson you learned, every Bible story that encouraged you, is a point you can bring to the table. Literally. When you share from your own experience, people feel your authenticity.

For Rodrigo and Saara, their church started in a similar way. They were sharing what they loved, their passion for worship, and leading a team. Then people started coming to their home. People wanted to share life and be family. People wanted spiritual parents. People felt loved, seen, and cared for by Rodrigo and Saara. They felt comfortable knocking on their door. Then after a powerful event with Heidi Baker, Holy Spirit began to move in an even greater way. People were so open, sharing, crying, and praying. Something was born, without them even trying. At first they felt unqualified to be pastors, but God taught Rodrigo through the life of David. David also started as a worship leader and became a leader and a king. In every season of life, David's identity was still a worshipper and a friend of God. Rodrigo and Saara also lead their church from this heart of worship and friendship with God.

Reaching Finland with worship and a new sound is something they are passionate about. Their freedom and creativity draw artists and others who might not feel at home in another environment. They have open doors in the music world reaching the unreached. When I asked their advice to artists, they simply said, to fall more in love with Jesus. "It's God and being connected to the real Source of all creativeness. He is the true Source of it all, and we should be brave enough to pursue Him as our Source." That is powerful advice for all believers!

Whatever giftings and talents come naturally to you are probably linked to your calling or purposes God has for you. Are there any areas where you have an open door? Maybe it is at your university or in a particular field or through art or music? It could really be anything you love to do, and God can use that to connect with people who wouldn't have any other chance to meet someone who loves Jesus.

11

Sergey Shidlovskiy

Organization: God Seekers Movement
Position: Founder and Leader
Location: Estonia

Personal Background

What is your favorite thing to do on your day off?

I absolutely love to be with my family. Every time I have a day off, I spend it having fun with my wife and children. We like traveling together, going to the cinema or to a restaurant. We also go to the gym together, not only for our health, but also family time working out and laughing together. I often don't get enough sleep with travels and busy schedules, so I like to sleep in on my days off.

If you could have lunch with someone who inspires you, whom would you choose and why?

In different seasons, it's different people. Today I would say Larry Sparks, the publisher for Destiny Image. We have been communicating about publishing my book in English, which will be titled *Penuel*. It is about my personal supernatural meetings with God and prayer. It's like fire in my bones to share this message God put on my heart and help others build their prayer lives and encounter God.

Choosing one person who has influenced my life is too hard. I will mention a few. The first is my pastor, Paul Zink. He is an apostolic leader over many churches including a Belarusian church I attended. He pastors New Life Christian Fellowship in Florida. They run a large school for grades 1 through 12 to provide high-level academic education with biblical foundations. This inspires me greatly for the prayer center I want to build in Estonia.

There are several covenant friends who inspire me greatly. Mike Bickle is the leader of International House of Prayer Kansas City (IHOPKC), a close friend, an inspirational man of God, and a pioneer of 24/7 prayer. I had the privilege of spending three months there learning many things, including English. Rick Renner is an American pastor of Moscow Good News Church, one of the largest churches in Russia, with thousands of members. It's unbelievable to me that God is using an American to have such an influence in Russia. My dear friend Jean-Luc Trachsel is the vision carrier for the Europe Shall Be Saved movement. He is a healing evangelist full of Holy Spirit fire for revival in Europe. It is an honor to work together for the harvest.

Additionally, there are several anointed men of God who inspired me through their ministries and with their books: Yonggi Cho, *Prayer: Key to Revival;* Benny Hinn, *Good Morning Holy Spirit;* and Tommy Tenney, *God Chasers.*

It is good to be inspired by many people. We can all learn from one another. What about you? How did you personally come to faith?

I met Jesus in 1994. I am from Belarus, at that time, part of the Soviet Union. Growing up, no one around me was a Christian. My father worked in a piano factory and my mother worked in a cafeteria. I'm from a very simple family of hard workers. When I was a teenager, I became interested in philosophy. I started reading philosophy books and thinking about the purpose of life. My family was shocked since they came from simple backgrounds without a lot of education. I began to question whether God existed. I started my own search to answer this question. I wrote many pages with my thoughts and reasoning. I understood everything has a beginning. All the trees came from the trees before them, and eventually, from one garden. People came from the generation before them, so tracing back, we must all come from one man in the beginning. I concluded that someone had to start all this. I also observed everything in creation is so logical and intelligent. We are surrounded by the evidence in nature of the existence of God.

I still remember my first prayer. I looked into space at the stars and said, "God? God? Are You here? If You exist, give me some sign. I want to know You. Reveal Yourself to me." That was my first prayer and is still my prayer today. I want to know God more and more. I want Him to reveal Himself to me. That is the most valuable prayer of my life for myself and for the nations. Salvation comes through the knowledge of God.

During that season, I came across a powerful and evangelistic book about the life of Job. It touched me deeply even though I was not born again yet. I am grateful for this foundation because it prepared me for real Christianity. Later, I met charismatic people who teach that if you follow God, you won't have problems. The reality is life is full of problems, but we can learn from Job that it's not the end of the story. Job gave me the courage to go through difficult seasons and trust God to bring me through to the other side.

Later, one of my Catholic classmates invited me to church. I attended Catholic church for two years and even considered becoming a monk, desiring to be fully devoted to God. God was speaking to me through dreams and a powerful encounter with Jesus. Then I went through a difficult season. New Age people came into our church and tried to convince me against Christianity. They had many rational arguments, and I became confused. I lost my peace and joy. I was incredibly discouraged for about a year, even to the point of wanting to die. Thankfully I was taken out of the situation because I had to complete mandatory military service in Belarus.

A fellow soldier preached the clear Gospel to me. He invited me to a charismatic church with about 200 young people. At that point, I was ready to hear the truth. Before that, even when other Christians would try to talk to me, I was very closed off. Then when I came to the point of wanting to die, I realized I was not going the right direction. I got through that crazy time, but I was so depressed and had very incorrect thinking. I needed God's restoration. I had a profound encounter with God that turned everything around.

Paul Zink, the bishop and spiritual father I told you about, came to our church. Just before he came to Belarus, he hosted Rodney Howard-Browne in Florida. Holy Spirit touched people with laughter and the strong presence of God. Paul ministered at our church in a similar way. Unfortunately, I was out of town; but after that event, I was invited to a meeting for potential leaders.

At the time, I was so depressed. I prayed for God to take away my depression and give me a spirit of joy. I walked out of the meeting into the warm summer sunshine, and the Holy Spirit came upon me suddenly. I started laughing and laughed for three days straight. Can you imagine? It was a shock for our whole church. I couldn't work. I couldn't sleep. It was like a physical workout. Then I was completely, absolutely free. Since that day, I have never felt depressed again. He healed me completely.

After that I attended five Bible schools, because I knew I needed good teaching and a biblical foundation. I was one of the best students. I also met my beautiful wife, Olga, in another very special "suddenly" from God. Now, we have been married for twenty-three years and have three children: Anna, Anastasia, and Andrew. God completely turned my life around.

Mission, Vision, and Lessons Learned Along the Way

Please tell us about your organization.

The first thing I will say is the God Seekers Movement is not just an organization, it is a movement. People and organizations join us out of relationship because they have the same heart and feel inspired about what God is doing. On the organizational side, we have a team and structure to accomplish the vision and mission God gives us, but the movement side is built from friendship and shared values. We are a network of friends around the world who are going after God. Our values are to seek God's face, listen for His voice, and obey everything He asks us to do. Our mission is to fill the earth with the knowledge of the Lord (Isaiah 11:9) and our vision is for spiritual awakening and reformation of nations.

Our strategy is to minister to Christian churches and society with the tactic of building a missionary organization, a media group, and a prayer movement. We have about forty full-time ministers. The ministry does not pay them. They live by faith through support from friends and partners. Our goal is to eventually have 1,000 full-time ministers. We also want to train many to serve around the world. Our heart is to train 10,000 or more and equip them for a season, then send them out prepared, equipped, and grounded in their faith. One of our goals is to raise up leaders for other ministries. We want people to go *through* our ministry, not just stay with us, but to follow Jesus wherever He leads them. We want our organization to grow as well, with the goal of 1,000 full-time team members. We have pioneered three bases: in Kiev, Ukraine; Moscow, Russia; and Azeri, Estonia. Our heart is to start more bases in key regions of the former Soviet Union.

How did you get started in ministry?

I was part of a charismatic church of mostly young people. I served at the church in whatever ways I could: first as an usher, then choir member, guitar player, and eventually a home group leader. I believe when we serve in any capacity needed, even if it is not our preference, that opens the way for our calling. Jesus teaches us the greatest in the kingdom of God is the servant of all.

Then, our church went through a difficult time because the founding pastor and his wife got a divorce. The bishop came in to choose a new pastor and approached me. I was 23 years old. Then right before the members meeting, he told me he changed his mind and another man would be the pastor. I was upset and confused. I really wanted to be the pastor, and I had told him that. The other man, Eugene, also spoke to him and said that I should be pastor. He didn't even want to be pastor. The bishop simply said, "No Sergey, you won't be the new pastor, Eugene will." He gave no explanation.

I closed myself in my prayer room for an entire day. It was my Gethsemane moment. I was in a dangerous place because I was so upset and offended. I didn't want to be obedient to my leader. About half the people from the church came up to me personally and told me they didn't agree with the bishop's decision. Some even urged me to start a new church; we could have had a church split over this. But I prayed all day. God spoke to me through Philippians 2:5-8: *"Let this mind be in you which was also in Christ Jesus, who, being in the form of God, did not consider it robbery to be equal with God, but made Himself of no reputation, taking the form of a bondservant, and coming in the likeness of men. And being found in appearance as a man, He humbled Himself and became obedient to the point of death, even the death of the cross."*

That was my rhema word from God, "You need to humble yourself." It was terrible, dark, and difficult. My old nature and new nature were fighting, but God won. I went to the meeting where they presented Eugene as the new pastor and told him I wanted to serve as his assistant. I decided it would be my victory. I served him as the best assistant I could be for one year. We ended up becoming best friends through the process.

Just one month later, in August 1999, God gave me one of the most significant revelations of my life. He gave me a message for the body of Christ about personal relationship with God, a revelation I have been sharing around the world for twenty years. Now, I have preached at hundreds of churches, I've been on television, and all of it from that summer in 1999. But I believe if I hadn't been obedient and humbled myself in the church leadership decision the month before, I would not have received this revelation from God. Our choices impact our futures and there is fruit from our obedience to God.

It's difficult to humble ourselves, but we have to fight for it. Even when we read our Bibles, we have to make sure we are humbling ourselves. Some people use the Bible to support their pride and justify their offense. It's possible to interpret the Bible to your own advantage and use it to support your own vision, but that is not how God leads us. We have to go before Him and let Him work in our hearts. My Gethsemane started out horribly, but God brought me through all the emotions to finish well. It is a fight to die to the flesh, but if we win, there is great joy, peace, and happiness on the other side. In my opinion, it's not possible to be truly happy without also being humble.

PRAYER AND ENCOUNTERS

That is a powerful testimony. I completely agree. There is great fruit to obedience and humility. Please share more about the revelation God gave you about a personal relationship with Him.

God changed my life and visited me. The revelation I received was about a personal relationship with the Lord. I always loved to pray and spend time with God. Even when I was first saved in the Catholic church, I wanted to be a monk. But over the course of that summer, I was going through a bad season in my spiritual life. I had lost my fire and my first love for God. I didn't know what was wrong, but something felt different. Looking back, I later realized it was because I was neglecting my personal time with Jesus. I still prayed at church and meetings with other Christians, but not alone in the secret place.

I was walking down the street one day and asking God to refresh me. I heard His voice very clearly. He said, "Seek My face." It was only one phrase, but I could also feel God's feelings. He was jealous about my ministry. He was jealous of the other good things in my life that were taking all my time and attention. I realized God can be jealous over the blessings He gives us when we prioritize those things above seeking His face. My calendar was very full of meetings with people, but I decided to put God on my calendar. I wanted to intentionally respond to His invitation. My wife and I scheduled two hours every morning to pray. Later we increased it to five hours a day.

We had a small apartment and a baby, so I prayed in the hallway. The secret place can be anywhere. We had great intentions, but it did not start off easily. I had to stand up and walk around, otherwise I would fall asleep. My wife would knock on the wall, and if I knocked back, I was still awake. If not, she came to shake me back to prayer. One of the biggest reasons I had success in prayer is because of my wife's faithful help. Through many terrible prayer times, mistakes, and falling asleep, we just kept on going, every day. Now I have shared this testimony all over the Russian-speaking world and on TBN Russia television. People are very encouraged hearing my negative experiences with prayer. As leaders, we need to be honest and share the struggles, not just the victories.

This journey changed our relationship with the Lord. It wasn't always easy, but we were genuinely seeking God. We were longing for real encounters like we read about in the Scriptures. We also read books by Benny Hinn and Yonggi Cho. We wanted those kinds of meetings with God. For one year, in 2000, we prayed five hours every day. We responded to God's invitation with our actions, not just our words. After about a year of being very disciplined, something shifted. I was so touched by Holy Spirit. I felt hungry and thirsty for God. I began doing personal prayer retreats with God outside the city. For the first time in my life, I prayed for 24 hours straight. People asked how it was possible, so I decided to model it. I prayed out loud in Russian for twenty-four hours straight with no breaks on live TV. I was praying and crying out to God for awakening the whole time.

People call me a prayer warrior or a prayer general, but I always correct them and tell them that I'm just a normal Christian. I like to be with God, and I am willing to pay the price to receive from Him. Prayer is the price we pay: our time, our energy, and our focus need to be on Him. We also need to be grounded in the Word of God to know Him. I don't like religious, traditional prayers in my own words. I like to be in His presence. I pray in the Spirit, not just in tongues, but catching the wave of what is being prayed in Heaven. You soar like an eagle. They don't flap their wings and work the whole time, they search for a stream of air, catch the wind and soar. We catch God's stream, otherwise it's just our prayers and our Bible reading. God's presence is the answer. We need to search for it every time we pray.

When God began to visit me, it was terrible sometimes, scary even, because the presence was so strong and overpowering. It felt more real than the physical world. One time, I saw Him like a person right before me. I prayed, "God, I want to know You. I want to be so close to You. I want to understand You more." Those weren't my phrases; they were His phrases to me and through me. I received the revelation that our hunger comes from His hunger for relationship with us. He initiates first. He wants to be close to us. This was one encounter out of many. I began to share and teach about my encounters in churches and on TBN Russia. After hearing my testimonies, many people had their own personal encounters. They too began to enter the Holy of Holies with the Lord. Everyone needs to find their own personal way into the Holy of Holies with God.

Yes! That is very true. Many people want to encounter God like that, but they haven't yet. For some people, praying for five hours seems impossible. What is your advice?

When people find it hard to pray for an hour, they are probably not praying by the Spirit. The key is to surrender to God, then prayer can be the most joyful time of our lives. Praying self-righteousness or self-prayers from your own strength is exhausting. We need the Holy Spirit to lead our prayers. We have to surrender to His presence and His prayers. Then joy comes in prayer. The other key is to search for yourself in the Bible. Find yourself on those pages, connect to the stories in a personal way. Find your situation, your emotions, your dreams, and your feelings. If you really do those two things, it will change everything.

One woman in Germany said she couldn't commit to praying for five hours a day. I asked if it would be difficult to pray for twenty minutes a day. She said yes it would be impossible. I suggested ten minutes, but it still felt too hard. She agreed to just five minutes a day of reading the Bible and praying for one year. I met her again ten years later, and she had been praying one hour a day for many years, truly enjoying God. It all started with five minutes a day.

One of the reasons we don't have success in our prayer lives is because we want to start with two hours a day. Maybe we do it a few times, then we stop completely. If we can just fully humble ourselves and start from zero, step by step, it will grow. In this way, we build a strong personal relationship with God. It's not about intercession moments, it's about relationship moments. The heart behind prayer is being a friend of God.

Some people think praying for hours a day is just for intercessors. What would you say to those who feel called to evangelism or business?

I prefer to talk about prayer in terms of our relationship with God. No matter what you are called to, everyone needs a personal relationship with God. It is not necessary to spend hours in prayer a day, although God does invite some people into this special relationship with Him. After that, they can share about what they learned and the fruits from their time with Jesus. But even the busiest people need time in the secret place with Holy Spirit every day. It is foundational for everything we do in the kingdom.

Relationship with God is our main value because God is our main value. We want to know Him on a deep and personal level. Some people are called more specifically to prayer ministry, but every one of us is called to have a close relationship with God. You are invited by God. He is waiting for you daily, nonstop. Put God and His desire to be with you first, and everything else comes second. Seek Him first.

How has this lifestyle of relationship with God through prayer transformed your personal life?

Through the prayers, my relationship with God changed. I changed. He fought with the idols in my life. He showed me that even things like my heart for success in ministry and my desire to see revival could also be idols. He has to be first in our hearts above even the very best desires.

God ministered to our family through prayer. My wife and I were emotionally distant from each other. Praying together absolutely changed our relationship. Now my wife is my closest friend in all my life. Our relationship was transformed through Song of Songs. I used to read it in a spiritual way, thinking about God. Then, I saw the literal way it was about a relationship between a man and a woman. I focused on learning principles of what Solomon did and how he felt toward the woman. I started doing my part in my marriage. I didn't worry about what my wife did or the woman's part. Through that, our marriage was totally transformed. My wife began to do her part too.

God also changed my relationship with my children. Every time my children would pray it was because I was pressuring them. I loved Jesus so much, and I wanted them to love Him too and pray. But they would treat it like a game. I used to get angry at them and tell them to take God seriously. I was so strict that I actually made them cry. Then one day, I saw a vision of people sitting in a circle, like in a recovery program. The question was, "Why do you hate God so much and why do you hate prayer?" My children were grown up and in this circle.

My heart was devastated. I waited anxiously to hear their answers. They said, "We hate God and we hate prayer because our dad likes praying and he always pushed us. We were always under so much pressure to pray. Now we hate praying. We are against prayer, and we are even against God." When I saw this vision, it was very sobering. It felt so real. I prayed and asked God to please save me and my family from that story.

Several days later, I read Genesis 32 where Jacob wrestled with God and was transformed into Israel. Just after that story, Genesis 33:13-14 was a rhema word for me. Esau asks Jacob to come with him. Then Jacob says, *"My lord knows that the children are weak, and the flocks and herds which are nursing are with me. And if the men should drive them hard one day, all the flock will die. Please let my lord go on ahead before his servant. I will lead on slowly at a pace which the livestock that go before me, and the children, are able to endure, until I come to my lord in Seir."*

God was showing me how to care for my children. The children set the pace. They needed to go slower, so the whole group went slowly. After that I told my children we could pray any way they wanted, but we would still pray together. One of my girls said, "I want to pray like birds." Well, I had heard of intercession, worship prayer, and spiritual warfare, but I had no idea how to pray like a bird! My children reassured me they could teach me. They began to jump on the couch and cry out, "Hallelujah, Jesus, we love You! We are birds who love you!"

I joined in, jumping on the couch and praying like a big bird. We prayed in so many different ways from then on. We were horses, trains, flowers, waters, anything they could imagine. For the horse prayer, all my children rode on my back and told Jesus how much they loved Him. In the train prayer, Jesus was the train conductor, and we were cars. We repeated, "Jesus, Jesus, Jesus, we love You, love You, love You."

Your children probably won't remember the prayers you prayed together or the verses of Scripture, but they will remember the feelings. They will remember the taste on their lips. My goal was to give them the taste on their lips of loving the Lord. Now they are in their teens and 20s and pray and read the Bible for hours a day of their own initiative. They truly love it. After all those years in the secret place during their childhood, today they each have their own secret place. We have to teach our children to enjoy God's presence and know Him personally. Praying together has the power to transform our relationships in our families. It's the way we can teach our children to build their foundation on God.

Ministry Focus

It's beautiful to hear the testimony of your children. You also mentioned that God transformed your personal relationship with Him and showed you that ministry could become an idol. Please share more about that revelation.

From 2000 until 2010, my ministry continued to grow more and more in the Russian-speaking world. We rented stadiums in

Kiev and held several events—with about 10,000 people—that were broadcasted live on Russian satellite television. I also traveled and preached at the largest churches in our stream. Then, in the middle of one of our big events, God called me to spend time with Him in the night. I walked around the outside of the stadium all night praying. Without sleeping at all, I went straight to the conference.

God spoke to me very clearly. He asked me to give Him my ministry the same way Abraham gave up his son Isaac on the altar. He asked me to cancel all our conferences, my TV ministry, my travels, and come to Him. It's a long story, but I obeyed. I canceled everything. I had seven people on staff, but I released them all. On Russian television, I announced I was canceling my whole ministry for a season because the Lord asked me to. People thought I was crazy. They thought this was a terrible decision.

One very famous pastor told me I would lose everything. He said when you're famous and well-known, you need to support your popularity and cultivate it. My response, "If this was my ministry I would lose everything; but it's the Lord's, and He can do what He wants. He can take everything in one day because it all came from Him anyway." God is even jealous of our ministries. We have to minister to Him first. He is our main ministry. It was not easy though. It's easy to tell you the story, but walking through it was very painful. Your personal garden is your responsibility. No one sees what is inside except you and the Lord. If you don't obey what He says, no one will know except you and Him. This was another huge opportunity in my life to be obedient, humble myself, discipline myself, and give my ministry fully back to God.

I laid down everything. My ministry, my team, everything. My income also came through ministry, so I lost that too. I lost everything except my wife. I have an amazing wife who supported me through it all. We didn't have money. Sometimes we had to fast, not by choice, but because we literally did not have money to buy food. I was one of the most famous preachers in the entire Russian-speaking world around the globe. Everyone knew my name. But no one knew what we went through in those years. No one knew we didn't have enough food or money for rent. It was a difficult season, a long, challenging few years. But God told me, if you will give Me your ministry in the Russian-speaking world, I will give you a worldwide ministry.

When Jesus died on the cross, He didn't just see the cross and hell. He saw the resurrection and Heaven ahead of Him. When God asked Abraham to put Isaac down on the altar, He had already given him the promise of nations. When God asked for my ministry, He also gave me a promise. He said if I would be obedient, He would use me around the world. He showed me my ministry would not only be for Russian speakers, it would be international. He told me it was easy for Him to give me a big ministry with a lot of people, but it was difficult for Him to break my heart, to break my character. He wants us to be broken, humble vessels completely surrendered to Him.

Again, it is a longer story, but God did exactly as He promised me. Our ministry is even bigger now than it was before. He connected me with people in the USA and other nations and opened the doors beyond the Russian-speaking world. We now have 40 full-time ministers on staff, and we do not support any of them financially. They all live by faith and God provides for them. Ten others are finishing their internships. We sense God is doing a multiplication work. God always keeps His promises even when it doesn't come in the way we expected.

God is so faithful! Thank you for sharing your story. Tell us more about your ministry.

We focus on teaching and training. Most of our team members are between 18 to 30 years old. We mentor and teach them through living life together. In Kiev we have a prayer room. It is not 24/7 yet, but that is the goal. We have an internship where people can come for a 5-month training. They can serve with us or go back to their churches and ministries. We work together with other ministries around the world.

Media is another area we are passionate about. We have our own TV channel, news agency, and radio station. We also work together with BOG TV (the Russian arm of God TV). There are worship teams on each base. They come together at various times for worship and creative trainings with musicians, singers, and dancers. The three bases are connected virtually and through face-to-face meetings back and forth. All the bases have weekly prayer meetings and we also have prayer retreats for three days each month.

You have three-day prayer retreats with your entire team every month?

Yes. We all leave our work and come together to seek the Lord. We fast and pray as a team. We have been doing this since 2006 when we started our first base, so almost fifteen years, every month. God gave me this revelation about giving Him 10 percent of our time, tithing our time. We spend hours worshipping and praying together as family. We have teaching and training for the team. During this time, we lay down all thoughts and plans about our ministry and focus only on God. This is the key to what we are doing. God comes first. It's all about Him.

I love that strategy! You shared earlier that God Seekers is also a movement, not only an organization. Who is involved in the movement and what does it look like to join?

The movement is spreading across the Russian-speaking world. There are houses of prayer, local churches, even some church networks that are part of the movement. As the leader, I am sensitive to build everything out of relationship, with trust, led by the Holy Spirit. I founded the organization, but in my opinion it is impossible to found or begin a movement. People have to be compelled to join you because of a common vision. Our movement grows out of our shared goal for awakening, revival, and transformation in our nations. When I speak about seeking God's face and what He did in my life, many people are inspired and encouraged. Even strong pastors and leaders want to join. I believe the Holy Spirit is inspiring and drawing them.

A movement is birthed when people are passionate about the same goal. If people are no longer inspired, the movement will end. Movements are not sustained by structure and organization. They are sustained through shared values, relationship, and inspiration. We have one value system—love God and love people. We want to see the entire continent of Europe reached with God's love, the Great Commission. As the movement grows, God transforms our hearts and we remain focused on the one goal of awakening. We are passionate for God, He is our goal and our motivation for all we do, and for who we are, individually and collectively.

Ministry is not like a business where consumers expect something from us. God is the owner of His ministry, and we seek His face, listen to His voice, and live obedient to Him. The people we are connected with are spiritual, prophetic people who seek God's face. I know other people who try to build up ministries through good marketing and good systems. They invite business trainers to their churches to teach them business models. While they pursue those strategies, I will continue to seek God's face in the secret place. All of my ministry is through revelation only. When I make decisions, when we plant a new base, whenever I take a key step, it's totally through revelation. These are just two different sides of Christianity. Of course, I am not against someone doing ministry another way. But I like my way more—ministering through relationship with God and through prayer, anointing, prophetic insight, and all from Him and for Him.

EUROPE FOCUS

What do you see God doing in Europe? What do you sense on His heart for the continent?

When I think about Europe, I think about men and women of God who will seek His face. Prayer and reading the Bible are instruments to be with God. I see this vision of God-seekers, like Abraham and Jacob. Those who will actually transform from Jacobs to Israels. We need the new Israels of Europe. I see young people. God is calling the youth and inviting them into relationship. Awakening in Europe is when people seek God, when they pray and hear His voice. It means revival. It means they receive rhema words in relationship and receive what God promises them.

God is looking for those who will be obedient. They will be the ones who do not focus on growing their own ministries or their own names. They won't just think about themselves and their fruit—they will raise up others. They help and raise up the ones beneath them to be even bigger than they are. This is true success in ministry and in the kingdom of God. When I pray about Europe, I sense we need more people who will go up the mountain and seek God, like Moses, and come back down with shiny faces and preach everywhere.

And are there any specific countries you see God is already awakening?

The former Soviet Union is definitely a region in which I see God moving. Since the 1990s when the Soviet Union collapsed, the doors have been open for the Gospel. This led to a major awakening throughout this region. I personally had the privilege of witnessing and being part of it. We have especially seen a great deal of openness in Ukraine with national leaders joining together to cry out for awakening. We continue to see powerful moves of God all across Eastern Europe. If God can bring awakening in a formerly atheistic empire, He can awaken any region!

I can also highlight Germany and Switzerland as places where God is moving powerfully. God is using people including: Jean-Luc Trachsel, with Europe Shall Be Saved; Ben Fitzgerald, with Awakening Europe; Markus Wenz with Holy Spirit Nights; and many others. Through people like them, we are seeing powerful awakening. We have seen fruit, for sure, but not the fullness. We all wait and expect so much more, something so much bigger. We long for a great movement of the Holy Spirit. That is what we long to be part of in Europe.

Amen! My last question is how can we work toward unity in the body of Christ?

First of all, we need to focus on a Person, on Jesus. If we look at our doctrines, we will be separated, divided by our beliefs. But if we focus on a Person and a relationship with Jesus, this will unite us. The example God showed me about unity among denominations comes from the last chapter of the Gospel of John. Jesus asks Peter if he loves Him three times. Peter replies three times that he does love Jesus. Then Jesus asks Peter to follow Him. As they walk, Peter sees John following and asks Jesus why he is coming. Jesus answers that it is not Peter's concern what John does, Peter just needs to follow Jesus.

When I read this story, I see it's not just about Peter and John, it's about two denominations. There can be feelings of competition or comparison, but Jesus's response is not to worry what the other is doing, just follow Him. Through this story, we learn how to walk in unity. We all follow Jesus and focus on Him. Another example comes from Acts 3:1. Peter and John, two apostles, came together in the temple for prayer. This shows us a powerful example for leaders. We build unity when we come together for prayer. Prayer is meeting with Jesus, and unity comes when we all draw closer to Jesus together.

LIFE APPLICATION—LAY IT ALL DOWN

Sergey has such a powerful testimony of faithfulness and obedience to the Lord. He follows God in a radical way with his heart and with his life choices, both big and small. It stands out to me that before he was promoted in ministry, God asked him to lay everything down not once, but twice. Now he shares his testimonies worldwide and many are inspired through his movement. People want to pursue their own secret place when they hear of his powerful God encounters. But before that, there were years of hiddenness and humility. There were very tough choices to follow God's voice when it cost him nearly everything. I believe the anointing and authority Sergey carries today came from those very costly moments.

The first was when his friend was given the pastoral position he wanted and expected. This was a fork-in-the-road moment. He could start his own new church, which many from the congregation were encouraging him to do, or he could submit to his leaders and serve the one chosen over him. Imagine if you thought you were about to be made the leader, and suddenly you are the assistant. Sergey wrestled with very real emotions in what he calls his "Gethsemane." It would have been easy, and it could have felt justified, for Sergey to start his own church. He could have even found some Bible verses to back himself up.

He pointed out that if our hearts are not humble, we can use the Scriptures to support our prideful choices. Because he chose to honor his leadership, serve his friend, and take the humble road, he was later promoted by God. He gained a lifelong friend and the church remained together. What would you do if this happened to you? Have you ever been overlooked or even humiliated?

The second time Sergey made a very hard choice was when he laid down his entire ministry to the Russian-speaking world because of a word from the Lord. People said he was crazy. He went through one of the hardest times in his life when he didn't even have money for food at times. But God honored his sacrifice and fulfilled His promise for a worldwide ministry on the other side of the desert. We often have to walk through a desert to get to our promises. If you're in the desert, keep going. I promise you, but more importantly, God promises, that He makes all things new. There will be a new season of breakthrough and victory if you cling to Him and don't give up.

God wants the first place in our hearts. Even our ministry or blessings from God can become idols when they have a hold on our hearts. God is jealous for our love and attention. He doesn't want anything else to take His rightful place. Obedience is very important to God. He wants a people who will literally lay everything on the altar for His sake. When we do, our "yes" carries great power and great breakthrough. Biblically we can see this example in the story of Abraham laying Isaac on the altar. God promised Abraham a son and a legacy. He waited long, challenging years for his promise. Finally, he received his son! Then God tells him to lay Isaac on the altar. What?! How hard that would have been, but Abraham obeyed. He knew His God could even raise the dead. God tested Abraham's heart and proved before Heaven and earth that He still had the first place above the promise.

Does God have the first place in your heart? If God told you to lay it ALL down on the altar, would you do it? Is it your ministry or is it truly the Lord's?

12

Sarah Breuel

Organizations: Revive Europe & International
Fellowship of Evangelical Students (IFES Europe)
Positions: Director & Training Coordinator
Location: Rome, Italy

Personal Background

What is your favorite thing to do on your day off?

We are just one hour from the beach, so during the summer we
love taking our boys to the beach for some sun and fun. We love
having a relaxing family day or evening together. I also love going
for a run.

*If you could have lunch with someone who inspires you, whom
would you choose?*

There are four women I admire, look up to, and have been
learning from, from a distance. The first is Heidi Baker, I would

love to get to know her and learn from her life. Second: Kari Jobe. I don't sing or play an instrument, but I am a worshipper. Her journey with God and the way she worships have always inspired me. I would love to get to know her. Third: Christine Caine. I like her because she imparts so much faith when she speaks, and she is so brave. And finally, Steffany Gretzinger, she is so on fire for Jesus!

Lunch with all four of those fabulous women would be incredible! Now tell us a little more about yourself and your faith journey.

I was raised in the south of Brazil with my two sisters. Our parents took us to Christian camps, and I loved Jesus ever since I was a little girl. I don't have a "before and after" in my testimony because I always genuinely loved God. When I was 9 years old, I first heard about cross-cultural missions. Although I was young, I already knew it was for me. I went forward for the altar call around the bonfire at Christian camp, and I truly meant it.

My father is a businessman. He encouraged me to study something else before digging into theology, which was good advice. I went to business school, where I also met my husband. We really felt God put us together. He also has a heart for the church and wanted to serve as a pastor, but wanted to study business first. After graduating, we moved to Canada for three years and studied theology. This was a special time for us, the first years of our marriage and also getting deeper into theology.

Now, I will get more into the organization I work with. When I was in university, I became familiar with International Fellowship for Evangelical Students (IFES), a campus ministry working with university students. There are different names for IFES in different countries. For example, Intervarsity in the United States,

UCCF in the UK, and GBU in Italy. During my student years, this organization had a big impact on my life. I loved seeing students sharing their faith. These are strategic years when God changes people's lives and trajectories. I got involved with IFES and have been serving for fifteen years now in various countries— first in Brazil, then one year in Norway, then in Canada, many years in Italy, and the last three years in Europe as a region.

I was working with IFES, but my husband and I struggled to discern where to serve in cross-cultural missions. It was a two-year process of praying into that. Then we both felt peace to come to Italy ten years ago. He had church planting on his heart, and I was passionate about student ministry. My husband pastors a church, and I work for IFES in the European region. We didn't plan it this way, but we have experienced a lot of synergy with the church plant and the student ministry working together.

Then my life was changed again after a God encounter when I was 30 years old. It was June 2013, and God encountered me in Dubai, calling me to be part of the planning team leadership for the Lausanne Younger Leaders Global Gathering. This gathering was in Indonesia in 2016 for emerging Christian leaders from 25 to 35 years old with national and global leadership potential. We spent several years planning and preparing for this powerful event. It was my first time leading in a global capacity, so I learned a great deal! After that, I took a nine-month sabbatical to rest and be with my boys and my husband.

After what I experienced, I was so hungry to hear from God again. I prayed, "God, I don't want to be spoiled, but ever since You spoke to me so clearly, I don't want to act on anything else besides hearing Your voice and knowing that Your hand is on something."

I was praying for five or six months not sensing something specific yet, but I wasn't anxious. I was happy to wait on God as long as He wanted. IFES Europe was planning an evangelism conference in Europe, and they asked me to lead it. This felt like a big privilege to me and included all the things I love—evangelism, Europe, and students. I told them I was waiting on the Lord to hear His voice. They were gracious with me and allowed me to take the time I needed to pray before making a decision.

Then in Oxford, God woke me up in the middle of the night. This was the second God encounter I had, and the first time I actually heard the audible voice of God. Unforgettable! He just said my name, nothing else. It sounded like a waterfall. I still remember it and get chills that He gave me that privilege. After that, I sensed to read Isaiah 54. Verse 2 stood out to me: *"Enlarge the place of your tent, stretch your tent curtains wide, do not hold back; lengthen your cords, strengthen your stakes"* (Isaiah 54:2 New International Version). I had been wanting to say yes to the invitation from IFES, but I was holding back because I longed for a green light from God. The verse really spoke to me. Then that morning, God used a woman from Ukraine to confirm again. She was leading a simple devotional time, and she sensed there was someone who wanted to say yes to something but was holding back. That was so direct! It spoke right to me. She shared that in Luke 1 Mary didn't know what she was getting into, but she said yes out of obedience. It felt like my answer.

That is the background for explaining what I am working on now. It is called Revive Europe. I was so hungry, but I suspected there were some things in my life that Jesus needed to deal with. A friend of mine read a book about forgiveness, and it changed her life, so I also read the book. It was about Matthew 18, the parable of the servant who had been forgiven much but doesn't forgive. The author encouraged readers to write a list of everyone they had not yet fully forgiven. I had twenty-seven people on my list! I couldn't believe it. I went through one by one, fully forgiving each one. In the end, I felt so free and healed. Jesus had dealt with some of the roots. I wasn't expecting this, but it was out of that experience that God released a hunger I hadn't had before. It was out of that forgiveness journey that I received a supernatural hunger for more of His presence, for being in worship and prayer for hours. I have always loved Him, but it feels different now. It feels like a personal revival.

Out of that came years of prayer and birthing the vision for Revive. We want to work in unity with other amazing ministries like Europe Shall Be Saved, the Lausanne Movement, Agape/Cru and many others. Our heart is to sow for revival in the student generation, that is the target group that Revive is committed to reach. It's a privilege to direct this process with twenty-five Christian organizations. The first event was for 5,000 students at the end of 2019 from all over Europe. Revive Europe is about going through a journey: "Revive our hearts. Revive our universities. Revive Europe!"

CAMPUS WORK

What does your campus work look like on a daily or weekly basis?

For the first four years in Italy, I worked as an IFES staff worker here in Rome with three large universities in the city. I worked alongside the students having Bible studies inside the campuses. We encourage students to be intentional about their friendships with seekers and bring them along to study the Bible. We focus on personal friendship and small group Bible study. We also have public mission weeks when students organize apologetic and faith-focused events on their campuses to reach out to other students.

Then I coordinated the Lausanne gathering for three years and now the Revive Event for the last two years. About 80-90 percent of my time is Revive itself, putting the team together, visioning, recruiting, program planning, fundraising, and logistics.

The other part of my job is evangelism training for IFES Europe. I travel and speak in different contexts and conferences about student evangelism through personal evangelism and small group Bible study. IFES is currently focusing on the "mission week" initiative. We work to become very visible on a campus for one week during each semester. This includes fliers, events, debates, very intentionally inviting friends, lunch bars, evening talks, open mic nights, being open about the Gospel, and reaching students on their journeys.

We have had about 200 mission weeks per year all across Europe in more than thirty nations. The students go all in. They are doing so much for evangelism. I am an evangelist at heart. The students are already doing so much, and the structures are in place. That being said, we often speak about how all fruitfulness comes from intimacy. Through Revive, we hope to bring the students to a deeper level of intimacy and prayer, dependence on and being filled with the Holy Spirit. God brought many student groups like Agape/Cru, Navigators, OM, YWAM, and others together to be part of Revive along with all forty European nations. This is already bringing unity on a regional level. We feel the focus on dependency and prayer is what Revive can add to the great work that is already going on. It is about depending on Jesus, not on how hard we work. That is our heart.

What type of evangelism training do you focus on?

We focus on personal evangelism and small group evangelism through building friendships. One of the key chapters I teach on is John 15. There are many wonderful techniques, but we need intimacy with God. My husband and I lead weekly seeker Bible studies where most of the people in the group are not Christians. We read stories of Jesus together and let Jesus speak for Himself. Over six to eight weeks, we create a safe place for students to ask questions and wrestle with what they believe. We pray that Jesus will impact people and that at least one person will start following Jesus. We have a one-on-one time with the most responsive person. Then when one person comes to faith, they become the best evangelist in the group. Their faith becomes contagious. We have baptized sixty-two people over nine years here. I am so grateful for all these people who have come to know Jesus. Another part of me longs to see more, where it won't just be one by one, but a wave of people knowing God.

Some people are intimidated about sharing their faith. How do you help people navigate through their fears?

Most people's biggest fear is personal rejection. We are afraid if we talk with our friends, we are going to look weird. I wrestle with this myself for sure, and it's been a place of dependence and learning. We encourage students to be themselves and share from their hearts. We talk about the verse: *"where your treasure is, there your heart will be also"* (Matthew 6:21). If we are worried about reputation, that can stop us from sharing Jesus with people. Instead, we ask for the grace to have enough boldness to choose to share Jesus, even if it might mean being rejected. We encourage people to share their faith in a really natural way. They tell their friends their faith is something they are passionate about, but to let them know if they prefer not to hear more. People are surprised how much a simple thing like this allows them to relax and have a real conversation. It gives us freedom to share our hearts.

WAITING AND SUDDENLIES

Please share the encounter you had in Dubai about leading the Lausanne Movement Global Youth Leaders Gathering. How did God speak to you and what impact did it have on you?

Whenever I start sharing, it's like I'm back in that place again. Before I answer this question, I need to give some background why airports are very significant in my journey. The background is that when I left Brazil to go to Canada in 2006, I was working in business and doing well. I left everything behind to go study theology and prepare for cross-cultural missions. When we arrived in Canada, for me it was such a crossroads. I remember sitting with my husband as the plane landed at the Vancouver airport, thinking there is no turning back from here. I cried my eyes out knowing it would be a three-year season, and our lives would never be the same. I remember well that it was at sunset. I remember asking God to be with me in the new season and thinking, *In three years I'll be back in this airport again to leave this country.*

In Canada, one of my courses was on Genesis. One story that really spoke to me was about Jacob leaving for Paddan Aram. When he left it was a sunset (Bethel), and when he returned twenty years later to cross the Jordan, it was a sunrise (Peniel). The professor was exploring how Jacob had Bethel and Peniel bookend moments with God. That stuck with me. When I had arrived in the Vancouver airport, it was a sunset. I sort of forgot about that until I was back at the same airport three years later in 2009 to leave after my studies. It happened to be a sunrise. It was so meaningful. I sensed God saying He was there with me. He had brought me there. Ever since then, airports have been tender places for me to listen to God.

Now to answer your question. Many years later, in 2013, I was returning from a conference in India. I had a layover in Dubai. I felt the Holy Spirit so thick as the airplane was landing, as if God was preparing my heart for the encounter I was about to have. Then on the screen of the plane, they showed a map of the world with arrows going from Dubai to many nations. God got my full attention. I was in a significant place, in an airport, in the middle of the world. My husband and I were talking about what they shared at the conference about putting together a planning team for the Lausanne Young Leaders Global Gathering.

About ten months before this happened, I sensed God clearly speaking that within one year I would be working part-time on a new project. I literally had no idea what it would be, but it was so strong that I even told my boss from GBU Italy. It sounded crazy, but I told him in faith. Just before the trip to India, my boss asked if I had sensed anything from God yet. I told him I hadn't. He was incredibly gracious to wait with me.

As my husband and I talked about the Young Leaders Gathering in that Dubai airport, my heart began pounding. I prayed, asking God if this was what He had been waiting ten months to show me. I sensed in my soul that He was saying yes, but I wanted something concrete. I wanted to hear clearly from God. I closed my eyes and it became very clear, "Open Isaiah 49." The passage was deeply powerful. It connected things from fifteen years ago, twelve years ago...it was as though it was written just for me, connecting things that no one in the world knew about. I was bawling because it was so direct. It was the perfect place, an airport, and the perfect word, Isaiah 49.

As I closed my eyes to thank God, it felt like a waterfall was flowing over me. I had experienced the Holy Spirit, but nothing like that before. It is hard to put into words how strong it was. It felt as though every muscle in my body was being filled with the Holy Spirit. It lasted for about fifteen minutes, just receiving and receiving. My husband was holding my hand as I was crying and receiving. After those fifteen minutes had passed in that waterfall experience, I knew that the Young Leaders Gathering was my calling. I was sure God wanted me to give myself to this. It was very, very special to me.

I think, looking back, God wanted to give a specific anointing for that task because those three years walking out the assignment were so incredibly hard. He wanted to get my attention in a place that made sense for me personally, an airport, in the middle of the world, with an encounter that He was preparing years before.

Wow, that is really beautiful! You shared that for the Young Leaders Gathering in Indonesia and for Revive Europe you prepared for each event for three years. Please share what that preparation process looked like and what your role was in preparing for these events.

The events were different. Both were challenging on the task level of putting the events together. Then there was the personal level as well, which was also challenging. Starting with the Indonesia Lausanne gathering, there was a stripping of my heart in the journey of preparing for it. For example, I knew after the encounter in Dubai that God was calling me to lead, but I was only 30 years old and this was a global gathering for 150 nations coming together. The other people on the planning team were mainly men. I am not the type to put up my hand and say, "God spoke to me." I did share briefly about my encounter with the global leader of Lausanne. He was excited and put me on the team. They had twelve young leaders, one from each region of the world. He said I could be the Latin American leader.

We had our team meetings, and things were a bit unclear. I knew I was called (and asked) to lead, but the team suggested an election instead. One of my friends even decided to run for the leadership role along with some confident young American men. I was confused, but I felt I had to release it and not strive for the position. I felt like David who was anointed as king, but it took a thirteen-year desert to get there. I wondered how this would all play out.

The elections took a whole month. It was very difficult, but then they chose me in the end. It seems these processes of releasing things in our heart back to God are more important than the outcome or position. Also, since I was officially elected by the team, it actually gave me a lot of authority with the others in the movement for the next two years of working together. God has us walk through things that at the time feel super painful but make a lot of sense when we look back on them.

That is one small story. Then there was fundraising, getting scholarships, and selections. We gathered people from 150 countries. It was especially challenging to organize bringing people in from Africa and the Pacific Islands. Coordinating all the logistics around bringing everyone together was overwhelming. It felt like a three-year pregnancy, but I knew God would do it. Also, since I was young, I had to learn a lot of lessons about leadership on a global level.

For Revive, it wasn't as stretching workwise, but this event felt by far the biggest faith journey. When I went through personal revival and started to dream about and pray for revival in Europe, I thought I was crazy. I didn't know anyone else praying for that. Now I know about Europe Shall Be Saved and Awakening Europe. I felt like Noah, asking for something impossible. IFES and the twenty-five other Christian groups we are working with are more conservative, so to be praying for revival felt a bit out-there. Our vision personally and for the event was "Do not hold back," so we dreamed for 5,000 people. The previous event had to be canceled for lack of numbers, so people thought this was crazy. It didn't make sense rationally. Over time, things came together, more and more registrations came through, and we saw God doing it. But in the beginning, it looked completely far away.

Then there was the area of fundraising. We invited participants from all around the world, and we wanted to help them get there. Our budget was 1.2 million euros, with a goal to fundraise 600,000 euros. As a young Brazilian woman, this felt huge. Then God started opening doors, and money started coming through. Organizations that hadn't given in 13 or 14 years despite many people knocking on their doors, were now giving to Revive. Other fundraisers in IFES asked me how the money was coming to Revive. I didn't have any answer other than God opening doors through prayer. I fully recognize that we stand on the ground that previous generations have been sowing. It still feels like a big test of faith, believing God will do what He said He would do even though it looks impossible and believing revival will break through in the student generation in Europe.

I have been filling my heart with faith, reading things from Heidi Baker and from Europe Shall Be Saved. That is not the environment I work in. We are pioneering vision for revival, but this is not a familiar topic for most of the organizations involved. Even the language could sound a bit "too charismatic" to some of these circles. I want to respect and honor where everyone I work with is coming from, which is not always easy.

Please share the vision for Revive.

We want to see revival in the student generation. I completely believe God will break through in Europe. Seeing Awakening Europe and Europe Shall Be Saved fills my heart with faith. The part of the puzzle we can facilitate is sowing for revival in the student generation, in the universities, which are very secular places where they make God too small. Our heart is to call the student generation to contend for revival. One strategy we embarked on was a 40-week prayer journey. Every Monday we focused on a European country to fast and pray for, and the students released a video about that nation.

The conference focus was Acts 1–5, studying how the early church was dependent on God and carrying the Spirit. The main themes were "Revive Our Hearts," "Revive Our Universities," and "Revive Europe." "Revive Our Hearts" is about encouraging the students to be honest and raw with their hearts, identifying idols in our hearts, and facilitating a place of worship, repentance, and prayer. Out of that place of repentance asking God to revive our hearts. "Revive Our Universities" is about being instruments in the university and students sharing their faith boldly. "Revive Europe" is about identifying idols in nations, repenting as nations and as continents, and asking God to breathe something afresh.

Many have a vision or a calling from God but do not know how to get from where they are today to the fulfillment of the dream. They want to be humble, but also to believe for the vision, prepare, and walk toward it. What is your advice about how to navigate this journey with God?

If you know the answer, please tell me! That's my biggest wrestle. God often gives us a picture of something far away. It can be amazing, but then how do we get from here to there? Sometimes it looks crazy. What I am trying to learn is the mixture of faith, just believing, and preaching to our own hearts that if God promised, He will do it. Otherwise, the obstacles would be too big. I think I would have quit many times if I didn't have the clear calling.

The second part is to walk it out without striving or trying to make it happen by ourselves. The verse I had was, *"Do not hold back, enlarge the place of your tent"* (Isaiah 54:2 New International Version). What I sensed about that was God wanted me to know He would do this. We don't turn back. We prepare for the vision He showed us. At the same time, even that can feel exhausting. We have to continuously remind ourselves God gave the vision. It is not going to be fulfilled through our striving.

We need to trust the journey and trust that the curves and obstacles are not surprises to God. In it all, He is molding our hearts. Our job is to keep our hearts pure and humble before God. That is even more important than the vision itself or how things play out. The vision won't look how you think in your mind, but God knows. When things don't come to pass or don't look like you thought they would, trust that God will not disappoint. He is good, and He is working for your good. Have a light heart and complete trust. We do our part and act responsibly to walk things out, but it is a dance of trusting Him more and more.

Have you gone through disappointments? How did you get back on track?

We go through challenges all the time. Literally every week! Working with teams, we find out quickly that relationships are not easy. It is incredibly important to honor one another, even when that is not always easy. Another important thing is to make sure that God is our Anchor. Our identity is not in the success of our ministry or our events. Even if we feel like failures some days, we continuously go back to that place of resting on God's word. Obedience to what He said, from a place of rest. I am still learning this myself. If God is our Anchor, no matter what waves come our way, we constantly fix our eyes on Jesus and get through the storms.

EUROPE FOCUS

What do you see God doing in Europe in this generation?

I think we, in Europe, have made God small. We have put God in a corner. Especially in the student world, we have been arrogant enough to think that we are smarter than God. I believe God is calling people to repentance: for this generation to repent of our ways, to repent of the idols we have, and to humble ourselves before Him and ask Him to intervene. That's what I feel God is doing, calling Europe back to Himself. It is the place of humbling ourselves before Him as in Second Chronicles 7:14: *"If My people who are called by My name will humble themselves, and pray and seek My face, and turn from their wicked ways, then I will hear from heaven, and will forgive their sin and heal their land."* This atmosphere of humbling ourselves and repenting, that's what I sense God is calling this generation to do.

Are there specific countries you feel God is highlighting?

Yes. It's almost like there are small fires in the student generation of places where God is moving. One of the dreams for Revive is to see these small matches coming together brightly. There are some specific places I see God moving. There is a student movement in Hungary that is seeing incredible things happen. It's exciting to see the unity and what God is doing in Austria through Awakening Europe. There are wonderful prayer groups in Finland. The work of Europe Shall Be Saved is pioneering this work for a lot of countries, with a ripple effect.

How can we continue to work toward unity and what does unity look like?

We must be very clear about what we are united for—Jesus and our shared desire for revival in Europe. We need to be gracious with our differences and not make them the main focus— but make Jesus and the longing for revival central. We can get together around these areas and have grace about the areas where we do not agree. We need to learn how to continue pursuing unity while understanding each other's differences. We also need to recognize the large differences country to country in the church landscape.

LIFE APPLICATION—THE SUDDENLIES OF GOD

I love the beautiful balance in Sarah's life of making wise choices in prayer, waiting on the Lord for confirmations, and getting swept into incredible opportunities through the suddenlies of God. Her trusting relationship with God grew deeper and deeper through each experience of following His lead. God is always speaking. He uses His Word, circumstances around us, other people, a sense within our hearts, and even His audible voice. As you follow Him and seek direction, keep your eyes and ears open to the creative and unique ways He wants to speak to you personally.

Let's dig deeper into the ways Sarah follows God and what we can learn. Sarah decided to serve with IFES campus ministry because her life was deeply touched through this ministry, and she loved the ways students were being impacted with the Gospel. This highlights an important way that God leads us. The ministries, people groups, and experiences that deeply touch our lives often speak to the direction God has for us. Pay attention to what moves your heart.

I also loved when Sarah saw the sunset as she landed in Canada. Then, three years later, she left with the sun rising, mirroring the story of Jacob that she learned about in theology classes. God loves to speak to us. That was a Daddy-daughter moment between Sarah and the Lord. It was His yes and amen that she was on the right track. Look and listen for those moments as you build your own history with God.

Other times God speaks through major encounters. Sarah's Dubai encounter caused her to join the Lausanne leadership team. Looking back, she thinks God spoke so clearly because it was a stretching and challenging three-year assignment. Often when God speaks very clearly about something, it's because there will be a long wait or difficulties on the path ahead. Those marking moments give us the strength and assurance to persevere and overcome. They also build our relationship with God as we lean fully on His voice and follow His leadership.

Sarah sensed God speaking to her about a new opportunity ten months before this encounter. She even took the risk of telling her boss. Then it was a long wait before that "suddenly" encounter. God often works through long seasons of preparation where we build trust and walk by faith, and then gives us sudden, clear moments of direction. After waiting and praying, Sarah saw the map of nations, felt God's tangible presence causing her to cry, and heard His audible voice saying her name. God led her to a passage of Scripture that continued to speak to her heart and confirm her assignment. He orchestrated everything so beautifully and powerfully. I love these testimonies because they remind us how real and present God is in our lives. He knows exactly how to get our attention.

God is the best leader. He has incredible opportunities for you too. Let this story stir your faith. Ask God for encounters of your own. Like Sarah, you can build your history with the Lord as you hear Him more and more clearly and follow His leadership.Sometimes receiving His "suddenly" requires waiting patiently and building your faith. Remember that God is faithful to fulfill His word and His purposes for your life. You can trust Him. You don't need to strive.

13

RAPHAEL ANZENBERGER

Organizations: France Evangelisation & NC2P:
National Church Planting Process
Positions: President & Leader
Location: Nice, France

PERSONAL BACKGROUND

What do you like to do when you have a free day?

I enjoy going to see the sailboats in the port of Nice.

What is your favorite Bible verse and why?

John 3:16. Because it was Billy Graham's favorite!

If you could choose, with whom would you dream of having a meal?

I would choose our French president, to tell him about Jesus!

Please tell us about yourself.

My name is Raphael Anzenberger. I am a father of four children. I am the president of France Evangelisation. I am a leader in the National Church Planting Process (NC2P). I am also the ambassador for abroad on behalf of the National Council of Evangelicals in France (CNEF).

MISSION, VISION, AND LESSONS LEARNED ALONG THE WAY

Please tell us more about the National Church Planting Process (NC2P) and your church planting work in France. This movement is generating powerful testimonies in many nations.

The movement is called NC2P, or National Church Planting Process. The mission is for countries to develop a nationwide vision to saturate all the sociological, cultural, and geographical spaces of the country with the Gospel. The history of the NC2P movement started in the 1970s. A man named Jim Montgomery had a vision to create a church planting movement in every nation of the world that would be shared by all evangelicals. This was called "The Dawn Vision." When he came to Switzerland, his vision was to plant one church per thousand inhabitants. At that time, the movement failed for various reasons.

Now there is a resurgence of this movement in Europe. Norway, Sweden, France, and Spain, which were not led by the Dawn Vision historically, are reflecting on how to develop unity in the body of Christ. The vision is for unity that leads to a real impetus for evangelism and discipleship on a national level. The goal is not to plant churches, but to disciple a nation. We are pursuing this question of how do you disciple a nation? This should include all sociological, cultural, and geographical areas. The goal is forming disciples at all levels.

The vision is defined in France with the slogan 1 for 10,000. In Norway they call it "Sendt." In Spain it is called "La Plaza." We join together as leaders from these movements to share our stories and learn from one another. There is a real convergence of these national-level initiatives. We decided to gather in person to share experiences. Our first meeting was in 2015 in Madrid, Spain. France shared our history, then Norway and Spain. From there, we grew from five countries to twelve countries in the movement. There is something really happening in Europe. Countries are building unity on a nationwide level and thinking about how to saturate all spaces with the Gospel. It is powerful.

There is so much power in working together and learning from one another! What is happening with NC2P now?

In February 2018, we held our second meeting in Berlin. This time we reached twenty European nations that are all pursuing this national vision for the Gospel. It was powerful to have the meeting in Germany and to see big, heavyweight nations getting involved. We saw something else really special beginning—countries are joining together to help other countries get started. For example, Norway and Sweden joined forces to coach Finland in starting their national process. Germany and German-speaking Switzerland are helping Austria begin. This is a wonderful cross-pollination throughout Europe.

I met with the leaders of the Swiss Evangelical Network about four or five years ago to share our story of developing the vision for one church for every 10,000 inhabitants. A holy jealousy rose up in my colleagues to not let France overtake them in discipling their nation. The Germans are jealous of Spain where a church is opened every three days. They want to know how it is possible. Nations want to learn from each other. There isn't funding or full-time staff, just volunteers. The countries are leading the way and the result is very organic development. The fruit of these movements is a 200 to 300 percent growth in church planting per year when this type of mission is implemented. It is absolutely extraordinary.

Dave Ferguson, the president and cofounder of Exponential USA, the largest church planting movement in the United States, came to our meeting in Berlin. We invited him as a speaker. When he saw the dynamic and heard the testimonies, he thought it was extraordinary. He said this is what he dreams for in the United States. Europe is inspiring the USA! We also had delegates from Africa, Latin America, and Asia. They loved seeing the continental dynamics and wanted to pursue similar synergies. Europe is educating Africa, Asia, and Latin America on how to start continental processes so that nations can come together for the evangelization of their continents. It is quite stunning, this story. I am writing my second thesis on this subject, examining and studying the internal dynamics. The World Evangelical Alliance even suggested that Europe can help other continents pursue this mission. Today, Europe is fertile.

Amen, we also see that God is moving in powerful ways across the continent as we work together. Another topic we are looking at is the shift from "maintenance to mission" in the body of Christ. How can we inspire this mission focus? Please share your thoughts on this topic from the French perspective.

I would say that French evangelicals have always had a focus on missions. I can point to a shift, or a point of change, in 2001 through the creation of the National Council of Evangelicals in France (CNEF). Before, we were living in a status quo with denominations working very separately. On one side, there were the Pentecostals, then the charismatics and the non-charismatics, then there were also the historical churches of the Baptist Federation. Eventually, there was a shift from everyone looking at each other with hostility and suspicion to an awareness that the Holy Spirit wanted to break this model and bring unity. There was also a renewal of the generations from a leadership perspective. New leaders were able to let go of the battles of the past and move forward.

The significant work of Daniel Liechti opened our eyes to the state of evangelism in France. From a geographical and sociological point of view, he especially emphasized places where the church was not at all present in France. This was a warning shot. Evangelicals were not happy to be 1 percent of the population in France with churches that were barely alive. In order for every man, woman, and child to have access to the Gospel, we needed churches in every area. This objective birthed the vision of planting a church for every 10,000 inhabitants throughout France. The consensus within CNEF from its foundation was based on the sense that we needed to create something that would transcend individual structures to fulfill the greater purpose. The shared mission supports the structure.

Is CNEF achieving that vision today?

Things are going very well. Currently, we are opening a new church every ten days. This figure takes into account the churches that are beginning as well as those that close, so it is a consolidated figure. Every ten days, there is one new church added to the total number across France.

This includes all evangelical denominations in France. When we use the term evangelical, we are using it in the broadest sense of the word. Churches with predominately immigrant background members account for about 20 percent of total growth. Daniel Liechti, the president of the CNEF's New Church Plants Committee, is a Swiss researcher, so he is cautious in his statistics. In my opinion, I think we can say over the last ten years, there is a new church planted every seven days or even every five days.

How close are you to reaching CNEF's goal to have a church for every 10,000 inhabitants?

We have one church for every 32,000 inhabitants today. We need to plant an additional 4,000 churches, to reach about 6,500 churches, in order to meet our goal of uniformly reaching the entire nation. We also develop learning communities where participants share their experiences in implementing this mission-focused vision into their structures. We have gone through a cycle of revitalization. We really see that the church leadership groups are taking this vision to heart. They want to do everything they can to bring this mission focus into their spheres of influence and accomplish this shift. It is very encouraging. It's a true signal that we've moved from maintenance to mission.

The initial research you spoke about showed that evangelicals were only 1 percent of France's population, has that figure shifted through your work?

Yes. The evangelicals are rather conservative with their figures, and they report the figure of 650,000, which is still 1 percent. However, others believe the figure is closer to 2 percent. Recently, though, we have seen a new phenomenon—the emergence of nominal evangelicals. This is a category that did not exist in the past. We have 150,000 people in France today who claim to be evangelical, but also report that they do not attend church. We have never seen this before. This speaks to those who grew up in church but left the church for different reasons. This is completely new.

So, another goal as you disciple the nation will be reaching those nominal evangelicals again. Why do you think the CNEF movement began in France in 2001? What were some factors that sparked this unity and passion for reaching the nation?

Actually, nobody saw this coming! The 2001 movement started with a movement of repentance. The country was in a political deadlock between the parties. Each party only represented about 30 percent of the population, so no one group could speak for the evangelicals as a whole. This division created confusion. There were also ego battles, but I don't want to go into those details. There was also a change of leadership.

Then there was this "warning shot" with Daniel Liechti's work of mapping the French evangelical population. That led to a wave of repentance. At one point, one of the leaders of the Evangelical Federation of France, which represented the non-charismatic movement, apologized to the Pentecostals on behalf of the organization.

They asked for forgiveness from the Assemblies of God for the way they had behaved toward them over the years. The repentance was focused on restoring relationships. The Assemblies of God formed a response where they also apologized. They repented for discounting their non-charismatic brothers and for saying because they did not walk in the gifts of Holy Spirit, they were not born again. (I am telling you what was said at the time.)

From there, the Federation of the Full Gospel asked for forgiveness from the French Evangelicals for the ways their teachings implied that other evangelicals did not have the full Gospel. This whole process was very spontaneous and felt Spirit-led. The sense was, "Now that's enough. You can't just keep claiming to be the body of Christ and continue to openly criticize other Christian groups." It was a huge breakthrough. This movement of repentance was true, deep, and sincere. It had such a strong impact to the point that the French Evangelical Alliance decided to stop its own activities to merge into the National Council of Evangelicals in France. They did not decide to dissolve the organization and become something new because of a mandate, it was truly led by the Holy Spirit.

The Evangelical Federation also changed its name to the Réseau Fraternel Évangélique Françai, "French Fraternal Evangelical Network." All of these shifts created a widespread political positioning and a new posture. We quickly realized that it could not just be about reconciliation. The vision would have to go beyond our own interests and be strongly mission focused. We created CNEF for the mission of proclaiming the Gospel and planting churches. Because of the in-depth process, it was clear that this mission would come first, above individual organizational missions. From that point on, we determined to keep this mission first and allow it to transcend our debates.

The writings from the Lausanne movement have helped bring a good theological background for unity, especially with Catholics and Reformed denominations. These writings, Lausanne 1, 2, and 3 and the Cape Town Commitment in particular, provide a framework and theological basis to work with. It is not simply activism. My Catholic friends especially appreciate these documents. They allow us to work together for a mission that has a theological framework, but is "bordered," if you will, by the texts of Lausanne. It is important to have a theological basis. It is also key to have fruit that remains. I believe, without a theological basis, our fruit will not remain. That is my opinion.

CHURCH PLANTING FOCUS

What are the challenges of planting churches in France today?

If you had asked the leaders of the denominations the question, especially five years ago, the answer, the winning trio, was money, buildings, and lack of pastors, in that order. Later, we realized that even if we had enough buildings, pastors, and finances, we still would not plant churches. Why? Because in fact, we lacked a fundamental element for which we had not accounted. We discovered that we did not have disciples in the parishes.

During this process of self-examination of the evangelical movement, we realized that training disciples was a key for church planting and growth. We also realized that we did not know how to train disciples. Consequently, we did not have any disciples, and we did not have mission-focused churches. Since church members were not disciples, they did not know what their callings were, so there were no people who felt like they had a calling to be church leaders.

We had a second realization as well: planting the same type of churches we already had would not get us where we wanted to go. We did not need 4,000 of the same church. Tim Keller's work has been a great source of inspiration for French churches. The goal is for churches that are strongly oriented toward society. These churches need to look different and carry a mission focus. This goes back to what I shared before about discipling a nation and reaching all areas of society.

To summarize, first, we did not know how to train disciples, and we need to train disciples. Second, we need to plant mission-focused churches that look different from our past model. Third, we need to review and renovate our funding model, especially through encouraging many more bi-vocational pastors and leaders.

Please expand upon this idea of bi-vocational leadership in the church as a way to facilitate church planting.

In the past, we had a limited model in terms of church leadership, with the pastor being a full-time, paid position. We made ministry a sacred function; but in fact, that led us to an obsolete economic model. Today there are many people who are leaders in faith, and are also part of society. They have secular professions in addition to their vocation as church planters, evangelists, or pastors. This is the model we need to pursue if we want to plant many churches.

As we developed a new mission together, our "winning trio" for church planting changed. It is no longer buildings, money, and pastors. *Our new trio includes disciple-making, mission-focused churches, and bi-vocational leadership.* Our new questions are how do we make disciples? What type of churches do we want to plant? How can we encourage bi-occupational ministers, leaders who also have a secular occupation? This also relates to the Ekklesia and the intersection between church and society.

What I am sharing with you is a very new road map. The federations are working together to pioneer something new to accomplish the vision. Historical perspectives and dynamics were not producing the desired outcome, but implementing new ideas takes time and can be challenging. It is interesting to see the different groups working together and learning from one another to get the new dynamic into the churches. Innovation is always on the periphery.

Today, we see more and more periphery expressions in terms of church planting or evangelistic movements and discipleship training that are slowly making their way to the center. I believe these models will become the new norm. While we have not reached the new standard yet, we are quietly moving in the right direction. I am sure of this. There was a definite awareness that continuing to produce what we had always produced would not get us where we wanted to go.

Please give us two or three concrete examples of these periphery expressions that you see becoming central.

The first example is related to the way we train church planting leaders. In traditional courses, people needed to leave their jobs and spend four or five years training at a Bible college. This doesn't work well for working professionals. We realized that to train church planters who also had another career, we needed to bring the training to them and accommodate their schedules. To facilitate this, we launched regional training centers. I ran the first training program in 2010. About four-fifths of the church planters were bi-vocational, meaning they also had a secular job. They had diverse professions including teachers, pilots, landscapers, and architects. They all felt called to plant churches. In fact, some were already planting churches before getting formal theological training.

Another part of our vision is to help people discover if they are called to church planting through weekend introductory sessions about church planting. Those who decide to pursue this are asked to join a training center. We train in theology and practical skills for church planting. As they go through the program, the students plant their own churches. They apply the training to their church plant and also receive personal coaching. This model gives them a strong support system. This type of model is very new and is working well. The churches are full! Because of its success, it is becoming a new trend. This also raises questions about traditional training. The essential point is that we have to bring the training to where it is needed, not the other way around.

Another example of a peripheral or newer model is in the area of discipleship training. We are called to train disciples who then train more disciples. In the past, we leaned upon classic teaching models. Discipleship was only through religious instruction, mainly Sunday morning preaching or classical theological training. Today we are shifting to a learning mode. In France, unlike French-speaking Switzerland, this is very new. The paradigm is shifting. People understand it is their responsibility to bring people to Christ and then to train them. This is not just the responsibility of the pastor.

There are also more resources available to grow in our own spiritual lives and to disciple others. In France, we developed the *disciples.fr* website as a portal to provide resources and tools for discipleship. The material is accessible for everyone to get training to make disciples. We have seen a phenomenon of a tenfold increase of those being trained, which is completely unprecedented. The training is multigenerational. It is fruitful in all environments, whether charismatic or non-charismatic, including Catholic environments, which have taken up certain elements of the trainings. We have reached four or five generations with discipleship training. That is a profound paradigm shift.

I will also share one specific example of creative church planting. In Old Lyon, Timothée Pomier planted a church that is also a coworking space. During the day, they use the building for coworking. They have morning and evening chapel where they have open prayer times. Many of the workers stay for the evening prayer times, even though many are not Christians. This rhythm of morning and evening prayer and using the space for coworking during the day has led to reaching a new demographic. The workers appreciate taking this break and reflecting on the day. They ask questions such as: Where was God? If you had to do it all over again, what would you do differently?

On Sundays, this whole space is transformed into a chapel for church services for about sixty or seventy people. It is a very interesting business model. They also have permanent exhibitions and invite companies to conduct training courses there. Using the church building for multiple purposes is leading to an unprecedented neighborhood dynamic. This is something new we haven't seen before. There are other examples as well with the Martin Luther King Center and the Ivan Carluer project in the Paris region. These initiatives are all based on the idea that the place of worship should become a place of life. It is not just about inviting people to church, but rethinking church from A to Z. It also means rethinking the sacralization of the church buildings. Not everyone wants to secularize a church building even for a few hours each day.

In summary, the periphery concepts that are proving successful are bi-vocational leaders, accessible resources for discipleship training, and innovative implementation strategies.

These initiatives sound creative and out-of-the-box. Thank you for sharing! What is the effect of church planting with new ideas on the centuries-old churches that already exist?

There is a challenge and an opportunity. We are in a real vocational crisis regarding pastoral positions. The demographics are troubling with my generation, Generation X, only holding 5 percent of the pastoral positions. The generation ahead of ours, the Baby Boomers, still make up 70 percent, but they are getting tired. There are a growing number of vacant positions, but the younger generation, Generation Y, the Millennials, do not want to take over these spots. They prefer to go into church planting. The older church leaders come to us and accuse us of accelerating their death by stealing the young pastors. That's when it becomes an opportunity. We need to help them understand that church planting will actually lead to more people becoming pastors. The more churches that are planted, the more people we can train to go into ministry and fulfill the pastoral needs of historic churches as well.

Trying to stop church planting will not lead to more pastors. It is obvious but can be counterintuitive. It is like when we made the transition of putting all the shoe stores together in the shopping malls. People said it was absolute nonsense and that instead of putting all the shoe stores in one place, they should be spread all over the city. Marketing studies proved that there was actually a 20 percent increase in sales with the shopping mall model. It's counterintuitive. The same is true for existing churches. Some think the church planting movement comes to steal pastors from them when in fact, in the long run, it provides more pastors for them.

Let's look at a church in Touraine for an example. This is the oldest church in the region, but they haven't had a pastor for four or five years. They thought they could not join the church planting movement because they didn't have a pastor. Interestingly, they made wonderful contributions to the movement through prayer, collaboration, and giving funding for church planting. Through that process, they discovered they were richer in human resources and talents than they thought they were. They had been seeing things from one viewpoint, but their perspective changed. It is very interesting.

The mindset shift happened as they helped us plant a church through a regional effort. They realized there was a difference between the pastoral position and the pastoral function. Even without one person in the pastoral position, a church body can still exercise the pastoral function. This actually made them rethink whether they needed a pastor in their traditional definition of the word. They began to redefine the role and evaluate what they really needed and wanted. They realized that they did want someone to develop vision and planning for the future, which is laudable, but the role they were seeking was actually more of a bishop position. Contributing to the regional church planting movement in their own way and on their own scale actually led this church into renewal. That is a powerful example.

Europe Focus

Through the Europe Shall Be Saved movement, we truly believe it is Europe's time. What do you feel during this season in Europe? From your experience, in your organization, where do you feel Europe is right now?

I would say we are at the end of a cycle. We are coming to the end of a Europe that is nominally Christian. For example, in the 1960s about 70 percent of Catholics were regularly attending church—today that statistic is down to about 4 percent or maybe 6 percent. As we reach the end of a cycle of nominalism, we find the churches that had become large, mainstream denominations are becoming churches of confession again. The people who remain in the congregations are the ones who are truly convinced of their faith.

The first sign I see of this new season is a much stronger collaboration between different denominations. In particular, we see Catholics and evangelicals working together toward the renewal of the desire to do missional work. According to Pope Francis, that is unprecedented. Sébastien Fath, a leading French social scientist, calls this trend "Kerygmatic Ecumenism," i.e., a unity around the Gospel being preached. (The descriptive term "kerygmatic" comes from the Greek word *kerygma,* meaning to preach or proclaim.) This is much broader than unity movements we saw in the past. It includes all those who are passionate about mission and evangelism, including both evangelicals and Catholics as well as Reformed movements and Orthodox groups. Here, we find a powerful convergence that is completely new.

The church is on a mission, which is termed "Missio Dei": "mission of God" or "sending of God." Unity is built around a common strong burden: the proclamation of the Gospel. The church cannot just be a structure and the vision cannot simply be maintaining what already exists. The structures must feed the vision of proclaiming the Gospel. We must be a church on a mission, as Jesus was on a mission. This is a point on which we can agree. We also understand we have differences that will remain fundamental theological differences. Then those who want to work together, which is a growing majority, find each other and unite around this element.

LIFE APPLICATION—THE WINNING TRIO AND OTHER STRATEGIES

It is powerful to see the unity in France and the collaborative effort to reach the entire nation with the Gospel. It all started with a drastic fact: only 1 percent of French people were evangelicals. That challenging news was a catalyst for many groups to lay down their past offenses and rally together to reach their nation. There was a season of repentance and rebuilding. Different groups realized they had judged and criticized each other instead of working together and loving one another. The repentance led to restored relationships and true unity. One new group was formed to work together for the mission of sharing the Gospel and planting churches. That mission was put above other agendas and individual organizations. The vision is to plant 1 church for every 10,000 residents of the country. These churches can be different styles and denominations, but together they will reach their nation.

Raphael brings us a big picture, nationwide perspective. This is an important viewpoint. Sometimes we are very focused on one local effort. We are passionate about our ministry in our city. This is beautiful, but Jesus also calls us to disciple nations. An important benefit of unity is that we can come together and have a much wider reach. As our ministries grow, it is important to meet with others and see how we can develop strategy that is intentional on a larger scale. This is also Jean-Luc's vision within the Europe Shall Be Saved movement. Our intention is to come together, learn from each other, and develop strategies to reach nations and the continent.

As we start a new strategy, we always learn a great deal in the process. Oftentimes, we have to reevaluate along the way, especially if we are pioneering. In the planning process, things sound wonderful, but when you execute the plan, it does not always go as expected! That is when we can come together again, regroup, and adjust. For Raphael and the NC2P movement, they learned great lessons and adjusted accordingly. In the past, the thinking was that money, buildings, and pastors were the keys to church planting. As they worked to reach the entire nation, they realized this mindset had to shift creatively. They couldn't be dependent on full-time, paid pastors with a building for every church and multiply quickly. Instead, they got creative.

Their new "winning trio" is disciple-making, mission-focused churches, and bi-vocational leadership. The more people within the church who take ownership of leading people to Jesus and discipling them, the quicker growth will happen. When congregants feel like they are part of a mission, they feel responsibility in a good way. In Raphael's experience, more and more people are reaching out for discipleship resources online. They want to learn, grow, and further the mission together. Another huge key was opening the possibility of pastors and leaders with full-time jobs. It allows leaders to reach different sectors of society and gives leadership opportunities to people who also have another job. This also helps with church budgets. To make this model possible, they changed pastor training to fit with job schedules and locations. This shows the practical ways of learning and adjusting to accomplish the vision.

God is creative, and we get to be creative too! What about you? How can you be part of reaching your nation? What is your vision? Are there creative ways to accomplish this? Could it require some out-of-the-box thinking? Are you willing to readjust along the way?

14

Hans Maat

Organization: The Dutch Protestant Reformed Church, Evangelisch Werkverband (The Evangelical Work Alliance of the Protestant Church of the Netherlands)
Position: Pastor and Leader
Location: Putten, The Netherlands

PERSONAL BACKGROUND

What is your favorite thing to do on your day off?

I like to work in the garden and do carpentry. I grew up in a city near Rotterdam, but now I live in a rural area that is totally different. No metros or trams or noise. As a leader, there are always people coming for healing prayer or to learn more about God and ask questions. It is important for me to have a silent place to be alone with God and myself.

I also love to spot airplanes, especially military ones. When I was a young man, I wanted to be an F16 pilot, but I was too tall to fit in the plane, 1 centimeter over the height limit. I was in the Special Forces and Stormtroops during my mandatory military service. Maybe that tells you something about my character. I'm still a little bit of a warrior. I'm steadfast. I'm soft too, though. I'm the type of guy who cries when my pet rabbit dies or even my goldfish, but I'm a fighter. Perhaps that's my role in the Church of Holland, not to fight with people but to fight against spiritual powers and principalities. I don't like religion, it's not my thing. We have a lot of religion because we are an old country with an old history of 1,600 years of Christianity. I am a reformed guy standing in the tradition of Luther and Calvin, the reformers of the Reformation of 500 years ago.

You're right, that gives us a good picture of your personality, a compassionate warrior. Please tell us who inspires you and why.

There are many people who inspire me. One who stands out is Corrie ten Boom. She is a Dutch hero. Her family hid many Jewish people in their home during the Holocaust, saving their lives. She escaped from the Ravensbrück concentration camp through a miracle and became a great evangelist worldwide. I met her once in my youth.

It is also nice to mention unknown people, like one of my relatives who was a Protestant nun, a deaconess. She really loved Jesus and football. We watched football on television, and then she told me about Jesus. There was so much love there. She is one of my spiritual mothers. I love my mother too, she was a faithful Christian; but the nun was so radical. Her nickname was "Sister Angel," because angels always saved her when she was in very dangerous situations. She lived a very profound life for God.

I also want to mention Leif Hetland and Randy Clark, because of their significant influence in my life. A lot of writers inspire me too. Church renewers like Martin Luther, Charles Spurgeon, John Wesley, and many others spur me on. There is a long list. My wife inspires me. She has a lot of patience, unlike me. She is wiser than I am. We are very different. Marriages are usually like that in the kingdom. God brings opposite people together in a beautiful way. I love her very much.

Please tell us more about yourself and how you came to faith.

I grew up in Vlaardingen, a city near Rotterdam. My parents were believers and raised me in the Protestant faith. I was baptized as a baby, then confirmed as a teenager. I attended Sunday school. Then when I was 11 years old, I had a personal experience with Jesus or an angel, I'm not sure. The entire room was filled with light, and I felt unspeakable joy fill my heart. My youth was challenging, so I think God visited me powerfully to help and encourage me. I believe that moment when I was 11 was my salvation moment. When I was older, I worked in youth ministry and did a lot of evangelism. I studied Theology and Educational Science. I was a primary school teacher as well. God gave me many creative talents, so I enjoy music. I started bands, and our songs are well known in Holland and Belgium.

MISSION, VISION, AND LESSONS LEARNED ALONG THE WAY

What is your current position in ministry?

I am, first of all, a "renewer," or a reformer, in the Protestant Reformed Church of Holland and beyond. I lead the organization

Evangelisch Werkverband (Evangelical Work Alliance). I have always worked on the countrywide level for the Protestant church, not for an individual congregation. First I worked in youth ministry nationwide, then I became the leader of the Renewal Movement. I have a team and a staff working with me. My role is to train and pastor the pastors and leaders in the area of the gifts of the Holy Spirit, to develop new concepts for discipleship, and to organize big events and conferences. We are church planters too, and we equip the saints in the local churches. The Protestant church has 2,000 churches in Holland. It is the mainline church since we are a Protestant nation.

In the 19th and 20th centuries, Holland went through a liberal period. Now we are living in a post-Christian time, which is totally different from the last era. A lot of older people are leading the churches, and they are very influenced by liberal theology. That has been a struggle for a conservative guy like me who really believes Jesus is here, among us, still working miracles. He is not just a concept or historical figure; He is very much alive! As a charismatic, it's not easy to be in the traditional church. I once told Heidi Baker, "It's a hell of a job," and she said, "No, no, no. It's a heavenly job." So yes, it's a heavenly job.

Through the Evangelical Work Alliance, our mission is to renew the church to get back to the source—Jesus! Maybe this is in an evangelical and charismatic way, but it is not about being evangelical or charismatic. It is all about Jesus in the center and living the kingdom in every area of life. It is walking in the power of the Spirit. In the Protestant tradition, the Holy Spirit is the unknown member of the Trinity. I was raised with "God the Father, God the Son, and God the Holy Scripture." We had no idea about Holy

Spirit and His active presence. Seven years ago, I discovered the Holy Spirit on my own because Jesus started to talk with me. He said something to me, and I had to do it.

That sounds like an interesting story, please tell us what happened.

I was in a restaurant in Amsterdam, with a long line of people who wanted their cappuccinos and cakes. When I got to the counter, the waitress asked me, "Do you believe in God?" I replied, "Yes, yes. Very much." I didn't really know what to say; I was surprised she asked the question. Then Jesus spoke to me, not audibly but very clearly, "Lay hands on her in My name and do it right now." I had never laid hands on anyone, especially not a waitress! I was calculating the cost because there was no faith in me, not even in my toes, to do something like that.

But I obeyed and asked her, "Would you allow me to lay my hands on your head and bless you in the name of Jesus?" She said, "Yes, I want that." Now I was sure this must be God because this was prepared. So for the first time in my life, fairly scared, I laid my hands on her and prayed a few sentences. When I touched her, she started to tremble and laugh and then cry. The whole restaurant became silent and turned to watch. Instinctively I realized this must be the Holy Spirit, although it was unfamiliar for me.

I knew Jesus already, but this was my first time doing something for Jesus at the prompting of the Holy Spirit. The waitress became a believer in ten seconds. In my ministry, I taught and used many methods for evangelism including the Alpha Course and friendship evangelism. It took years to bring someone to Jesus, and now in ten seconds I saw the power of God working. I could not believe it, but she believed it.

The waitress had never been to a church, she wasn't raised Christian, her parents were not believers. She was totally secular. I asked her, "Do you really believe in Jesus?" I could not imagine it was possible in ten seconds! She was sure, so I connected her with a good Christian organization. They helped her to discover more about faith and baptized her. That was my first powerful and conscious experience with the Holy Spirit.

God threw you right into the deep end. What happened next for you?

Some colleagues heard about my experiences in the media, and some were excited while others were skeptical. They described the charismatic movement as a world full of weird people with strange behavior. Then my friend David ten Voorde, a reformed charismatic pastor, invited me to visit a Global Awakening conference in London with Randy Clark, Leif Hetland, Todd White, and others. I was still very afraid because of what some people said about charismatics.

As a Dutch Reformed leader, I felt behind on everything and timid, but I went anyway. I told the Lord that He could do anything with me. It was a dangerous prayer, but I was ready for more. At the conference, my friend and I were skeptical about the woman in front of us. She was screaming and shouting, manifesting in the Holy Spirit. We weren't used to that. Normally, we would take people acting like that to the psychologist. I prayed, "God, I am a Protestant, and we don't like this, but we need an encounter with You."

On the second day, there was a prophet from London, Andrew Chapman, who called me out of the crowd of about 800 pastors and prophesied over me for a long time. Most of the things he prophesied began to happen directly when I got home. I began to speak at some of the largest conferences in Holland including Opwekking, "Revival," just as he prophesied.

On the second day, Leif Hetland spoke. He ministers the love of the Father in a very special way. Whenever he looks at me, I experience the deep love of the Father that affects me profoundly, and I usually fall to the ground with the power of Holy Spirit.

On the fourth or fifth day, Randy Clark was laying hands on everyone in an impartation session. He said I needed a "quicker anointing" for what was to come. That became true. When I went to churches to preach, teach, and equip people, miraculous things began to happen, which was totally new for me. Also, after I speak, some people are visited by the Holy Spirit in the middle of the night. They have supernatural encounters after simple prayer, and sometimes their lives also change drastically.

For example, recently I spoke at an Evangelical Convocation. The church members were afraid to evangelize on the streets. I encouraged them to just try sharing their faith and prayed for the Holy Spirit to empower them. The next week, they went on the streets with 200 people to share the Gospel. They normally don't dare to do things like that, but they did. I want to be used as a fire lighter; so when Holy Spirit shows up, I am very delighted.

Your life radically changed in a moment. First when the waitress gave her life to Jesus, then at the conference in London. How was it with the people around you after those experiences? How did they react?

It felt like turbo speed, "a quicker anointing," as Randy prayed. My wife and children wondered what was going on with me. They were surprised when I started praying for people and seeing miracles, people with cancer healed. My children thought it was strange and were embarrassed to go to church with me on Sunday. It can be hard when you start stepping out with Holy Spirit because people don't know what happened to you. They can't recognize it because they don't have it themselves. That happens a lot in the Christian world.

My wife is a quiet, tender woman. She was curious, but she wanted to be next to me, not behind me. I was running, and it caused a gap between us. But the Lord is good and graceful, so He touched my wife too, also through Leif Hetland. He didn't know anything about her, but he prayed for her in a restaurant, and she fell to the ground under the power of God. She didn't like that because she is always charming and put together. She was lying there and couldn't move. She had her own personal encounter with God. That was good because for the few years between my encounter and hers, there was a gap between us in that area. She is a prophetic woman, and she is very friendly, so people feel secure with her.

My board saw that I was changing and that wonderful things started to happen within my ministry. At the same time, they themselves were often cautious. They encouraged me in this new direction but were not always part of it themselves.

What was the biggest revelation for you personally after you experienced the power of the Holy Spirit?

The secret was not directly in the power or the healings. The secret was that I now realized Jesus is the Good Shepherd who speaks to His sheep, and they recognize His voice and follow Him. That John 10 passage took on a completely new meaning after my experience hearing His voice and seeing the powerful effects of following Him. I saw that there are works God has prepared for us to do (Ephesians 2:10). The Holy Spirit started speaking to me constantly. A lot of miraculous things happened when I received words of knowledge, words of wisdom, and saw healings and deliverances.

I remember one Sunday morning service when, as the elders led me to the front, a woman began screaming louder and louder, but she did not raise a hallelujah. She was demonically oppressed, and she reacted because of the anointing. The enemy confronts Jesus in you. We're just flesh and blood, but with Jesus in us we're powerful. I remembered Luke 4, when Jesus was in the synagogue and a man possessed by demons shouted, "What do we have to do with You, Jesus? Do You want to destroy us?" I knew Jesus in us is stronger than the one who is in the world. We delivered her after the service.

Another time, I was preaching in a morning service, and a grandfather and grandmother asked me to pray for their 7-year-old granddaughter who was battling cancer. She had tumors in her intestines. I prayed Psalm 103:2-4: *"Bless the Lord, O my soul, and forget not all His benefits: Who forgives all your iniquities, who heals all your diseases, who redeems your life from destruction...."* Within one week, the child was healed and had a totally cancer-free health report. I had just prayed for the grandparents from the pulpit. I said, "I believe. I have enough belief, like a mustard seed, that Jesus heals cancer."

My ministry looked completely different. When I realized there is more, I wanted it. For me, the biggest keys were, and still are, listening to His voice and waiting on the Lord. I spent months praying, often during the night. I felt dried up in my theology and in my own ability. But more and more, God began to move through my life. I also experienced acceleration in seeing God's power in my life after impartation from Randy Clark and Leif Hetland.

STEPPING OUT ON A PERSONAL LEVEL

What's your advice for people who aren't as familiar with the Holy Spirit? How can they begin to experience the Holy Spirit in the ways we read about in the Bible and in the ways you have experienced Him?

My personal experience is, "Get it." Get it for yourself, that's the first step. If you don't know where you can get it, come to us, or people like us. Pray for it. Dedicate yourself. Do not resist verses such as Matthew 10:8: *"Heal the sick, cleanse the lepers, raise the dead, cast out demons. Freely you have received, freely give."* I want to freely give all I have received. I love to teach about Holy Spirit. I love to lay hands on pastors. I love when they experience the power of God and get electrocuted by Holy Spirit. Since they are often very rational, when I lay hands on pastors, I always touch their heads.

My second piece of advice is to testify, share the stories of what God has done in your life. God will touch people through you. I constantly pray for the people close to me. All the people around me, including my board, are now testifying. What we are building is still fragile, but we are building. The enemy is a reality too, so do not wonder when you have to suffer and when people ignore you or even criticize you. People can argue with theology, but they can't argue with your story. When you testify, God does it again and again and again. That's the secret of testifying. Find examples from the New Testament and the Old Testament to confirm what you are sharing personally.

I would also advise you, especially if you are a pastor, to surround yourself with people who have similar beliefs and passion for God. Then you need to stay humble and teach in a quiet and friendly way. You need to approach people in a wise and tender way. When you prophesy, use words people can relate to if they are not familiar with the prophetic. Don't say "Thus says the Lord..." Say something like, "I have an impression as I pray for you."

Please tell us a testimony of stepping out in faith.

I will start by sharing that it takes courage to step out in faith and ask your waitress if you can pray for her. But after walking in this for about eight years, I can say it takes more courage to do this in a very conservative or in a very liberal church. The Protestant Sunday morning services follow a very specific format. That's liturgy. It is risky to deviate from the norm in this context. When I ask if someone has a bad left knee and needs prayer or if I get a prophetic impression about someone in the room, it takes courage to speak it out. It is unexpected to minister like this. The first time was about seven years ago.

I preached a normal sermon. I did not say anything about praying for people. Then, after the service, I was meeting with the elders. There were twenty people lined up outside the door wanting prayer. There was a couple with a difficult marriage, a man with cancer, parents with a sick child at home...people with a variety of prayer requests. We were all very surprised because this was not normal. I knew this was God. I sensed Him telling me this would happen every week from then on. I have to say, it really does happen every week after I preach. I pray for people and see God do incredible things.

Since you asked for a specific testimony, I will share a big one with you. I preached at a church and after the services, the elders brought a woman for prayer. "Sue" (not her real name) was very unwell and could not walk, her muscles were not strong enough, and she had a lot of other physical problems. Her three children had the same condition, weak muscles and tiny legs. They needed wheelchairs and had to attend a special school for disabled children.

When I prayed for Sue, I sensed that she had a very painful childhood including incest, pornography, and other issues. I asked if she had forgiven her parents. She said she had no relationship with them and never wanted to see them again. I told her that if she would forgive them, Jesus would fully heal her body. Unforgiveness can open the door to sickness in our lives. She agreed to forgive her parents and Holy Spirit touched her.

Her husband was at home, glad for a few hours alone. He was burned out, exhausted, and unhappy in the marriage from the constant pressures of their situation. When I prayed for Sue, her husband (at home) felt the power of God. He fell on his knees and prayed for the first time in years. He prayed for his wife and children to be healed.

At that same moment, I was praying for Sue in the church and started to prophesy over her saying, "The Lord will come this week in the middle of the night, and you will feel His heat and warmth and love. You will be totally healed. The next day, you will lay hands on your children, one by one, and Holy Spirit will completely heal them." I don't know why I had the courage to say all that so boldly, but I declared it.

On the following Tuesday, Holy Spirit came and completely overwhelmed her, just like I had prayed. She was totally healed; and in the same week, her children were totally healed. They needed a truck to come and take away all the wheelchairs from their home. Now the children attend normal school and their muscles are so strong they can run ten kilometers. The doctors couldn't believe it—four sick people healed in one breath. These are the types of things we experience.

Wow, that is so powerful! Praise God. It can be scary to step out in faith like that and give a word of knowledge. Sometimes people are worried about what will happen if they get it wrong. Do you have any stories or advice about that concern?

Fear of failure. Yes, I understand. It is difficult, because it's not nice when you meet a stranger and you give a word that doesn't resonate with them, or something like that. You can feel like you're making things up in your head. It happens to me too. Sometimes I get it wrong, but I just keep going. Don't let it discourage you from trying again. I like to teach people to do the little things. We can all encourage people in a normal way. When you ask to pray for someone, just start off praying something normal and encouraging. Then, often after the third sentence or so, Holy Spirit will give accurate information through your prayers.

You can begin with something like, "It is wonderful to meet you. I see you are a lovely woman, and I see something special over you. I believe God wants to encourage you today...." Maybe you don't have any prophetic words for someone, that's alright too. Maybe you are scared to speak, but you can still help people. We can all do something to share God's love. We shouldn't over-emphasize healing, deliverance, prophesy, discernment, and gifts of Holy Spirit. Those are part of the overall package, but there is more. We can all be people full of compassion. Don't be afraid. Pray for courage.

Some situations require the gift of faith. That is when you receive faith for God to do a miracle in an impossible circumstance even when others don't believe. This is supernatural, and it is a gift from God. Not everyone receives the gift of faith. Other people have other gifts. Again, we can all share God's love in many ways. If you send a postcard with the right sentence, it will be a blessing for the person receiving it. It does not have to be miraculous to love people. God is the God of the natural and the supernatural, and it fits together. A lot of the beautiful work of the Holy Spirit is actually very normal.

BRINGING THE SHIFT

How was it for you to introduce Holy Spirit and miracles into the Protestant church?

Because I have a leadership role in the Renewal Movement organization, it was not very difficult to introduce the Holy Spirit and miracles. A lot of people already believed miracles are possible and recognized them happening in places like Mozambique and Latin America. Then they saw me, their leader, walking in these miracles in Holland. They wondered what was happening with curiosity and were positive at first. I later faced some controversy as well.

In 2015, I decided to host a conference with Randy Clark, which we called "There is More." Randy carries an anointing for revival, and he's a fire lighter. I needed that for our country. When he came, we saw very large angels around the building. They were six-feet-tall blue angels, which symbolizes renewal, so we knew we were on the right track. There was also a lot of criticism, a lot of skepticism, and a lot of resistance all over the country about Randy coming since he was a catalyst of the Toronto blessing. He is a revivalist; he is also an extraordinarily well-educated theologian and an experienced pastor. Thank God I invited him because it broke open so much.

I am grateful to Randy Clark, Paul Martini, and Richie Selzer from Global Awakening for bringing a change in the climate. I believe this has benefited the whole body of Christ in the Netherlands, though I also felt a lot of criticism, resistance, and spiritual attack over it. Despite all that, I knew I had to share about signs and wonders and about the works of the Spirit. The conferences brought a breakthrough. I love it when people say, "That event was the turning point of my life. I have never experienced such a powerful change before."

The first conference was the most powerful one. About 800 pastors attended, along with leaders from different organizations and denominations. A lot of people were touched there. We had the conference two more years after that. I'm glad I could make that contribution to the Netherlands, and I know there is more to come.

During those first years after my encounter with the Holy Spirit, I had to learn lessons directly from God. I was very naïve. It was like a playground of experiencing things and putting into practice what I was learning. After I met Randy and Leif in 2013, and later Reinhard Bonnke, Chauncy Crandall, Robby Dawkins, and Todd White, I started to read charismatic books and tried out what I read. I teach others whatever I learn straightaway. That is my way of living.

As a fire starter, have you been able to help churches shift from maintenance to a mission focus in their congregations?

I have seen that shift, but it is not simple. There are the more ecumenical believers, the more conservatives, the more evangelicals. When we try to bring a shift, it can be shocking how the pastors and elders react. Sometimes pastors even burn out from trying to keep the different groups in their congregation unified. It's not easy to integrate or continue this completely new lifestyle or to take people to a deeper level, into a mission-focused life. A lot of churches are not equipping the saints, they just preach sermons without any further expectations.

I think I'm stimulating something new among Christians across the country, a message of hope and faith, of natural and supernatural, of joy and simplicity. Of course, I am not the only one, but we have a very unique and exciting position within the institutional church. It is a learning process to combine the tradition and liturgy and the wild and spontaneous works of the Spirit. Dr. Andrew Wilson from the UK puts it this way, "We need to learn how to be eucharismatic." Dr. Sam Storms from Oklahoma City also helped us navigate this, but we need more good examples.

The first thing we need in order to shift from maintenance to mission is hunger and thirst for the power of the Holy Spirit. I regularly quote the Bible verse, *"My soul thirsts for God..."* (Psalm 42:2). Each one of us has to feed that sentiment, to bring thirst, to bring hunger—then God releases the gift of hunger. Maybe we are preparing the ground for the time you are talking about, when pastors can bring their whole congregations from maintenance to mission. For now, I see pockets of people responding and grabbing hold of our message.

It is very important to equip people after they are touched by the Holy Spirit. We have to equip them and help them because they have a lot of questions. In Holland, we are always thinking with our heads. We struggle to live from our hearts or from our feelings. The enlightenment of the 18th century made the rational so important, but this can make it harder to understand the supernatural. We have to teach people how to live out what they experience.

What does this equipping process look like? How do you do that?

I work with a team of equippers to equip the local churches through training courses or weekly evening sessions in the congregations. The courses include teaching about the Holy Spirit based on the Word of God. Then we practice doing what Jesus did. We also plant churches and organize conferences.

In my opinion, the key for revival, reformation, transformation, or renaissance is to bring renewal within the tradition. That is the key for many European countries. When the traditional church starts to fly, the whole country will change. The economy will change. The government will change. Everything will change. In Holland, even our king and queen and prime minister are members of the Protestant church. I love the Pentecostal movement and the charismatic renewal, but we must discover how influential, traditional Christians from every level of society can get involved in a movement of the Spirit and experience the living God personally. This will change everything. Jean-Luc Trachsel and the Europe Shall Be Saved movement are also very aware of this dynamic. Jean-Luc is a forerunner to bring transformation in this way, and that is why I love this movement.

At the beginning, you mentioned briefly that you started famous bands in Holland. Please share about this part of your life.

I started bands in Holland with a clear concept of integrating contemporary music styles into the traditional practice. In 2004, when I was leading a youth ministry in the Netherlands, I started a band called Sela. The youth in the band were between 18 and 20 years old. They were very talented musicians, but also humble and not after a platform. We had a good base of thousands of youth. I helped with writing lyrics that express faith, specifically about experiencing God in a direct way, but also deeply anchored in God's Word and theology.

I also worked closely with a Dutch Gospel singer named Kinga Bán, beloved in Holland. Tragically, she died of breast cancer at the age of 37. We wrote more than one hundred songs together as Sela; I personally wrote about sixty of them. My most popular songs are well known across Holland and Belgium. The influence of my songs helps me to underline my message of Word and Spirit, suffering and victory, dependence, and Christian authority.

My songwriting feels familiar to that of Charles Wesley. He was a revival preacher and a songwriter too, so I am in good company.

Do you still write songs?

Yes, but last year I only wrote three songs. That is not enough. I would love to have a band like Jesus Culture or Hillsong for Europe. I want to see the European worship movement rise up. That is one of my dreams. But there are more beautiful initiatives. It is my job to listen to Jesus and to do what He says. Nothing less and nothing more. We will see.

Hans's friend who was present for the interview chimed in to tell us a bit more.

Hans is an artist like David was an artist. David has had more influence through his Psalms than he did through his kingship. Hans's personal influence is very great through his work in the Protestant church and through his music. His influence as an artist is amazing. One of the songs he wrote, "Ik Zal Er Zijn," "I Will Be There," has been streamed over 6 million times. That is huge for a Dutch song. Holland is a small country with 17 million people, and 6 million of them have streamed this song from YouTube, that doesn't even include Spotify or other mediums.

Europe Focus

What do you see God doing in Europe in this generation?

We are hopeful for Europe because this is an old continent, and the Lord has already done so much from a historical perspective. We went through the Dark Ages and the Enlightenment. Those periods were tough for countries in Europe, the enlightenment especially, for countries in Western Europe like France, Germany, Holland, Belgium, Denmark, Sweden, and Norway.

We live in the challenging time of post-Christianity. So many people do not know who Jesus actually is. They really have no idea of the spiritual background of Easter or Pentecost. At the same time, people are longing to experience the supernatural. Their heart's cry is "there must be more," and we know, yes, there is more! They feel there must be something more to life, something between Heaven and earth. The younger generation, not hindered by bad experiences with the traditional church, asks fundamental questions.

We live in incredible times. The COVID-19 pandemic once again made visible how vulnerable we are as Western civilizations. Trend watchers who are not Christians themselves interpreted this period as "biblically apocalyptic." I expect a move of God and a lot more opportunities to share the Gospel. We have an open door to share a living Jesus. But I also expect in the coming decade more persecution and struggle for Christian values. It is my calling, along with many others, to express real faith and uncompromised dedication to our Lord Jesus Christ. We are called to demonstrate the kingdom by the power of the Holy Spirit in evangelism, healing and deliverance, mighty signs and wonders, which have been so neglected for centuries by the church.

What I sense from God and have received from prophetic voices is to bring Pauline truth into the theology and to establish the morality and truth of the kingdom. This is not just for me, but many others as well. We are building bridges between denominations, but also fighting religion. We need to get down on our knees and receive new instructions from above for the completely different, beautiful church of the future. We have to raise up fresh apostolic counsels to bring leadership and guidance to the people of God within our nations.

I especially believe in young generations, because I think they will carry a great anointing for the harvest. I am ready to help young ministries and prepare their way like a John the Baptist. I also see more and more awareness of the kingdom of God. I love kingdom theology, with teaching about how we can shift culture and influence government, economy, and media. It is not just church in the midst of our four walls, but in every area of society. I'm praying for hunger, and it's coming. It's rising. When the Word and Spirit come together, it will be an explosion.

Are there specific countries you feel God is really highlighting?

We are beginning to discover the Holy Spirit again in large countries with predominantly Protestant or Catholic backgrounds, for example in Germany. Our recent history is a history of secularism (declining churches), and for many reasons it is the reality in Western Europe especially. What we see are upcoming renewal movements, especially evangelical and charismatic. We see people, especially young people, longing for more, for personal experiences with God.

The Netherlands is a small country with 17 million citizens on a tiny piece of earth. But we have a big economy, relatively speaking, and relationships worldwide. Because of our location, we are a gateway for everything. We are very tolerant and very democratic, and work with everyone. Our ideas and principles have had an impact across Europe and the world. Spiritually, Holland is coming alive now, but we need much more and especially more help from abroad. We need provision, and we need prayer. I love the charismatic movement, and I love the international approach of Europe Shall Be Saved.

To reach the continent, we still need a process of multiplying from Heaven. We need to reach city by city. To reach all these congregations is a process of multiplying. We can't do it on our own, we are not strong enough. But our God is mighty, and we need support of people from abroad too. For hundreds of years missionaries took the Gospel from Europe to the ends of the earth, now the very continent that sent people out is in need of Jesus again. Now we need people from all around the world to support us with prayer, provision, and help. It is a call back. That's why I love Awakening Europe and Ben Fitzgerald with his initiative, "The Call Back."

As I travel more, I do see Holland is farther along than some other places. I am fully expectant for revival to rise here over the next ten years. I believe it will be revival and reformation together. I see God moving in culture through a cultural reformation. I see the Holy Spirit moving in a very broad and integrated way, touching our nation. But most of all, we need to evangelize, inside and outside the churches.

LIFE APPLICATION—JUST GO FOR IT!

Go after the Holy Spirit! Hans is a fiery, passionate, Protestant Reformed pastor. I love this story because it combines God's sovereignty and the power of pursuing God and cultivating hunger. Hans grew up in traditional church without teaching on the Holy Spirit. He didn't see people walking in supernatural power in his personal life. Then there were two encounters. First as a child, light filled his room and he was filled with unexplainable joy. That visit from God, even as a young child, marked him and strengthened him for hard years in his youth.

Next, he heard Holy Spirit ask him to lay hands on the waitress. That was completely outside of anything he had ever done or seen modeled. Again, God sovereignly invaded his world. The waitress asked him about Jesus and then she wanted prayer and gave her life to Jesus in ten seconds. After years and years of faithfully serving God and reaching out to people, one sovereign encounter changed everything. That is beautiful and important. God is very real and alive. He is working and speaking and wants to encounter us. I don't know why it happens so intensely for some people as it did for Hans, but I do know that what is written in the Bible is available to all of us.

After this powerful sovereign moment, Hans took steps to follow Jesus. He went to a conference that was completely out of his comfort zone. He began to pray for sick people and even call out words of knowledge in the traditional church. People were unfamiliar and uncomfortable with this, but God began to move. His children were embarrassed to go to church with him and his wife was curious but uncertain until she had her own touch from God. Some colleagues feared and judged what was going on. Yet he pressed on. He invited passionate speakers to come to his country and saw powerful breakthrough. He read books and learned and tried things out. He prayed for more hunger.

There is a very important connection between our willingness to pursue God and asking Him to move through our lives as He promises in the Book of Acts. We need to be willing to go after it, and we can't be ashamed of the Gospel. We also have to be willing to "fail" sometimes or be criticized. When we put aside fear of people, we have many more opportunities to touch their lives with God's love and power.

I also love that as Hans shares powerful testimonies of cancer healed and miracles; he also reminds us that a simple postcard to a friend with words of encouragement can deeply impact someone. Paying for a coffee for a friend, stopping to greet a homeless person and buying some food for the person, all these "little things" are also the Gospel, love in action. It is the natural and the supernatural working together.

Our own personal stories and testimonies also have great impact. As Hans points out, no one can argue with your life and your experiences. As you share how God met your needs, provided for you, and showed you His love, your friends and coworkers will begin to wonder if it can be possible for their lives too. As I wrote in the "Introduction" of the book, the testimony of Jesus is the Spirit of prophecy. When we share what God has done, there is faith that He will do it again—and He will!

Well, what are you waiting for? Where can the natural and supernatural move through your life today? Who needs a word of encouragement? Who needs a healing prayer? Open your heart to hear Sweet Jesus and follow whatever He says.

15

WES HALL

Organization: Gospel Forum Church
Position: Pastor and Bible School Director
Location: Stuttgart, Germany

PERSONAL BACKGROUND

What is your favorite thing to do on your day off?

Spend time with my kids and Carol, my wife. We enjoy swimming, cycling, and going to the movies. My son and I are big *Marvel* movie fans. Whatever is on the schedule with the kids, I'm there.

If you could have lunch with someone who inspires you, whom would you choose and why?

I am a huge history buff, so I will choose John Wesley. He is one of my favorite heroes. In fact, I was named after him. He led what is probably the most long-lasting and sustained revival that led to national transformation. I am inspired by how he believed

God for his nation (England) and saw his nation transformed by the power of the Gospel. He was steady. His ministry was not based on massive events. It was based primarily on preaching the Gospel in small groups, discipling people, and creating a network of believers who did the work of ministry where they lived.

If I think about someone from my lifetime, it would be Reinhard Bonnke. I had the privilege of meeting him, but I wish I had been able to spend more time with him. He is a great inspiration. He had so much impact with the Gospel in his generation. He is German but attended Bible school in the UK, so he embodied the connection between those two nations, which have worked together in revival over the years.

What ministry are you part of now?

I am part of Gospel Forum, which is a large charismatic church in Southern Germany, in Stuttgart. It is the largest church in Germany, but that's not why I am involved. I am part of it because the Lord called me there. I am part of the senior leadership team of the church. My primary role is leading our full-time discipleship Bible school called the Revival Training Center.

Please tell us a little bit about yourself and how you met Jesus.

I grew up in England in a Christian family. My father was a farmer who went into full-time ministry when I was 6 months old. He is an evangelist. He was part of the overspill of the 1970s revival that became known as the Jesus People Movement. That outpouring touched the United States, had massive impact there, and then leaped over to Europe with many young people getting saved. My dad got saved, filled with the Spirit, and started preaching the Gospel almost every weekend. Then he was offered a position as a youth minister and felt the call of God. He sold our successful family farm and went into full-time ministry. My dad's life was marked by, "There must be more." That was always his cry, as he pushed for more of God. I grew up with that same sense of holy dissatisfaction.

I wanted to experience more of God, not just go to church on Sundays. I wanted to see the power, the signs, the wonders, and the revivals I had read about in history and in the Book of Acts. That said, it was not always easy growing up in a ministry family. If the Lord wanted me in ministry, He would have to make it very clear. I studied law and worked in a large, global corporate law firm in London for a number of years. During the day I was a corporate lawyer, but in my free time I was leading worship and the Lord was drawing my heart into the place of prayer. My strong passion was revival, and every revival I studied was birthed out of sustained corporate prayer.

I was searching for a place to really learn how to pray when I discovered Mike Bickle and the International House of Prayer in Kansas City (IHOPKC). They were holding prayer meetings three times a day in their church throughout the 1980s and 1990s and experiencing the supernatural. In 1999, they started IHOPKC with prayer and worship 24/7, which was pretty uncommon back then. I remember thinking, *If there is a place on the earth doing 24/7 prayer, there is going to be revival.* I wanted to learn from them. I asked the Lord if I could go and He said no. About a year later, in 2000, the Lord spoke to me in a very supernatural way and said, "I want you to go to Kansas City." At that time, I didn't want to go anymore, but I felt it strongly from the Lord.

I joined a group of about forty young people who were praying night and day in a little trailer. The only jobs were leading worship or leading prayer. People know IHOPKC today as a large international prayer ministry, but at that time most of the prayer meetings were just two people in a room playing guitar and praying. Our mission and rallying cry were to keep the fire on the altar. We learned this from Count Zinzendorf and the Moravians, one of the longest 24/7 prayer and missions movements during the 1700s in Germany.

Over time, the ministry grew. I helped to establish and build the Bible school, which, while I was there, grew to 700 full-time students. It was a school of ministry with a curriculum based on prayer. But my passion was not to build a Bible school, my passion was for revival. In 2009, we experienced just that. Holy Spirit visited our community in a profound way, starting in one of my classes in November 2009. We were meeting every night, six hours a night, in a community revival. Over ten months, we saw 8,000 written testimonies of healing, 2,000 people baptized, and people equipped with boldness to preach the Gospel at a new level. There were also 195 nations watching on live stream.

That is powerful! Let's talk more about that later; but first, how did you get from Kansas to Germany?

As a family, we had prophetic words about Europe. From about age 18, I felt drawn to Germany and sensed God wanted to use me there and in England. Over the years, the Lord opened doors for us to minister in England and Germany that we could not have opened for ourselves. We developed strong friendships in Germany and prayed about longer term ministry there, but I wanted a clear sign from the Lord. I didn't just want to go do ministry.

When I was in university in the 1990s, I studied in Germany for a year. During that time, I became familiar with three well-known ministries that the Lord was using powerfully. I had zero contact with any of them. I prayed and told God that if He opened a door with one of those three, I would take it as a sign that it was time for our family to move to Germany.

At the end of that season of awakening at IHOPKC, I went to England with my family and a team of students. Mike Bickle sensed and prayed that God was going to open a door in Germany during this trip. During one of our ministry meetings in England, a German youth leader and his girlfriend came from Berlin—and she was healed. Then they attended our young adult conference in Kansas City that December. It was a huge event, and I walked right by the German youth leader. He yelled out my name and shared the testimony of his girlfriend's healing. His entire church in Berlin was touched by what the Lord did in Kansas City through me and the revival. He invited me to minister at their church— one of the three I had prayed about!

Within three months, God opened doors to visit all three ministries. Between 2012 and 2015, our family traveled and ministered in Germany and England each summer. By the end of 2015, we sensed a transition. In the midst of that, Peter Wenz, the pastor of Gospel Forum, invited us to Germany. He told us if we felt led to move to Germany, he would love to have us on their staff team. We prayed about it but didn't hear anything right away. Five months later, the Lord spoke to me and my wife powerfully through a series of dreams and encounters and said, "It is your time to go to Germany." I reached out to Peter, and he also felt it was the right timing. We sold our home and belongings in the US and flew to Germany in May 2016.

That is a big transition. Was it challenging to move your whole family to Europe after living in the US for so long?

I studied German in school but hadn't spoken much for twenty years. Carol knew no German and our four children had no German language training. They were born in the US and homeschooled there; but in Germany, homeschooling is illegal. Not only did our children have to attend formal school for the first time, they also had to study in a foreign language. It was a tough transition. We experienced culture shock as a family.

We'd been in IHOPKC for fifteen years, a very unique and awesome place in Kansas City; then suddenly we were living in Southern Germany. New language, new culture, and new schools presented many challenges. It was an intense time, but the Lord also gave us such favor with leading the Bible school. We had a tremendous group of about forty students, and the Holy Spirit started moving from day one.

MISSION, VISION, AND LESSONS LEARNED ALONG THE WAY

Please share more about your work at Gospel Forum.

I am part of the senior leadership team. I lead the full-time Bible School, a one-year program with a second-year option. The focus is on discipleship, studying the Word, building life in God, and helping students find their calling. The Lord is really meeting us in this role. I taught in a Bible school for about fifteen years in the States, but I never had a group so in love with one another and with the Lord than that first group of students in Stuttgart. That was a kiss from Heaven. It confirmed again we were in the right place at the right time. Many are now serving the Lord either full or part time in significant leadership roles.

It sounds like you walked through transition and challenge, but God confirmed you were where He wanted you. Please share insights about hearing God and following Him into your calling.

The Lord spoke to us very clearly in supernatural ways to go to Germany. I've learned over my life and from my study of the Bible that when the Lord speaks so clearly, it's usually because it's not an easy assignment. Some people think if the Lord speaks clearly, it will be easy, but it's often the opposite. It is probably going to be difficult and you need to hang on to those prophetic words. One of the reasons for the audible voice and the clarity of God's voice is actually to equip our hearts and stabilize our hearts for challenging times ahead when we will want to give up.

Biblically, Moses heard an audible voice. Everyone wants to hear the audible voice of the Lord so they can know the will of God for their lives. They think if they knew with such clarity from God, it would be easy. No. Moses heard an audible voice from the Lord emanating from a burning bush. His assignment was to lead two million people, stand before the most wicked person on earth, and command him to release a nation that had been in slavery for 400 years. That's not an easy assignment. Then Moses had to lead all those grumbling and complaining people through the desert for forty years. And then he didn't even get to walk into the Promised Land.

I remember the Lord spoke to me so clearly about going to IHOPKC. A couple of months later, I was experiencing some tough challenges. I was sitting in my room evaluating. I got a pad of paper and put a line down the middle. Column 1: "Reasons why I should go home." I filled the page. I was so discouraged. Column 2: "Reasons why I should stay." There was only one reason: God spoke clearly.

A lot of people get excited to go into ministry, but serving the Lord is opposed by the enemy. The problem is if you do not have confidence that God really called you, you will quit easily. We overcome by the promises of God. Paul told Timothy to wage war according to the prophecies that were spoken over him. The prophecies and the promises are actually tools that we wage war with when we have difficulty, when the enemy opposes us. I learned that principle twenty years ago.

In Germany, even in the last three years, there have been a dozen times when we wanted to pack up and go back to the United States. But we knew God spoke to us. He made it so clear that we are supposed to be here. We are not going to quit. For me, it's an anchor to my soul to remember the promises of God and to thank the Lord that He spoke. David was anointed as king by Samuel, but after receiving that promise, he went through really difficult times. First Samuel 30:6 says, "...But David strengthened himself in the Lord his God." That's really what we have to do—strengthen ourselves in the Lord when we are going through tough times.

That is a powerful revelation. You said you heard God speak very clearly about Germany, but you also mentioned earlier that He put this on your heart from age 18. How do you know when it is the right timing for what God is showing you?

Revelation 3:7-8 (New International Version) says, *"...What he opens no one can shut, and what he shuts no one can open. I know your deeds. See, I have placed before you an open door that no one can shut...."* A lot of people go around knocking on the doors and trying to push the doors open because they have a calling. That may be true, God might have shown you things that you are called to do, but we don't always know the exact timing for the fulfillment of those words. I personally advise waiting for God to open the door for you. If God is speaking something to you, then He is going to open the right door at the right time.

If you push your way through a door that isn't open yet, you have to defend that open door. Bill Johnson has a great way of phrasing this, "Whatever you gain through self-promotion, you'll have to sustain through self-promotion. When our promotion comes from God, He sustains it." The way you get there is the way you'll stay there. If you force your way through, you live out of a place of war rather than a place of rest. It is better to wage war with your promises in the place of prayer and wait for God to make a way. Just stay faithful to what God has given you in the season you are in.

And does one's calling or ministry have to be big?

No. We are not called to bigness. God didn't call us to be famous, He called us to be faithful. If God calls you to do something big for Him, then do something big. But you will not be rewarded based on the size of what you do, you'll be rewarded based on whether you are faithful to the assignment. I believe there are many things God wants to do on a large scale, but your part is to be faithful in what God gives you when He gives it to you. Those who are faithful in little, will be faithful in much. God always wants to give us more, but it is the reward for being faithful with little.

But just to counterbalance that point, some people get a false humility when God has called them to a big task. I am thinking of the Gideon-syndrome: *who am I that You've called me to do this big assignment?* When God is the One who puts you on the platform, your job is to be faithful there. Your job is not to say bigness is or is not important, it's to do what He calls you to do when He calls you to do it. Maybe that's leading a group of four friends in a prayer meeting or a Bible study. Maybe it is something small. But maybe He will also ask you to do something big.

People often ask me to lay hands on them to give them my teaching anointing so they can teach on stage like I do. I ask them where they are teaching now. They are usually confused by that reply. I continue explaining that the reason I teach on the platform isn't because I did a class to qualify me to teach on a platform. It's because I have been practicing my teaching gift my whole life. I taught in small groups or wherever else I had the opportunity. Over decades I've been teaching and preaching, not just on platforms. I have also immersed myself in the Word of God. If they want me to lay hands on them to give them my Bible knowledge, I suggest they read their Bible. Read your Bible, share what the Lord teaches you, and that's how you get to the next level.

Zechariah 4:10 says, *"Who has despised the day of small things?"* There truly is something in our Western culture where we despise smallness because we think big is important and more significant. I love what the Lord says to Zechariah about the significance of smallness in context of the restoration of the temple in Zechariah 4. There was a huge crisis because they started to build, but the foundation of the new temple was so much smaller than Solomon's temple. They started to weep because they were disillusioned with how small and insignificant it seemed in their eyes. They quit building for sixteen years because it didn't look how they expected.

Then God tells them again, You need to build THIS temple because I am going to fill THIS house with My glory. It goes on to say that God rejoiced when they got out the plumb line, the measuring tool to begin laying the foundation accurately. Most people would only have a party when they saw the finished temple, but God rejoiced to see the plumb line, the commitment to build according to His pattern. The Lord rejoices when you say yes in the day of small beginnings, even when no one else sees you. What is significant in God's eyes is often very different from what is significant in our eyes.

Please tell us about a time when you were discouraged or disappointed and how you regrouped.

For me, it was the times in life when people I trusted and looked up to disappointed me. In most cases, it was due to the fact that I had made a person into something more than he or she actually was. We have this desire for heroes in our life. We make heroes out of men and women who are just men and women. It is fine when we see them from a distance, but if we get close to them, then we see their cracks, and that is going to disappoint us.

What helps me regroup in that kind of situation is to recognize that no matter where someone is ministering, they are simply a weak and broken human being. We all have weaknesses, each and every person. Often our weaknesses and broken places are actually what enable us to be where God called us. It's kind of the flip side of gifting. There is a gifting and there is a corresponding weakness. It helps to ask God for His perspective. Paul writes, *"From now on, we regard no one according to the flesh"* (2 Corinthians 5:16). Personally, that verse teaches me that I do not want to evaluate people according to their human weakness and failings. I want to see them according to how the Spirit of God sees them. God knew their weaknesses when He chose them. They disappointed Him before they disappointed me, in that sense. And yet nevertheless, He chose them. That helps me to forgive and love and receive from them.

Don't allow disappointment to make you bitter. Disappointment can rob our joy, but bitterness can destroy our souls. Again, ask God to let you see people through His eyes and love them the way God loves you.

Sometimes we are disappointed because we wanted to go in a certain direction, but someone seems to come against us. It can feel like they blocked the call of God on our lives. *If it wasn't for THAT person, I would be happy and fulfilled.* The reality is that no one can block God's call on your life. If God has begun a work in you, if God has called you, He is going to get you in the right place. No one can withstand the will of God and the purpose of God in your life. This is another way to strengthen yourself in the Lord— remember that if God called you, He is going to follow through. If He didn't call you, you don't want to be part of it anyway.

That is a great point. Sometimes we worry about what other people think or say about us. Please speak into that fear.

Disappointment often has to do with where your reward is. Often our reward is focused on the recognition and praise of other people. To live for the praise of others is a very dangerous way to live, but it's the way most live. That puts such a pressure on you to perform and to be something that you're not. It prevents you from being weak and vulnerable before other people. Typically, if you're living for the praise of others, you will shy away from being connected at a deep level to avoid exposing weakness or being criticized. Criticism is the opposite of praise. This is very sad because you were created to be connected, not just with God, but with other people.

This is a crisis among many Christian ministers. Truly, the greatest desire of the human heart is to be seen and known and loved and accepted. That's why some people strive for the platform. Often that's why we strive for success, because we want to be seen, loved, and accepted. But we don't find it at that level. If you're living for those with the greatest influence and the greatest potential to reward you and to recognize you, you will always be striving. You will never be at rest. Instead, we can find confidence and a firm foundation in relationship with God, the greatest Person in the universe.

If you have confidence that you are known and loved and accepted by God, just as you are, it settles the issue of praise and acceptance once for all. The greatest thing we can understand is what Jesus understood before His ministry, complete acceptance. Before He did anything, the Father said, *"This is My beloved Son, in whom I am well pleased"* (Matthew 3:17). That declaration made His love and ministry authentic, real, and acceptable. Jesus told His disciples in John 15:9, *"As the Father has loved Me, I also have loved you; abide in My love."* In other words, the way God the Father loves Jesus, God loves you. When you embrace this truth, you will know you are loved and successful.

Live from the basis of God's acceptance of you so you can clean toilets, be on a platform before 20,000 people, be a successful businessperson, or be a mom at home with your kids and know you are already successful. You can settle the issue of success in your life before you even start. That mindset causes you to live from rest rather than from striving and pressure. It enables you to open your heart to other people like nothing else.

Revival at IHOPKC

You shared earlier about revival breaking out in Kansas City in one of your classes at IHOPKC. Tell us that story, please.

The Lord said at the beginning of 2009, "I am going to visit you with wine like I visited Toronto in the 1990s." We didn't know what that was going to look like. The director of the Bible school and I decided to steward that word by asking the Holy Spirit to come in every class until He came. As a school, we continuously prayed for revival for about six months. Then it happened.

During our student chapel service, we always allotted time for testimonies. One young lady shared about how God delivered her from pain in her stomach. When traveling in Montana, God set her free from the self-hatred she had ever since someone attempted to rape her years earlier. When God healed the trauma and delivered her, all her pain left. As she shared, the Holy Spirit came on her, and she started laughing. We began ministering into that area in our students, and the student chapel time lasted about an hour longer than usual. In the middle of that, I sensed the Lord whispering, "It's starting now. It's starting now, and you're going to have extended meetings." We already had 24/7 prayer and worship at IHOPKC, but I knew the Lord meant we were going to have revival meetings. I spoke to the director of the Bible school about what happened in our chapel time and he told me to let him know what happens over the next few days.

On Monday, we invited the Holy Spirit to come again. There was no teaching in the class. It was more like a deliverance service and the joy of the Lord was sovereignly poured out. The same thing happened on Tuesday. By Wednesday morning, I walked into the classroom and the glory of God was there. Students showed up at 8:30 to pray, when normally they strolled in at 9:10 for their 9 o'clock classes. They were praying for each other and receiving deliverance and healing.

We basically had to have testimony time every couple of hours just to figure out what God was doing. That Wednesday, November 11, 2009, the class started at 9 in the morning with about one hundred students. By midnight about 2,000 people were in the room. Young people were being taken up and having visions of Heaven. God was healing bodies. People's vision was healed. People were delivered from fear and shame and all kinds of issues. We ended up meeting six hours a night for the next ten months until we sensed the Lord saying to pause the meetings. At that point, we felt Him say that what He wanted to release had taken hold in our community, and we would continue to receive it without the daily meetings.

So some of the keys to what you experienced were having a prophetic word, praying consistently and passionately for that word, and believing for that word corporately?

Yes, and making space. A lot of people miss the move of the Spirit simply because they are too focused on their own agendas. They don't make space. They have a plan. They have two hours and want to get through everything they want to cover, but they miss the Holy Spirit. The Holy Spirit knocks on the door and waits for us to open it, but often we have too much going on behind the door. We aren't ready.

For me, it started with a slight impression that we were going to have extended meetings. I felt Holy Spirit leading me to make space in my classroom. I had a full lesson plan, packed with content that I wanted to teach the students. We were recording the classes for our online school. I could have easily said, "I don't have time to just worship and wait on the Lord as a class." But I gave the space and the Lord took hold of it. It is cooperation with the Holy Spirit, which requires vulnerability—what if nothing happens? If you don't take the risk and give the space, you will never know. That is what we learned in our awakening season.

EUROPE FOCUS

What do you see God doing in Europe in this generation?

The youth of Europe are looking for reality. They see that success is not found in economic success. I think there's a tiredness in the society with the political system, with economics, and there is a search for something that truly satisfies. What we need to understand about Europe, particularly regarding the millennials and younger, is that we are living in a post-Christian culture. We are living in a culture that has sought to satisfy itself with money and with political solutions, but the political solutions are not working. The economic solutions are not working, and so there is a weariness that leads to an openness. There is a search for reality. We know that search for reality can only be met by the Gospel. This has led to an openness for the authentic Gospel like never before.

The thing is, people want more than becoming a number on a church seat. What this generation is crying out for is to be known, loved, and accepted. We have to preach a Gospel that results in people being connected within the body of Christ. This is a time of tremendous opportunity for sharing the Gospel. It's also a time when the church has to recognize the generation in which we are living. It's not like previous generations.

We are living with a generation that doesn't just want a decision at an altar. They want something that is really going to take hold and transform their lives in the day-to-day. More than anything else, they do not want a church to attend. Rather, they want something they can be part of, where they can share their lives. Vulnerability and authenticity are the cry of this generation. That is not going to be found in a decision card for Jesus, although that's the first step. It will be found as they find the life of God in the body of Christ.

I think that's why we are, in many ways, seeing a move away from people wanting to be part of traditional churches or even big churches. I see it in the worship movement as well. We've had the big worship movements, worship bands, and arrangements. Now, I hear young people saying they just want a guitar and a piano. They want something simple, but deep, authentic. There is an ache and cry in their hearts to connect with God. It's not about the show, it's about connecting with God. We are living in a time, because of the cultural setting, of great opportunity. That being said, the church needs to recognize the hunger and respond. We can't be caught up in programs or topics that are not answering the cry of people's hearts.

In addition, there are many in European churches who know much about God, but have no deep personal experiences of God. The Lord is calling His body to recover intimacy with Jesus, to become a lover before a worker. I like the quote, "We are called to be human beings, not human doings." God wants us to recognize who we are and grow in the revelation of that relationship. Often, we say we are children of God, but are we developing relationship with our Father? We are the bride of Christ, but are we developing relationship with our Bridegroom? A lover will outwork a worker every time. We need millions of workers in the harvest field, but simply being called to a task is not enough to carry us in the task. We need to be in love with the One who sent us, Jesus. That's what will motivate us even unto death.

And what about unity? What does unity look like in the body of Christ?

Unity looks like relationship. It looks like deep relation-ship. What does unity look like in a family? It is not the family all dressed up nice on a Sunday morning, sitting in the front row together. There must be genuine love and relationship. The stan-dard of unity is John 17:11— *that they would be one as Jesus and the Father are one,* in family. It's common purpose. It's common destiny. It's not high fives once a year when we are all sitting in a room together, but then we go and do our own thing.

Unity is when we love one another deeply, we honor one another, and we fight for one another. It is the *koinonia* (Greek for communion or fellowship) of the New Testament: you belong to me, I belong to you, and therefore my calling is to fight for your destiny even when your calling and destiny are different from mine. It's not just being part of the same church or using others to fulfill our own dream. I see God is moving in this area, building deep relationships across boundaries, across denominations. We need to know one another, and love one another, and trust one another more. We need to move from saying we have unity to actually living unity.

Are you hopeful for Europe?

Definitely, I am very hopeful. It's going to be challenging. There was a prophetic word in the 1980s that said the Lord is going to change the understanding and the expression of Christianity in a generation. I think the Lord has to change the understanding and expression of the wineskin that is going to carry the new wine. What we have called "Christianity" is not going to survive the shakings in society. The Bible says two things are going to happen parallel: deep darkness and great light. Jesus says in Matthew 13 that the wheat and the tares are going to grow together at the harvest time. That means with the harvest time, we can expect to see more harvest but also more weeds. We have to examine and strengthen our root system so it won't be choked by the weeds. The light in believers has to be more than a philosophy or a message we repeat to others. We can't just say, "Jesus loves you. God has a plan for your life." Those words have to be our reality. They have to be real and living and deep in us.

And are there any specific areas you see God highlighting?

The two areas I am focused on that the Lord has highlighted to me are England and Germany. There are many prophetic promises about these nations. Plus, the whole history of the church in Europe has been so impacted by these two nations. They are wells of revival called to impact all of Europe. Germany, the land of reformation. England, the land of revival.

LIFE APPLICATION—GOD REJOICES IN YOUR YES

People ask Wes to lay hands on them to receive the "teaching on the platform gifting." They want instant promotion, instant calling. Throughout the interview, Wes teaches us about the small beginnings. His teaching gifting led him to teach in conferences, but it started out with many years of teaching in small groups, at Bible school, then in larger contexts. He studied the Bible to teach God's truth. When we are faithful with the little things, God gives us more. But "big" is not the goal. Being in front of a crowd is not the definition of success. It will not fill the longing in our hearts to be seen and known. We need to find our acceptance and identity in God. He speaks approval and love over our lives because He is our Father, not because of what we do. Then, just like Jesus, we pray, seek Him, and follow Him wherever He leads.

God cares about relationship and our obedience to His voice, not the size of our work.

Regarding Wes's calling to Germany, we see these same principles. Wes studied German in school. Later, he and his family took ministry trips to Germany. He asked for God to speak and confirm. He waited on God's timing. He did not push open the door. A German youth leader's girlfriend being healed in England was one key that opened a door in Germany. God can do anything in any way. Don't worry, He is God! And no one can stop your calling and your destiny. You get to choose whether you will listen for His voice and obey. You get to choose if you will start with small faithfulness and watch God work in and through your life. Is there a yes cry in your heart?

Another lesson is that when you hear God very clearly and receive many confirmations, it will likely be a challenging assignment. It might take a long time to be realized. You might face giants on your path. We see this throughout the Bible. Look at King David. He was the youngest brother out tending sheep. His father didn't even call for him when Samuel came to anoint a king. He was the unlikely choice, yet he was God's choice. He spent years killing bears and lions, worshipping beneath the open skies before he was ever in the public eye. Even after he killed Goliath, there were years of obscurity and emotional, spiritual, and physical battles. When Saul was still king, David would not harm him or take his position by force. He waited for God's promotion. He honored and respected his leader, flawed as he was.

When God calls you, He will make a way for you. If it gets challenging, remember David, Moses, and the heroes of this book. You are in such good company. Don't let the enemy lie to you and say you are off track if it's taking a long time or if others don't recognize you. Listen for God's fatherly voice speaking perfect acceptance and love over you. You start from a place of approval before you do one single thing. And God rejoices when you say yes in secret before anyone else sees you. As you faithfully follow, no matter how small it seems, you will fulfill the amazing calling of God over your life. Watch and see what the Lord will do!

CONCLUDING THOUGHTS

As you finish reading this book, be filled with faith, courage, and fresh inspiration for your own God-dreams. Fall even more in love with Jesus and be full of hope for His great plans for you. The most important thing any of us can do in life is to wholeheartedly follow Jesus. He is our Source. He is the Leader of our lives. I love Psalm 37:5 (The Passion Translation), which says, *"Give God the right to direct your life, and as you trust him along the way you'll find he pulled it off perfectly!"* That's our God. As we follow Him, His glorious plans unfold in our lives and in our nations.

Revival and awakening start with our own hearts being awakened to His love. We become more and more passionate for others to know Him and for His power to come and change our nations. We believe Him at His word, and we step out in faith. We come together with others and honor what each one carries. We work in unity and answer Jesus's John 17 prayer. We believe that nothing is impossible for our God. We are already seeing this in Europe with amazing moves of God. We know there is so much more to come. Join us in Europe or take hold of this passion wherever He leads you.

Continue to pray for your city and nation; prayer is a major key to revival. Join with others and seek God for what He is doing in your region. You don't have to know the full plan to take the next step. Kingdom visions often start with what touched your heart and sparks your passion. Then they grow and grow, as you stay connected to Jesus. Eventually, you'll look back and see that God had a magnificent plan all along, even when you felt like you didn't know what you were doing! He knew. He is right there with you every step of the way.

As we see in these stories, following Jesus does not have to look a certain way or use a specific model. God is creative and diverse, so His body is creative and diverse in who we are and how we express His love to the world around us. God is writing a story with your life that only you can live out. He is for you. He placed dreams and desires in your heart. He has purposes and assignments prepared just for you. You will carry them to completion as you follow Him step by step and join with others in kingdom family. Some steps are glorious, others are painful. He sees your faithfulness. He hears your every prayer.

If you've walked through disappointments, you're not the only one. Follow the advice you've read and trust God to heal your heart. Find your identity in Him alone. If you've made mistakes, run back into Daddy God's arms and remember that His mercies are new every day. Wherever you are, God sees you and knows it all. Go back and read the stories that touched you the most. Apply the keys to your own life.

Be strong and courageous. You have a destiny and a purpose on earth. Your dreams are part of God's glorious plans. Together, as we each do what we are called to do, we will see awakening in ourselves and our nations. Arise and shine, full of Jesus. Take your place in the harvest of nations.

About the Author

Laura Taranto's greatest joy is to be a trusted friend of God and live for Him. Her passion is to inspire people to know who they are and to courageously dream bigger. She loves to prophesy destiny and hope. Through writing and speaking, she shares the stories of what God has done to bring inspiration and strength to others.

Laura is the founder and leader of Be A Witness, an organization dedicated to raising awareness and ministering to refugees. God is powerfully reaching many who came to Europe to escape war and crisis in their nations. Laura lived in Europe for two years, working with the Europe Shall Be Saved movement and Iris Germany. She is now based in Florida and continues to minister in the nations.

Laura earned her master's degrees in macro social work and international public health from Boston University. She is ordained by Iris Global. Previously, Laura was Heidi Baker's executive assistant, working with her in Pemba, Mozambique, and internationally. She loves to see Jesus transform the most desperate situations with His great love. Laura believes and prays that many people from around the world will join the move of God in Europe!